THE THIRD SIDE OF THE DESK

GREG CONWAY/73.

THE THIRD SIDE OF THE DESK

*How Parents Can Change
the Schools*

HANNAH S. HESS

GREG CONWAY/73.

CHARLES SCRIBNER'S SONS, NEW YORK

Library of Congress Cataloging in Publication Data
Hess, Hannah S
    The third side of the desk.
    1. Home and school. I. Title.
LC225.H38   370.19′31   72–7946
ISBN 0–684–13081–5

This book published simultaneously in the
United States of America and in Canada -
  Copyright under the Berne Convention

1 3 5 7 9 11 13 15 17 19 H/C 20 18 16 14 12 10 8 6 4 2

Printed in the United States of America

This book is dedicated to my mother, Ruth Spier, who helped me survive the system, and to my husband, Walter, who helped me fight it.

CONTENTS

ACKNOWLEDGMENTS

Thanks to Barbara Rosen, Billie and Arnold Dolin, Jane Mills, Ellie Cohen, Sandy Rosenblum, Janet Potter, Pat and Sam Nowell, Jo Butler, Laura Bryant, Judy Browne, Rose Thompson, Sondra and Ted Thomas, Alice Fields, Edith Rood, Jamie Dietrich, Sheila Collins, Jay Shulman, Creola Kelly, Blanche and Ray Gandolf, Jim Finkelstein, Lola and Sy Salter, Dick Earle, Olga Cassiz, Thelma Callaway, Hester Giddings, Bernice Hudson, Rose Brundage, Nora Wainer, Beulah Sanders, Aida Maxwell, Linda and Stanley Grover, Ruth Solar, Bettina Olivier, Marlene and Howard Pascan, Margot Harwood, Rudi Collins, Paula Kopelman, Elizabeth Levi, and all the other parents who made the events described here happen. Thanks, too, to all the dedicated teachers who not only helped to change the school, but who, amid all the turmoil, carried on EDUCATION.

Special thanks to Shelley Alpert and Terry Berl who first gave us their plan for the open corridor school, to Ann Braver, Jane Ortner, and Jacqueline Sanders who taught the first classes, and to Professor Lillian Weber who guided the program in its beginnings. And personal thanks to Jane Ortner, Andi Salsberg, Norma Morris, and Harriet Cohen who provided security and education for my children while I was engaged in the battle.

And to Dorothy Dandridge, an educator and a lady, who kept the school running and all of us sane during the lockout.

And to all the children at the school.

And to Rhoda Karpatkin and Marie Ford of the Local School Board.

And to Sid Morrison.

For their help, advice, and encouragement, thanks to Andre Schiffrin, to my sister, Elizabeth Stern, to Bernice Gross, and especially to Walter, whose wise and patient criticism helped shape this book.

And thanks, too, to Kathy, Maggie, and Sam, who bore up while I lived and wrote it.

THE THIRD SIDE OF THE DESK

Though the events described in this book are all true, and as accurate as minutes of public meetings and my own recollections can make them, the names of all the people involved, except well-known public officials, have been changed.

INTRODUCTION

I have seen the New York City public school system from three sides of the desk: first, as a student, where in addition to the fundamentals that school is supposed to teach (but which, in fact, it does not always succeed in doing) I absorbed many attitudes that I carried with me, largely unmodified, when I approached school from the second side of the desk—as a teacher. It was not until I saw the school system as a parent—from the third side of the desk—that these attitudes changed.

The keystone of the educational system (private as well as public, I suspect) is that only effort, application, and a modicum of intelligence are necessary to achieve success. Along with these virtues, cleanliness, punctuality, physical presence (euphemistically called attendance), and a surface politeness are generally sufficient to earn for the student a high school diploma, at the very least. In short, comformity to the middle-class ethic is what is stressed in our schools; and it was this general attitude that, along with my academic credentials, I brought to my own classes.

I was a shining example of the American success story. I started school as a non–English-speaking student. I received none of the bilingual assistance that is beginning, but barely, to be offered to children today. For me it was sink or swim in English, and presto, I swam. True, I had sympathetic teachers at the outset. True, I came from a home where nothing less than success was expected of me. True, I came from a tradition where Jews were many things, and most recently those things had certainly been viewed negatively; but Jews were not academic failures. Therefore, clean, polite, punctual, and hard-working, I succeeded. Not all my teachers were sympathetic. In any school one cannot entirely escape the bigots and the

1

incompetents. Nevertheless, I learned and I succeeded; and if I could do this, then anyone could.

Still, as a teacher, I could not escape the fact that some children did not learn. I did my best. I was, I think, sympathetic. I cared. So did most of my colleagues at the high school where I taught. And yet, some children did not learn. Who was to blame? Certainly not the sympathetic, caring teacher who knows that if you work hard, apply yourself . . . and all the rest. Who was to blame? That, then, depended on your bias. It could be the child himself, his uncaring parents, his general background ("some of 'those people' never even read a newspaper" or come in on time or do an honest day's work or whatever); or for comfortable liberals like me, it could be society as a whole that placed "those people" in a position where success was almost made impossible. That some of the poor, the black, the Puerto Ricans did succeed only proved that "with hard work . . ." and so on. The one factor that was never responsible for a child's failure was the school (though for us high school teachers a faulty elementary and junior high school education was, perhaps, a contributory cause). What never occurred to me or, I think, to most of my colleagues was that even if our diagnosis of the cause was accurate, diagnosis is hardly enough. If a doctor diagnoses appendicitis, it then behooves him to act on that diagnosis. We would not long tolerate a doctor who let his patient die while standing by, saying "He can't help his pain. It's his appendix." And yet most teachers do just that. They are there for the students who will learn anyway. For the rest, the schools *may* diagnose the cause of failure, but they do not, in most instances, effect a cure. And so generation after generation of children die in our schools; and the fault continues somehow to be theirs, while the schools go on smugly with their business as usual. They are prettied up periodically and with great fanfare by this or that pilot project or innovation, which in the end changes the conditions of failure not one iota, and which finally gets so dissipated that it is meaningless.

But this simple, yet basic, insight did not come to me until as a parent I saw the school system in a way I never had before. The account that follows describes how I, a fairly conventional, "liberal" teacher, was changed by my encounter with the stupidities of a fairly typical school, and how that change in me, and in parents very much like me, in turn changed the school. I did not go into the school bent on revolution. In fact, I first approached it with the same deference and respect that most middle-class people have for their institutions. If our ultimate activities were revolutionary in nature—and the removal of two unsatisfactory principals, the selection by the parents of a capable one, and the implementation of the open-classroom program at the school are all revolutionary in the present educational structure—it was only because the circumstances allowed no other sensible response. And so, as a parent, I was radicalized by these experiences, because I refused to accept any longer the premise that the school cannot be an instrument to change the pattern of failure for so many children. And thus radicalized, a small group of parents and teachers worked together to change the school from one that served the system and the teachers into one that serves the children.

Since the book covers only about three years, the story of PS 84 is obviously not over, but I think it does demonstrate that where people are willing to accept responsibility change is possible and that once schools are willing to accept the nature of the child—any child—and stop alibiing, education may even be possible.

ONE

"Don't Push Your Children"

When my son was born, hot on the heels of his two sisters, it became clear that our two-bedroom apartment was no longer big enough for us all—at least not if we were to remain reasonably sane and civil. And since Walter had long been singing the praises of life in Manhattan (where we had both grown up), we decided the time had come to make the move back. We were lucky enough to find an apartment in the West Side Urban Renewal area, and we agreed that if the local school were at all viable we would take it. One of my friends knew the guidance counselor at PS 84 and suggested that I call her, which I did. The conversation was quite reassuring.

"It's a new building," she said. "There are some excellent teachers, and we just got a new principal. Your daughter will do fine. We don't have IGC* classes any longer, but there are enough bright middle-class kids so that it works out. Why don't you come and see the school?"

"That would be good," I said. "Could I come soon?"

So we set up an appointment for the following day. She told me to stop in the office to get a pass, and they would direct me to her office. Then she hesitated and, almost with embarrassment, added, "If anyone asks who you are, say you're from BCG.†"

It seemed an odd request, but I didn't give the matter too much thought at the time.

The following day, gray and threatening rain, I left the kids with

---

*Intellectually gifted children.
†Bureau of Child Guidance, the Board of Education arm that allegedly ministers to the emotional needs of the children in the public schools.

a friend and took the train into Manhattan. I got off at 96th Street and Central Park West and walked down to 92nd. The day did nothing to lift my spirits. The buildings seemed cheerless and cold, and the park across the street, barren of leaves and people, was equally uninviting. The side streets, as I passed them, seemed untouched by the promise of urban renewal, the buildings either partially tinned over or in the last stages of decay. Garbage and abandoned cars decorated the streets, and mounds of black snow were studded with litter and dog waste. It hardly seemed like the kind of neighborhood in which any sane person would want to raise children. Still, I walked on, turning west into 92nd Street.

The school was a three-story shiny yellow brick building that stretched for half a block, ending in a city playground with gaping holes in the concrete. I walked in and was hit by the smell—a compound of dampness, steam heat, chalk, tomato soup, and children—that pervades every school I've ever entered, summer or winter. I had no trouble finding the office, and when I asked for the guidance counselor, I was given a pass and directions with no questions asked.

Peering in open classroom doors as I went up to the second floor, I was somewhat reassured. Teachers were in front of the classes, teaching. The kids were in their seats, presumably learning. There was no sign of chaos. The halls were fairly unlittered, the walls free of obscenities. (I had no occasion then, of course, to go into the bathrooms or up to the third floor where the older children were.) The few kids I saw in the halls seemed to be on some kind of business, not just loitering. No one, that I could see, was heaving furniture at anyone. If this was a blackboard jungle, it was not apparent. I reached the guidance office, where I was greeted cordially.

"Hello, Mrs. Hess. How are things at the Bureau?"

For a moment I drew a blank, until I remembered her warning and answered that things at the Bureau were unchanged. (I'm sure they were, too.) Then she turned to an eight- or nine-year-old boy who had been sitting in her office and asked him to leave since she wanted to talk to me privately.

"Go back to your room Robert, and I'll get you when I'm finished," she said.

The boy left. She closed the door behind him and with a conspiratorial air said, "We've just gotten a new principal, and I don't

know how she feels about parents. The last principal didn't welcome
them in the school. That's why I told you to say you were from
BCG."

"Why didn't the old principal want parents in the school?"

"Oh, it was a political thing," she said. "I really wasn't too involved."

This seemed rather strange to me, since I assumed that a guidance counselor would of necessity deal with parents, but I didn't
press it.

"How's the new principal?" I asked.

"Too soon to tell. She's only been here three days, but so far
everyone seems to like her. And she has some new ideas about
teaching reading. That's one of the big problems here, though of
course not for the middle-class kids."

"Is the school safe?"

She assured me that it was and repeated that for children like
mine (whom, of course, she had never seen) there would be no
problems.

"The kindergarten classes are very good here," she told me,
"except for one teacher. And we think she's retiring in the fall. I'll
take you down to see her—I'll make up some excuse."

I followed her down the stairs and down the hall to a room
presided over by a sweetly smiling elderly lady who was introduced
to me as Mrs. Winter. (Since I assumed that I would not be able to
request a specific teacher when I registered Kathy for kindergarten,
her name came under the file-and-forget category, though I would
later recall the introduction well.) We exchanged a few trivialities,
then I told the guidance counselor that I should be going and
thanked her for her time. In parting, she ostentatiously asked me to
give her regards to someone at BCG.

On the whole, the school had impressed me favorably—certainly
enough so that it could not be a reason for turning down the apartment. The children I had seen seemed happy; and from what I had
been told kids could get an education there. That was as much as
anyone could hope for from a school. The one thing that had struck
me about the children was the contrast—the blond, John-John
Kennedy haircutted kids in Danskin outfits versus the others in the
hand-me-downs of their brothers and sisters; but they all seemed
mixed together in the classes, and diversity was one of the pluses
of the neighborhood. Altogether I felt cheered as I left; and though

the sun was still not shining, somehow things seemed less bleak on
the return walk to the subway.

And so once again we became Manhattanites. That was the end
of March. The next few weeks were spent in getting to know the
neighbors and the neighborhood, and I was so busy that I had little
time to think about school. In May I took Kathy, her birth certificate,
and her arm (proof of vaccination) and registered her for kindergarten. Like any other new parent I was thoroughly browbeaten,
though politely, by the school secretary (all of whom must, I am
sure, take a course in the art of intimidating parents and other lesser
forms of life). Kathy got a lollipop, and I got the information that
I would shortly be invited to a tea for new parents at which I would
have a chance to meet the principal, ask questions, and see the
school.

In due course I got a letter inviting me to said tea. On the appointed morning I substituted a respectable dress for my blue jeans
and joined a group of about twenty other new parents in the school
library. I was immediately struck by the fact that the group was
predominantly white and middle class. The rich diversity of the
neighborhood—proclaimed in all the speeches and articles about
the upper West Side Urban Renewal area—was glaringly absent.

The principal arrived, a very large, stocky, middle-aged lady in a
loose-fitting knit suit and space shoes. Her glasses hung from her
neck by a chain. She introduced herself and her assistant principal
for the lower grades and began to tell us that though our children
were now entering school we should not make them feel that we
were abandoning them. We should walk them to school daily and
pick them up, because they still needed us. She also spoke, I remember, about her own daughter, now grown, and how fast the time had
passed, warning us to cherish these few years of our children's
childhood. She then went on to say that we should not push our
children. They would all learn in time if encouraged but not pushed.
To this end, she told us, the school had decided that reading would
not be taught formally until the second grade. It had been found,
she said, that most children were not ready to read till then, and
pushing them earlier was bound to backfire and result in all sorts
of blocks and problems. Kathy was already reading simple books,
but I certainly did not want to be a pushy parent, so I held my peace.

After a few more exhortations to leave our children alone but to
be interested in them even if they answered our "What did you do

in school today?" with "Nothing," we were invited to ask questions.
The questions were as inspirational as the introductory speech,
dealing mainly with whether our children would be in the morning
or afternoon kindergarten and why (it was done by age, all children
born before June 1 attending the morning session and the others
going in the afternoon, though why this should be so was not explained), how we would know in whose class they would be, and so
forth. Finally the principal urged us to become active members of
the parents' association, a bit of advice I suspect she later regretted
having given. We were invited to return with our children to visit
the kindergarten classes, and then we were dismissed.

I spent the summer in Central Park and in some of the activities
of a group of mothers with preschool children who decided to
organize to make our building's community room usable for the
children on cold or rainy days. The person with whom I was most
impressed at the first organizing meeting was Anne Best, who
seemed both sensible and sensitive. For one thing, she expressed
my own feelings about too many rules and regulations—that the
more of them there are, the more trouble you let yourself in for.
    "A few sensible rules—like don't destroy things or hurt anybody
—should be enough to start, and if you find you need more later,
you can always make them up as you go along."
    This seemed to reflect the general attitude, and we managed to
get along quite nicely, and our children, too, on that basis.
    I didn't get to know Anne very well for quite a while. She lived
in the other building of our co-op. Her kids, both boys, were somewhat older than mine, so I used to see her with a book on the grass
in the park while I pushed swings in the playground. Also, I found,
she was president of the PS 84 Parents' Association, so she was very
busy; but on the few occasions that I spoke to her, I liked her. She
was bright and funny—and had convictions that she stuck to, even
when these convictions were unpopular. She was also outspoken
and rubbed some people the wrong way, partly, I think, because she
knew so well who she was that it never occurred to her that what she
said could be misconstrued. It was through Anne, finally, that I
really became involved at PS 84.

TWO

"There's No Such Thing as a Disruptive Child"

September 1967 came, and the newpapers screamed "School Strike." As a teacher I had been involved in the beginnings of organized unionism, including the struggle among the old TU (Teachers' Union), the HSTA (High School Teachers' Association), and the UFT (United Federation of Teachers) to be the collective-bargaining agent for the city's teachers. I had belonged to the UFT at first, but their campaign literature was so offensive that I quit and joined the TU, which was, of course, promptly trounced. At any rate, after the demise of the TU, I supported the UFT because I felt that only through unionism could teachers become a force for educational change. And so when the teachers had gone on strike in the fall of 1961, I had gone from my obstetrician's appointment to join the picket line in front of my school, demonstrating my solidarity with my colleagues.

Kathy's first day of school dawned bright and clear, though of course she was not going. We did walk over to the school to show the teachers that we were with them and to walk the line with them if they wanted parental support. There were about ten teachers picketing in front of the school, all of them young. I asked them how many teachers were striking or at least honoring the picket line. They told us that only about half of them were out. The others felt that they were professionals and could not abandon the children. Since for years teachers have been beaten down by their professionalism—while they keep on punching a time clock in a most nonprofessional way—I was not terribly impressed by this argument. I was struck, though, by the enthusiasm of the picketing teachers and by the warmth with which they spoke to their children—both those who went in and those whose parents were honoring the strike. Several of the picketing teachers said that they, personally, had voted against the strike because they felt that the issues were not serious enough to warrant such drastic action, but once the strike vote had been taken, they felt honor-bound to support the union. They were rather bitter about those of their colleagues who had gone in—understandably so. It may be a cliché that in union there is strength, but it is much harder to fire an entire faculty (or, at least, to make *everyone's* life difficult by giving them garbage detail) than to single out those few who have taken a stand. The picketing teachers expressed the fear that since the principal was not herself striking, she would make their lives unbearable when the strike ended.

One of the parents was handing out fliers announcing that there would be a speakout that evening to hear how the community felt about the strike.

"Isn't the community for the teachers?" I asked.

"I'm not," she said. "They should be in school. They have an obligation to the kids."

Since it sounded as though it would be an interesting meeting, I went home and arranged for a sitter.

That night Walter and I went over to the school. The auditorium was fairly crowded when we arrived, but we found seats near the front. (Auditorium seats always fill from the back down—a hangover, no doubt, from our school days, when to be up front meant to be under the too-watchful eye of the teacher.) I looked around and saw, here and there, a familiar face. Unlike the tea for us new parents, tonight the "community" was much more present, though by no means in proportion to their numbers in the school (about 40 percent Spanish-speaking, 30 percent black, and 30 percent "other"). The "other" was still very much in the majority in the auditorium, and very much the most vocal.

Anne called the meeting to order, asked whether anyone minded that it was being taped (no one seemed to) and whether anyone wished to have the speeches translated into Spanish. Silence.

"Ask it in Spanish," someone called out, and one of the Spanish parents repeated the question. Several hands went up shyly. Thus I attended my first bilingual meeting, and I was embarrassed by the rudeness of some of my fellow Anglos who kept up a steady stream of chatter during the Spanish translation.

The first few speakers were rather mild, expressing for the most part some ambivalence about the strike. They did, they said, support the teachers; but on the other hand, what about all those children who had to be in school because their parents worked?

"Are we babysitters, or are we teachers?" someone called out.

"If you were teachers, you'd be in school where you belong," someone called back.

A blond young man rose and got the floor.

"As district-chapter chairman of the UFT, I'd like to urge all of you parents to support us," he began.

"When did you ever support parents, Joe Gelber?" someone shouted. He ignored the jibe and continued.

"We're not striking for ourselves. We're not asking for more money. What we're asking for are the kinds of conditions that will improve education for your children. Smaller class sizes, more MES*, and help for disruptive children so they won't keep your kids from learning."

For some reason this caused the meeting to erupt. There was a great deal of booing, catcalling, and shouts from various sections of the auditorium, all swelling into an indistinguishable roar. Anne called for order several times, and gradually the people subsided.

"Listen," said Anne, "if we don't give everyone a chance to speak, there's no point in having a speakout. Please, let's try to respect each other's opinions."

"When he respects children, I'll respect him," called a woman toward the rear. She wore slacks and a dashiki and no makeup, and she looked very angry.

"C'mon, Irene, we'll listen to you, too, but we can't have everyone talking at once."

Irene subsided, and finally it was possible for the meeting to continue.

*More Effective Schools—a category set up in schools that had the facilities to provide extra services, such as additional teachers, more free periods, and the like. Though this program had been intended for ghetto areas, MES ended up in many middle-class schools, which was a misuse of Title I funds. There had been conflicting studies as to whether all this additional expense produced better educational results.

A black man, also very angry, began to speak. "My child has been in this school for three years," he said. "And the only thing she's learned is that teachers are racists. When I come to school I'm treated like dirt, and they tell me that it's not the fault of the school that she's not learning. Well, dammit, whose fault is it? I send her here to learn, and if the teachers can't teach her then let *them* get out. I'm not supporting any teachers. If they can't teach thirty children, who says they can teach twenty—if they're black children. I'm sick and tired of all this talk about improving conditions for our children. Hell, every time the teachers get a new contract, it's supposed to make our kids learn better. All it does is make life easier for the teachers. My kid's going to school where she belongs; and any time those teachers want to come back and teach, she'll be there waiting for them." He sat down amid cheers and applause.

A large black woman rose. I recognized her as Edna Garrett, a leader in the National Welfare Rights movement, whom I had met once at a Board of Estimates meeting to which I had gone to support a low-cost housing project. Edna spoke slowly, softly, but with great feeling.

"My children have been in this school for five years," she began. "And no one has ever given a damn about them. They wanted to put my son in a junior-guidance class, and I let them because they told me it was the best thing for him. He'd be in a small class, and he'd learn. Well, he's been there for two years now, and he hasn't learned a damn thing. They say they're striking about disruptive children. Well, let me tell you, there's no such thing as a disruptive child. There's only disruptive teachers."

"Tell 'em, Edna" and "That's right" came from all over the auditorium. I was stunned. I had never attended a parents' association meeting before. When I was teaching, teachers were neither invited to, nor expected to attend, such meetings; and if parents were hostile to teachers they must have swallowed it during open school night. I was taken aback by the anti-teacher feelings that so many parents were expressing. Maybe things had been different in my school.

Florence Steinberg rose. A short woman with a fiery, highly emotional style of delivery and a voice that if necessary could reach the back of Shea Stadium without electronic assistance, she lives in our building and was at that time president of the parent association of PS 75, another elementary school in our district. She is also very

active in Stryckers Bay Neighborhood Council* and has long fought
the good fight in education, housing, welfare, civil rights, and peace.

"Edna's absolutely right," she began. "I went into my school
today and I taught a class. That's right. I scabbed. I didn't have any
hesitation, because strikes aren't sacred. This is a bad strike, and I
can't support it and I won't support it. And I'll be back at 75 tomorrow teaching those kids until their teachers come back. As for disruptive children, I taught those kids all day—and I'm not a teacher.
I never took any fancy education courses. But there wasn't one
disruptive child there. They were all well-behaved, and they did
their work. Maybe if teachers really taught—and really gave a damn
about their kids—they wouldn't have to worry about disruptive children either."

She sat down to a thunderous ovation. 'Oh, come off it, Florence,'
I thought. 'How can you compare a one-day stand—especially on
the first day of school—to classroom reality? People behave better
during blackouts and other unnatural events, too. You ought to stay
there for a couple of months and then see if there still is no such
thing as a disruptive child.' But I didn't say it. After all, I was new
in the community, and I didn't feel like getting lynched. Irene, the
lady who had interrupted Joe Gelber, was now speaking. I didn't
catch her full name because I had been engaged in my mental
debate with Florence.

". . . in the labor movement when you were in diapers, Joe Gelber,
and believe me, as a good unionist I know there are some strikes I
wouldn't support. Did you support the Southern railroad workers
when they struck to keep blacks out of their unions? There's nothing
so sacred about a picket line. And as the white mother of a black
child I can tell you that everything Edna and John said is absolutely
true. This is a racist system, with racist teachers, and till they learn
to care about all children, I'm not supporting any UFT picket line.
I'll be in that school tomorrow, and every day till the strike ends."

"Oh, good grief," I said to Walter.

Again there was wild applause. A few people got up to support
the teachers, amid boos and rude remarks. Several teachers also
spoke, asking the parents to support them. They were shouted

*An umbrella group of organizations in the West Side Urban Renewal area.
SBNC was actively engaged at the time in trying to get housing for the poor
who were being displaced by the renewal.

down with comments like "Did you support my kid when his teacher said no black or Spanish kid was smart enough to be in an IGC class?" All the anti-strike speakers took pride in crossing the picket line, thereby showing their contempt for Albert Shanker and the union and their solidarity for the black and Spanish children in the school.

I decided I had to say something. It wasn't the first time I'd spoken before a hostile crowd; and though I knew I wouldn't win any friends tonight either, I felt I had to speak. Shaking somewhat, I raised my hand.

"I'm fairly new in this neighborhood, and I don't know much about PS 84," I said.

"Then why don't you sit down?" someone called.

"But," I went on, trying to keep the shaking out of my voice, "before I had children I was a teacher for six years. I'm not crazy about Al Shanker and the UFT, but sometimes you have to make choices between two less than perfect alternatives. If you go in and cross the picket line, you're saying to the Board of Ed that you support them and their policies. They're not going to look inside your heads and read that you're saying 'a plague on both your houses.' They'll just count your bodies and use you. Well, I'm not willing to be used by them. If I have to choose between entrusting my children to the Board of Education or to the UFT, then I'll have to opt for the union. Sure there are lousy teachers, but there are more good teachers in the system than there are good people in the 110* bureaucracy, and since I can't sit on a fence, I'll go with the teachers."

I sank back into my seat and watched the shaking in my hands subside. "Good girl," said Walter. Irene had the floor again.

"Since you're new in this neighborhood, maybe you shouldn't be making any decisions. I've lived and worked in this neighborhood for over twenty years, and I've been involved with this school for four of them. And let me tell you there's hardly a teacher in this place that I'd trust my kid to. And that goes for all the black and Spanish parents. The union isn't going to change this system. The only way anything is ever going to change in the schools is through community control. When we elect the Joan of Arc governing board

*The New York City Board of Education offices are at 110 Livingston Street in Brooklyn.

and make teachers accountable to parents, then maybe you'll get some changes. In the meantime anything else is a bandaid. If you care about your children, you'll get involved in this community and work for community control with us. But till then, maybe you ought to just listen to what the community is saying."

Well, it wasn't a lynching, but it sure was a putdown. Several other people spoke, but it was pretty much the same theme, with minor variations—a recounting of how their individual children had been damaged, a citing of the appallingly low reading scores, of the fact that although the classes were, allegedly, balanced (both ethnically and intellectually) there was still, in fact, tracking, with all the bright and well-mannered children in the top classes in each grade, and all the others—the slow, the disruptive, the nonconformists (mainly the poor, the black, and the Spanish-speaking)—in the bottom classes. And the kids were definitely labeled and aware of who they were. There was also more talk about the junior-guidance classes, originally designed as a sheltered environment for the students who couldn't make it in a regular class. These classes were small—no more than eight children to a class—and they were supposed to offer, in addition to individualized instruction, all the psychological and physical services that the school system had to offer. They were also supposed to be balanced between withdrawn and acting-out children, in the hopes that this mix would be beneficial to both groups. In fact, according to all the speakers on the subject, the classes were nothing more than a dumping ground for children who presented problems to their teachers. The children in the classes were all black and Spanish, they were placed there not on the basis of psychological tests or other objective evaluative tools, but on the basis of teacher judgment. And since many of the teachers who put kids into these classes were not, according to the speakers, sympathetic to black and Spanish-speaking children (to put it mildly), their placement was, obviously, suspect. Furthermore, once in these classes, nothing happened. The kids didn't learn. They received no psychological services. They served their maximum term of three years, and were dumped back into the lowest-track class afterwards, further behind academically and (if they were truly disturbed to begin with) no less disturbed at the end. It was not an encouraging picture.

Then a tall, slim woman with long black hair and piercing eyes rose.

"I want to say something, but since I was sure I wouldn't remember it all I wrote it down." She then began to read and I noticed that the paper in her hands was shaking badly. Obviously I was not the only one with coffee nerves. I tapped Florence, who was sitting in the row ahead of me, and asked her who she was.

"Her name is Toni Diamond," she whispered. "She's one of the best teachers at 84."

I sat back and listened, not only to the words, but also to the obvious emotion behind them. At times her voice almost broke, at times it went to a whisper, but everyone listened attentively as she read. What she spoke of was a vision of a new school system, one in which the bureaucracy of the Board of Education would give way to an alliance of parents and teachers who would make the educational decisions. She said that teachers, like children, were the victims of the present system, that they were held in the same contempt by the bureaucracy, and that it was this that killed everyone's spirit, to the death of education. And she pleaded that parents and teachers should work together to change not only the form but the substance of education.

When she finished there was a moment's pause—followed by general applause. I'm sure she didn't change many minds (maybe not any), but I think they were applauding her because of her sincerity and because of who she was. Another woman rose, very young, her hair cut in a Sassoon, her skirt mini.

"Hi, I'm Nancy Calvert, and I have two kids in this school. I'm also a music teacher here. I can't say it as eloquently as Toni, but I certainly agree with her." She then continued to tell us that Mrs. Diamond, she, and a few of the other teachers were running a Freedom School at Goddard-Riverside Community Center, as an alternative for those parents who wanted to honor the picket line but who needed to have their children in school or who wanted them to attend.

"It won't just be a babysitting service, either," she assured us. "There'll be classes according to grade, and we'll be teaching." Shortly afterwards the meeting ended. Walter and I walked home with Florence, and I voiced to her what I had thought earlier. She agreed readily that her one day's experience was not typical, but still maintained that the disruptive-child clause was another weapon by which teachers could rid themselves of children they couldn't, or wouldn't, reach. I had to agree that the clause, as interpreted by the union, could do that, and I would certainly fight it on that basis. Still, I could not cast my lot with the Board of Education.

"And I've honored too many picket lines to be able to cross one of my colleagues'." Those words were to haunt me a year later.

The next morning I told Kathy to get dressed for school.

"Is the strike over?" she asked.

"No, but there's a school that's open as long as the strike lasts, just around the corner from PS 84."

"Will my teacher be there?"

"I don't think so."

"Why not?"

'Because she's a scab,' I thought, but aloud I said, "Because she thinks teachers shouldn't strike. She thinks someone has to be there to take care of the children who come to school."

"Should teachers be allowed to strike, Mommy?"

"That's a hard question to answer, honey. Teachers are people like everyone else, and sometimes it seems the only way to get people to listen. Teachers shouldn't have to strike, but if they believe what they're doing is right and no one listens, then sometimes it's what they have to do."

I'm not sure I convinced Kathy much better than I convinced the people the night before. It's a difficult thing to explain to a child the necessity for strikes.

"Why can't I go to my real school," Kathy asked, "if my real teacher is there?"

"Because I think the teachers who are striking are right, and I don't want to do anything to hurt them."

"How will it hurt them if I go to school?"

(If you think this was turning into a rough session, you should have heard the one on the subject of how babies are made.)

"Well, if enough people stay away from school maybe it will show the people who run the schools that they should listen to the teachers. And then the strike will end more quickly."

"Is my real teacher wrong?"

"She doesn't think so."

"But do you think she's wrong?"

"Well, I don't agree with her, but everyone has to do what she thinks is right."

The classes in the community center—the Freedom School— were set up according to age, but since there were fewer children and teachers than in the normal school the divisions were not so rigid, so that kindergartners and first-graders were together, second- and third-graders, and so forth. Kathy came home every afternoon happy and enthusiastic. What is more, when I went to pick her up each day, I found the teachers surrounded by kids, talking, showing them things, listening. There was none of the mad dash to escape at the sound of the bell that is a traditional part of school. Some of those kids would stay as long as the teacher was willing to stand there and then would follow her, still talking. Quite a switch from the battle of wills I had sometimes had to engage in to finish a sentence once that bell had rung ("*I* dismiss you. The bell is only a signal for me." And then they'd sit at the edge of their seats, poised for the takeoff when I relented, victorious?) These kids had to be pried loose like barnacles. Was it the lack of compulsion of the Freedom School that made the difference? Were the children who attended it those apple-polishing kids that always hang around the desk halfway into your lunch period? Or was there something else happening that made them want to stay? At the time I only wondered.

Then the strike ended, and the school year began officially. Teachers and children left the Freedom School and returned to what? An institution belonging to the Board of Education.

THREE

Kindergarten: "She May Be Reading, But That Doesn't Mean She's Ready"

Kathy went to school every morning at 8:40 and I picked her up at 11:20. Her teacher was Mrs. Winter, the elderly lady with blue-gray hair and syrupy smile whom I had met on my first visit to PS 84. She loved Kathy, which was not hard since she is a girl (a prerequisite for success in the early grades) and, what is more, is bright, friendly, and cooperative (except at home, where she is like everyone else's child) and takes school very seriously. Of her life at kindergarten I got only glimpses. If I were early to pick her up, I could, on most days, hear her teacher screeching halfway down the hall, though as soon as the door was opened to greet the waiting parents, the teacher would emerge with her smile in place. Every day the children came tumbling out with a gargantuan piece of completed work. The teacher preparation must have been immense, for these objects were always made by the teacher. The children's task consisted of coloring in, in appropriate shades, the body of the thing. At Halloween it would be a pumpkin, at Christmas a Santa Claus, a hatchet for George Washington's birthday, so that I began to suspect that holidays were invented to supply the kindergarten curriculum. In bad months, when no holiday, major or minor, could be celebrated, and when no president had had the foresight to have been born, the time was filled with coloring mittens or spring flowers. For Mother's Day the teacher made each mother a picture frame, and in the fall she made each child a kite. The children were not allowed to use a pair of scissors or to staple. If they ever used paints, or any media other than crayons, I never saw the results. And the pattern, I found, prevailed not only in Kathy's class, but in all the kindergartens

19

except one. What is more, it was not limited to PS 84, for when I spoke to one of my friends in Queens one day, and she told me that her daughter was sick, she said, "Diane is so upset, because she was in the middle of making her fireman's hat, and she wanted to finish it," and I realized with a start that Kathy had that day also made a fireman's hat. It's rather chilling to imagine that all over the city, on any given day, all the kindergarten children are mindlessly coloring the same object.

In addition to the objets d'art that she brought home, Kathy brought home the judgments of her teacher as to who the "good" and the "bad" children were. It didn't take me long to figure out that all the "bad" children were boys and that they were all either black or Spanish. One boy in particular became the class patsy; and even when every other child did the same thing, the children would turn and say "I'll bet Jose didn't bring his Easter egg" or whatever.

Then there was reading readiness. Now remember, the children at PS 84 were not taught reading until the second grade, but they were made "ready," so that by the time they came to second grade they would all roll into reading like a ship off the launching slip. (Alas, in reality it didn't work out quite that neatly, as witness the reading scores.) This reading-readiness material consisted of rexo-graphed pages, sometimes somewhat blurred due to mechanical failure, of simple objects. The children were to circle the object that was different or to draw lines connecting the two similar objects. Later in the year, as the material grew more complex, they had to connect the objects that began with the same sound. The only trouble with this was that Kathy was a fanciful child, and half the time, instead of circling or connecting, she would choose one of the pictures that appealed to her and embellish it to suit her tastes. When I went over it with her, she'd say, "Oh, I know that one is different, Mommy, but isn't this a pretty picture I made?" And how could I disagree? Which led us, finally, to a conference with Mrs. Winter, who told me, "Well, Mrs. Hess, she may be reading, but that doesn't mean she's ready to read." Putdown number three for the pushy parent! After a while, of course, Kathy learned to do what was expected of her, and she could connect and circle with the best of them. IBM may consider that progress, but we were less than en-chanted as we noticed that her imagination was being squelched and she was becoming less and less inventive.

One day Carole Arnowitz, one of the women in my building, who was a member of the PA Executive Board, approached me.

"We need a class list from every class—names and addresses of parents—because we want to do a mailing about the Joan of Arc Governing Board elections. Could you get us a list of the parents in Mrs. Winter's class?"

"How do I do that?" I asked.

"Just ask the teacher. The principal said she couldn't give us the parents' names and addresses. She says it's against Board of Ed regulations."

"Everything's against Board of Ed regulations," I said. "Will the teacher give me the list?"

"Mrs. Wachtel said we could ask the teachers."

So I went dutifully to my teacher and explained my mission.

"Oh, I couldn't do that, Mrs. Hess."

"Mrs. Wachtel told the PA it was all right if the teacher gave it to us."

"But Mrs. Hess, it's against the rules."

I said nothing, for the simple reason that she spoke with such reverence of the rules that I could think of nothing to say. I would have felt as though I were asking a religious to break one of his vows.

"Unless," she went on, with a coy, conspiratorial smile, "you were the class mother. The class mother is entitled to the class list. Are you the class mother?"

"What's the class mother?" I asked brightly.

"Oh, it's not a big job, really. She gets people to go along when we go on trips. She doesn't have to go herself. She just gets people. And sometimes, if we need help with a project, she gets volunteers. Things like that. It really isn't a big job. Would you like to be the class mother?"

'Not particularly,' I thought but didn't say. Instead, I hedged,

"Well, I can't just appoint myself. Wouldn't I have to be elected by the other parents in the class?

"Oh, I don't think that's necessary. I'm sure I could designate you class mother—and if any other parent wanted the job, then I suppose you could have an election. But in the meantime, Mrs. Hess, you could be the class mother. And," she added, dangling the carrot, "you'd have to have the class list so you could call parents for class trips."

"Well," I answered, "I don't want to do anything undemocratic. Let me check with the PA and see what their policy is, and then I'll let you know."

I went back to Carole and reported the conversation.

"Okay," she said, "I've just appointed you a class mother. We really need those lists. If we're going to get a decent turnout for the election, we've got to get a mailing list."

And so, by executive fiat, I got my first job (a most impressive one, to be sure) in the Parents' Association.

A few words about the Joan of Arc Governing Board. After IS 201 was built in a location that would insure, forever, a segregated school, the people of Harlem realized that the Board of Education had, in fact, reneged on its promise to integrate. Consequently, they (and people in other ghetto areas) said that if the schools were to remain segregated then, at least, they should be run by the communities in a manner that would serve their needs. The struggle for community control was on. There was a battle when IS 201 opened about the appointment of a principal. There was a boycott of the school, the community prevailed, and the principal appointed by the Board of Ed was withdrawn in favor of one of the community's choosing. Shortly thereafter, the Board of Education (which is always quick to adopt someone else's good thing—and as quick to drop it before it can be properly evaluated) decided to choose four areas of the city as demonstration districts for community control. The four districts chosen were the IS 201 Complex, the Two Bridges Complex*, the Ocean-Hill Brownsville Complex†, and the Joan of Arc Complex. Ocean-Hill and 201 were almost entirely black in composition, Two Bridges was a mixture of Chinese, Puerto Rican, black, and a small percentage of whites. The Joan of Arc Complex was the most integrated of the four, not only ethnically, but economically as well. It included Joan of Arc Junior High School and its four feeder schools, PS 75, 84, 163, and 179. Of these four, only PS 179 was predominantly black and Spanish-speaking, while the other three were more nearly like PS 84 in composition. Furthermore, because of the urban-renewal struggles, most of the area's residents were fairly well organized and politically sophisticated, and there were several strong community organizations that

*On the lower East Side.
†In Brooklyn.

could be counted on to insure broad community participation in a school-board election. The other three communities proceeded, almost at once, to elect community boards. The people in the Joan of Arc Complex decided that if the election were to be meaningful and if the participation of the large numbers of poor—black, Spanish, and white—as well as the politically savvy middle class were to be insured, then before the election could be held there would have to be a good deal of political organization. The West Side Committee for Decentralization was formed for the task of organizing for the election, led by, among others, Norma Hill, Stephanie Hale, Irene Martins, Florence Steinberg, and Sonia Plowden. While the organizing was in process, the Board of Education decided that three demonstration districts were sufficient and withdrew its commitment from the Joan of Arc Complex. In spite of this the community decided to go ahead with its organizing. They tried to enlist the support of the West Side legislators who, as usual, took a firm position on the fence. It was because of this organizing effort that mailing lists of parents were essential, since it was obvious that the parents must be informed if they were to make intelligent choices regarding their children's education. It had been decided that only parents would be allowed to vote in the election, since theirs was the most direct stake in the schools.

Armed with my PA mandate, then, I returned to Mrs. Winter, and good as her word, she gave me the roll book so that I could copy the class list, saying as she did so how glad she was to have me as the class mother. After I got the list, I returned the roll book, with thanks.

"Oh, Mrs. Hess," she said, "now that you're the class mother maybe you can help me." The hook had been right behind the bait, apparently: it's called *quid pro quo*.

"There's a little girl in my class whose mother works. She can get her to school, but there's no one to take her home, so she doesn't come to school. It's a shame. She's a lovely girl—just your daughter's kind. If you could look over the addresses, perhaps you could find someone who walks that way, and who could walk the child home. There's a grandmother at home, but she can't get out. Perhaps you can work something out. The mother is willing to pay whoever does it."

"I'd offer to do it," I said, "but I have two smaller children, and I really can't make that kind of commitment."

"Oh, I wouldn't expect *you* to do it, Mrs. Hess. But perhaps you could find someone who walks that way."

I agreed that it was certainly a shame that the child was missing school and promised to try to find someone. And indeed, after checking the class list, I found that one child lived several houses down the street past the little girl's house, and the mother, a lovely, shy woman by the name of Mrs. Ferrer, readily agreed to take on the responsibility. Mrs. Winter was delighted. I was a success in my new job, and the little girl began to attend kindergarten. She may have been Kathy's kind of child, but Kathy never noticed, and I don't think they ever said two words to each other. But then, the class was not particularly conducive to social intercourse, since the children were glued to their seats coloring most of the time and conversation was not encouraged. Small wonder that squirmy children have a hard time of it!

Open-school week arrived, and, dutiful mother, I went for my conference. I was told that "Julie" was a wonderful child.

"Kathy," I said.

"Oh, of course," she said. "She's so bright, and so nice. A real delight."

Delight or no, her name remained Julie throughout the year, even to the last day, when Mrs. Winter said to her, "Julie, it's been a pleasure having you in my class." "Julie" took it in stride, treating it as a big joke, perhaps because she's always liked that name. The reason for the mixup was quite simple. There was another little girl of Kathy's "kind" in the afternoon kindergarten; and though they did not look at all alike they were both white, bright, and girls. A natural mistake.

Also during open-school week the parents were invited to come to see the classes in actual session. I left Sam at home with a neighbor (Margaret was in nursery school) and, along with several other parents took my seat in one of the chairs that, even as a kindergartner, probably could not have accommodated my long legs. We watched what was, I suppose, a typical morning. The children sat straight in their chairs. Mrs. Winter sat straight in hers. She smiled and in a condescending falsetto asked, "Now, children, what holiday are we celebrating next week? Let me see those hands." Several went up, and one child was called on to say "Thanksgiving."

"That's right. And why do we celebrate Thanksgiving?"

This time there were no hands raised.

"Come, children. Who settled America?" No hands. "The Pilgrims, right?" The children nodded soberly. "Was it easy for the Pilgrims when they first came here?" That was a simple one, and several hands and backsides rose. "No," said the chosen boy. "That's right, Freddie, it was very hard for them, wasn't it, class? They had no food, no houses. And they had to work very hard. Now, does anyone know why the Pilgrims carried guns?"

If anyone knew, no one was telling. "To shoot the Indians," she answered herself. I almost left then and there, but breeding will tell —and so will curiosity. I really wanted to find out how it all came out.

"Well, boys and girls," she smiled, "the Pilgrims managed to find food and to build houses, and when the next fall came they were so grateful to be alive and so happy that their harvest had been good that they decided to have a big party. They even invited some Indians. And whom did they thank?"

"God," someone called out.

"Oh, Harry, you must raise your hand or I can't hear you. Now, whom did they thank?"

This time Harry raised his hand.

"Yes, Harry?"

"God."

"That's right, Harry. They thanked God. And that's why it's called Thanksgiving. They were giving thanks. Now, who knows why we eat turkey at Thanksgiving? Yes, Margot."

"Because it's good."

"Right. But why else?" I wondered whether it had ever occurred to her that some of her children might not eat turkey at Thanksgiving or at any other time. I'm not sure that welfare checks and government-surplus foods recognize the holidays quite as fully as the school system.

"Because that's what the pilgrims ate?" someone asked. The teacher beamed.

"Now," she said, "let's sing that nice Thanksgiving song we've been practicing for our mommies and daddies."

She rose and moved slowly to the piano, and they began to sing a song that, tuneless as it was, I recalled from my own early education. Continuity is a wondrous thing. After that it was milk and cookie time, and Kathy had a chance to shine. She had been appointed "sink monitor" (the job description reads "the person who stands at the sink and finks on the kids who throw their straws into it instead of into the wastebasket"), and she performed her chore without a hitch. The actual drinking of milk did not, of course, go as smoothly. There was the inevitable spillage (Jose, naturally) to the accompaniment of shrieks from Mrs. Winter. She included all of us parents in a comradely scowl and, eyes rolling heavenward, shoulders shrugging, and arms thrown out, let out her breath in exasperation and said, "He's always spilling something."

Poor Jose didn't fare much better when we were invited to accompany the class upstairs for its art lesson. Someone got pushed, though not, I noticed, by Jose. Still, he was in the vicinity and got screeched at for his manners. By this time I was strung tight (I wondered how the kids managed to keep their cool in the midst of the constant shrieking or controlled, clenched-teeth smile), and I looked forward to a period of relief in the art room. It was Mrs. Winter's free period, and after shepherding the children up the stairs, she vanished. As we went up she confided to me that it was most unfair of the art teacher to make these little children go all the way up to the third floor (I thought it must be a welcome change from sitting cramped at their tables) when it would be so much easier for her to come downstairs. Though she did not say so, I suspect that Mrs. Winter's complaint concerned her climb more than the children's.

If I had thought art class would bring relief, I was soon corrected. After another catechism of the upcoming holiday (though this time the children knew the proper responses—hooray for education!), the art teacher, a young blonde woman in a smock that almost hid her pregnancy, handed out 8" x 11" sheets of colored paper and three crayons per child and asked them to make a Thanksgiving picture. The girls set to work diligently. Most of the boys were finished after making a few quick scrawls. The teacher spent the rest of the period (was it only thirty minutes?) trying, unsuccessfully, to keep them in their seats. They were very inventive in their mutiny. Some of the boys began to karate chop the crayons.

"Oh, boys, what's your name? You mustn't do that. The crayons are your friends . . ."

She trailed off despairingly as more boys joined the fray. Papers began to fly. So did the boys. Several of them were, by this time, wrestling on the floor. I looked at my watch. So did the art teacher.

Ten more minutes to go, and by now half the boys were rolling on the floor. The girls still worked at their pictures. Finally, the teacher could stand no more. With eight minutes left till relief came, she collected what remained of the crayons, collected the pictures, and lined the children up in the hall where they all squirmed in line, or rolled around in the hall, until Mrs. Winter puffed back upstairs for them. The quiet tension of the kindergarten room seemed a haven by then—for me, at any rate.

On my next visit to the kindergarten, when we were all invited to watch the children's Christmas show, I was expecting less and my expectations were met. It was more of the same, with jingle bells. There was no mention made of Chanukah, which does happen to fall around the same time as Christmas and which some of the children celebrate, at least nominally. There was much talk of Santy Claus—by Mrs. Winter—and what he brings good little boys and girls (alas, poor Jose again). There was much talk also of white Christmases. Never once did she ask the children how they celebrated Christmas in Puerto Rico, whether snow and Christmas were inextricably bound, nor did she ask whether any of them knew any Spanish Christmas songs. What a wonderful opportunity it would have been for a Spanish-speaking child to have taught his classmates something of his culture! I exchanged *sotto voce* comments on the program with the mother sitting next to me, a pretty black woman who subsequently confided to me that her son ran a close second to Jose in incurring the teacher's displeasure, and I was glad to find, at least, that I was not alone in my objections to the class.

"Mrs. Hess, could I see you for a moment?" Kathy's teacher asked one day when I came for her. "We're going on a class trip, and we need a few parents to go along. Could you get some for us?" I agreed to try, and spent the afternoon calling people, all of whom were unable to make it. I couldn't go myself because I had no place to leave Sam and because I could not be certain that the bus would return in time for me to pick up Margaret. The next morning I met Mrs. Ferrer and asked her whether she could accompany the class. She was not certain but said she would let Mrs. Winter know. I reported my efforts to Mrs. Winter, mentioning the fact that Mrs. Ferrer was a maybe instead of an unqualified no.

The morning of the trip I met Mrs. Ferrer as I was leaving school. She was dressed for travel, with stockings, heels, and makeup instead of her usual cotton housedress.

"Oh," I said, "I see you're going. Have a good time."

She smiled at me and we parted. Twenty minutes later, after having taken Margaret to nursery, I again met Mrs. Ferrer. This time she was leaving the school.

"Aren't you going?" I asked, puzzled.

"They're not leaving yet," she answered.

"But they must be leaving soon, if they're to be back by 11:20 Why don't you go back and wait?"

She shrugged, and I didn't want to push, so I went about my business. But when I returned to pick up Kathy there was Mrs. Ferrer, with all the other parents, waiting for the delayed bus.

"You didn't go?" I asked needlessly.

She shrugged and smiled apologetically. When the bus finally returned, I followed Mrs. Winter inside and asked why Mrs. Ferrer hadn't accompanied the class.

"Oh, Mrs. Hess," she said, "I knew she wanted to go, but we already had so many parents from the other classes that we really didn't need her. If she had asked, of course, I would have let her come, but as long as she didn't, I thought it was just as well."

I was speechless with fury. The only proper response, at that point, would have been to punch her in the nose, but, alas, I'm too civilized. So I stood there and said nothing and finally turned and left. Walter was furious, too, when I told him, but with *me*.

"You mean you didn't say anything?"

"I was speechless."

"Oh, come off it. You should have told her off."

"I know—but I was really so taken aback that for the life of me I couldn't think of anything to say—and Kathy and some of the other kids were around . . ." I added lamely.

He was right, of course. I should have said something then and there.

"Next time she asks me to get parents for a trip I'll refuse. I'll tell her that after the way she treated Mrs. Ferrer, I wouldn't subject anyone else to that kind of insult. And then people wonder why Spanish parents stop being involved in the schools. It doesn't take too many things like this to do it."

"Don't tell me," said Walter. "Tell her."

"I will. Next time she asks me to get her some parents."

But she never asked me again, either because they never needed parents again or because she didn't like the "kind" of parents I found for her. So I never got to tell her what a terrible thing she had done, and I'm sure she never realized it on her own. I can imagine my mother in a similar situation. My mother, after a lifetime of rejections, is very sensitive to slights, real and imagined, and had she been in Mrs. Ferrer's shoes I know she would have reacted the same way. She wouldn't have pressed forward either. She would have withdrawn, hurt, and would never have come near the school again unless summoned on official business. I had been amazed at the speakout by the tremendous hostility against teachers. I was beginning to understand the reason.

FOUR

A Principal Sets the Tone
of the School

"How come you never come to PA meetings?" Anne asked me one day.

"I never knew they had any," I answered.

"Well," she said, "we're having a little trouble with publicity. It's hard to get fliers out. Listen, we're having a parent-faculty conference on reading this afternoon at three. Why don't you come?"

"I'll have to see if I can get a sitter. Where is it?"

"In the library. Try to come. Mrs. Wachtel is going to give us last year's reading scores for the school."

The library was about half filled when I arrived. There were, perhaps, fifteen parents present and about an equal number of teachers. Since this was not the regular monthly faculty conference, attendance for teachers was voluntary. Most of the teachers who were there were under thirty. Many of them were the same ones who had been on strike and who had been teaching in the Freedom School. Kathy's teacher was not there, nor were most of the others whose concern for the welfare of their children had been too deep to enable them to strike. Their concern, however, obviously did not extend to a discussion of the school's reading problem—at least not on their own time. And though they were not, at that time, members of the union (they became staunch unionists and worshipers of Albert Shanker in 1968), they were all well aware of the contract that stipulated only one after-school compulsory meeting per month.

The sun streamed in through the large windows, reflecting off the glossy covers of the illustrated books on display on the shelves. Children's art decorated the walls. There was a low buzz of conversation, and cigarette smoke curled lazily upward into the shafts of sunlight. I found a seat amid the parents who sat, for the most part, separated from the teachers. Again I noted the absence of black and Spanish parents, though by this time no longer with any surprise. Also by this time I recognized some of the teachers and some of the parents from the few meetings I had attended and from simply passing them on the street. But I still felt pretty much like an outsider and an observer.

Anne, who was chairing the meeting, called it to order and said that, in addition to a presentation and discussion of the reading scores, there would be a discussion of the after-school study center and that that part of the meeting would be chaired by Sonia Plowden. She then introduced Mrs. Wachtel, who, after a few brief introductory remarks about reading tests in general, proceeded to read us the scores for each grade. She seized her glasses from the chain around her neck, put them on, and pulled herself up to her full six feet as she said,

"These are the scores for the Metropolitan Achievement Test for grade three."

"What about the second grade?" someone asked.

"Since we just begin reading in second grade, we don't test the children; so we have no scores for them. Now, for grade three . . ." As she read, we took notes. The picture was uniformly bleak. In no grade were more than 50 percent of the children reading on or above grade level. In the upper grades, where many of the middle-class children transferred to private schools (both because inner-city school problems intensify as the children get older and because their parents feared the junior high school scene and wanted to insure their children's admission elsewhere), the scores got worse, so that although there were still some children reading several years above their grade level the rate of retardation in general had increased. In other words, children were falling farther behind as their schooling progressed, and more of them were doing so—as many as 60 percent of the upper-graders. And when one stopped to think that a sixth-grader reading on a second grade level would go into junior high school because he had already been left back once, was thirteen, and therefore was mandated for promotion, it was most discouraging.

"Why are so many children reading below grade level?" was one of the first questions.

"There are many reasons. First of all, there may be a physical problem. The child may have poor vision or poor hearing. Or he may have a language problem. Or he may come from a home where no one reads. This is *so* important. When my daughter was growing up, she always saw us with books, and naturally she couldn't wait to read. I can't emphasize enough how important that is to your children. And then, of course, some children are late bloomers and get off to a slow start. Once they start, though, they catch up in no time."

'Tell that to the mother of a dropout,' I thought.

"Some children," she continued," who are perfectly normal have emotional blocks that keep them from learning. Very often we find they've been pushed too much, from too early an age. That's why we don't teach formal reading till second grade."

Considering the scores, I shuddered to think what the results would have been if reading had been started earlier. I also wondered, irreverently, whether if we eliminated formal reading instruction altogether the picture would not be rosier. Since no one would be taught (and, therefore, tested) no one would be reading below grade level. Perhaps that was the ultimate solution, but I refrained from suggesting it. Meanwhile, Mrs. Wachtel was droning on.

". . . look at the comparative scores in *The New York Times*, you'll find that our school did no worse than most of the schools in the district. And further," and she treated us to a forced smile, "you must realize that things aren't really so terrible, After all, if 50 percent of the children are reading below grade level it also means that 50 percent are reading on or above level. That means half of our children are reading as well as, or better than, the city average. That's a pretty good record. Besides," she continued, pulling her trump card, "you must remember that with a bell curve you always have to have 50 percent above average and 50 percent below average. So we really come out right."

I shook my head in disbelief. Granted I'm not a statistician, but I did learn something of bell curves in college; and though it's true that the distribution in the general population will always fall as she said, there was nothing that I had ever read that said the distribution could not start at grade level. Failure was not irrevocably written into the curve. Then, to belie even her statement that everything was as it should be, she ended her recital with the homily that, of course, there was room for improvement. Now, if we fell right smack into a perfect bell curve and if that was where we should be, then where was the room for improvement, without destroying the curve and causing all those statisticians to tear out their hair? All in all, it was a stunning performance. As fascinating as the lecture in statistics had been, her evaluation of the reading problem was equally fascinating. (What problem? We're right on center.) Of all the contributory factors to low reading scores, the one factor that was conspicuous by its absence was the school. Uncorrected physical problems (why did they go uncorrected if they were known?), emotional problems and blocks (where was the Bureau of Child Guidance?), the perennial poor home environment—all were causes of a nonexistent failure. Only the school was blameless. I ventured a question along those lines and was told about the remedial reading program and the TESL* program.

"And of course if we find a child has a physical or emotional problem we refer him. But after all, there's only so much the school can do."

There we were again. The school, which is charged with educating the children, is the only faultless one when they remain uneducated. Remedial and corrective programs are all very good; but perhaps if the schools were educating the children to begin with, they might not be so necessary—especially since they are so rarely successful.

Having disposed of the subject of reading, the meeting now turned to the after-school study center. Sonia Plowden, a tall, gangling, dark-haired woman, who was at that time very active in the Stryckers Bay Neighborhood Council and in the West Side Committee for Decentralization, told us that the center was funded out of the Title† programs. The purpose of the center was to give remedial help to those children who were behind in their studies. Since the money came from Title funds, the children who were intended as its primary beneficiaries were the poor. However, for some reason, as the questioning soon elicited, very few of them were availing themselves of the opportunity. The reason for this also became quickly apparent. Staffing of the center, in accordance with the UFT

---

*Teaching English as a Second Language.
†Federal money allotted under the Elementary and Secondary Education Act (ESEA) to remedy academic retardation in poverty-group children.

contract, was by strict seniority. The teachers who wanted the jobs and had been in the school longest were hired. And since, it developed, these were the very teachers who were not reaching the children from nine to three, it was small wonder that the children did not choose to return for another dose of failure after school. Sonia was having a rough time of it, mainly from Irene Martins, who kept asking the hard questions that gave me this information.

I left the meeting feeling very depressed. On the few occasions in the past that I had seen the principal, my feelings about her had been fairly neutral. She had seemed, at least, like a pretty decent type—not overly creative or innovative, given to the usual clichés and jargon, but then, so are most principals I've met. I had not been impressed by her performance at the the tea for new parents, but she had indicated, I thought, some feeling for children. But at this meeting I was appalled. And this was the new principal for whom everyone had had such high hopes. That she was an apologist for the status quo was not too surprising, but that she seemed so inept was. And yet it was she who was entrusted with the education of over nine hundred children!

Many people feel that a principal is really unimportant, that if you have a school with good teachers (a big if) all that school needs is an efficient administrator, a super paper-pusher to see that supplies come in and that the million and one forms that are such an integral part of administering a school are properly filled out and sent back to some other administrator elsewhere. I have never agreed with that theory, for I feel that a principal must set the tone of the school. He must give direction to the teachers (even good teachers), encourage excellence, and come down heavily on teachers who are not performing their functions properly. Even with the New York City tenure system, where people, once they are off probation, are locked securely into their jobs (practically the only way a tenured teacher can be fired is if he rapes a child on the stage of the auditorium in front of at least twenty unimpeachable witnesses who are willing to testify against a colleague), it is possible for a good principal to put pressure on teachers. There are always undesirable assignments to be doled out. There is always the threat of frequent, even daily, observations. Lesson plans can be meticulously checked. And in extreme cases there is always the threat of an unsatisfactory rating. On the whole principals use these weapons sparingly; and where they do use them, it is often for political rather than for pedagogical reasons. But they are, nevertheless, tools that a good principal can use effectively. Furthermore, a good principal can let her teachers know just what is expected of them and what will not be tolerated. In a school where a principal makes it quite clear that bigotry will not be tolerated, teachers (who are a most accommodating breed) will mend, if not their morals, at least their manners.

But from the performance I had witnessed that afternoon, I had to conclude that this was not a good principal. And I had heard from various teachers that she was capable of making their teaching lives miserable. Supplies were withheld for long periods of time. Teaching materials met undue delays in the rexograph room, so that by the time they were returned the need for them had long passed. Innovations were vetoed.

Nancy Calvert tells the story of trying to teach her music class some Kurt Weill songs and receiving a frenzied veto because the songs were not on the prescribed Board of Education list. On another occasion, a Bach Cantata was similarly vetoed, this time because it violated the separation of Church and State. When Nancy took that one to the District Superintendent he asked, "What's that? Piano music?" Small wonder, then, that the good teachers felt thwarted and stifled at every turn. On the other hand, the teachers who made the racist remarks, who, year after year, sent only black and Spanish children into Junior Guidance classes, whose children tuned out or dropped out and whose reading scores nosedived, continued to bask in the approval of the principal.

On one occasion a mother asked me to accompany her to the principal's office to complain about the fact that her son's teacher had slapped him. This was the second such incident with this particular teacher. We had learned that on any occasion when we went to school with a problem we did not go alone, and so I went along. Mrs. Wachtel conceded that the teacher had on the previous occasion hit the child and had admitted it. She had been warned (though not in writing) that this must not happen again. On this occasion the teacher denied the episode; and Mrs. Wachtel, without talking to the child or to the other children in the class, accepted her word for it.

"You see," she said to us, "just because a teacher is honest and admits a mistake, she is harassed. No wonder teachers deny things."

It is this kind of attitude that makes teachers feel they are immune from the laws that govern most of us. Corporal punishment violates a bylaw of the New York City Board of Education!

A principal sets the tone of the school. Every morning, when I brought Kathy to class, we would pass the older children lined up in the yard or, in inclement weather, in the lunchroom. Strict silence was enforced by means of whistles blown shrilly into microphones. An occasional bellow would also be transmitted to some malefactor at the back. These sounds, and the accompanying tensions, would follow us as I led Kathy to her room. (Kindergartners were spared the lineup for their first year.) Once the children were sent upstairs, all hell broke loose. After standing coiled for ten to fifteen minutes, they were ready to spring; and heaven help anyone who got in the way of their charge. It resembled a stampede more than a school. And of course the period of repression at the start of the school day carried over into the classroom, so that the children were already angry and resentful.

On mornings when we were late, we could watch the late line. Trembling children waited rigidly while they were interrogated by a thin-lipped woman with a whistle around her neck.

"Why were you late?" she would spit at them through clenched teeth and would wait while they paled, most of the time too terrorized to answer. She scared *me*. I fully expected her to stop me, on many a morning, and ask for *my* late pass; and all the days of my junior high school nightmare, peopled by her spiritual sisters, came back to haunt me.

The trouble with fear as a disciplinary tool is that it is only effective as long as the object of fear is in the vicinity. As soon as she leaves, things return to normal, or worse. A child after such an interrogation would not be any easier for his classroom teacher to deal with as a result. Those teachers whose classrooms were also armed camps managed to contain their children, but those who were not as strong had a hard time of it. Children who are characterized as "animals" by their teachers (and treated accordingly) tend to live up to those expectations. The lunchroom, supervised by aides rather than by teachers, was unqualified bedlam. Food was thrown through the air; children were shoved; the place was a mess. All of it tended to confirm the theory that the children were animals and the adults their reluctant keepers.

After hearing Mrs. Wachtel's sanguine acceptance of reading failure as the normal condition, I began to understand somewhat the overall tone of the school. And I did not like it.

FIVE

"If the Parents Don't Care,
Why Should the School?"

The school year continued. I attended an occasional meeting, but for the most part I was busy with other things. Since Kathy was apparently happy at PS 84 (though I was not), I did not spend a great deal of time there. I took her to school, I picked her up, I attended conferences when asked; and if I got a notice of a meeting, I went. That was the extent of my involvement. I had paid my $1.00 in dues, so I was nominally a member of the Parents' Association. I really had no great desire to become more involved, since my concept of a Parents' Association dated back to the time when I was in school and the PA was a do-good organization that provided sneakers and glasses for the deserving poor and ran cake sales to provide the funds. All the magazine articles on PTA's had done nothing to make me change my basic image; and though it is true that at the few meetings I had attended that was hardly the tone, still I did not feel that the PA was more than a discussion club (not a very polite one, at that); and I didn't have enough spare time to want to waste it on a powerless, frivolous outfit.

So the year wore on. It was early February when I got a notice saying that because of parent-teacher conferences class time would be shortened, for a period of two weeks, for kindergarten and first-grade children. These children did not get report cards, and this was the only way to let their parents know how they were doing. The kindergarten children came at their normal time, but were to be picked up at 10:30. The first-graders were to report an hour later than usual. I didn't give the matter much thought, beyond that it was a pain in the neck for me, because no sooner had I delivered Kathy to school than I had to take Margaret, and no sooner had I dropped Margaret off than it was time to pick up Kathy, and by the time I got home and took off her clothes it was time to put them on again and go out to get Margaret. All this with Sam in tow in the stroller. It was also a particularly cold February, which made the whole thing even more of a nuisance. But that was the way it was, and every day I got on my merry-go-round and looked forward to the peaceful afternoons in the community room with fifty or so children tossing blocks at each other.

One morning—the temperature was in the low teens, and a fierce wind was blowing so that the block-and-a-half walk to school seemed endless (the chill factor, that marvelous invention of the weather bureau, must have been minus something)—we got to the playground in front of the school, and I saw a little black girl standing near one of the benches crying. She couldn't have been more than seven or eight. She was wearing a shabby coat and hat; and the tears were freezing on her face. I asked her what was the matter, and she stood mute. The street was deserted. An occasional child scurried by, head down against the wind, hands jammed into his pockets, and dashed into the first open school door. I was half frozen myself, and Kathy's nose was as red as Santa Claus'. Again I asked the little girl what was wrong, and still she didn't answer. I asked her whether she went to PS 84, and she nodded. I put my arm around her shoulders and began to propel her gently toward the school, saying that in that case she should come with me and cry inside, if she must, because at least it was warmer there. Wordlessly she let me nudge her along while I continued to chatter just to keep her moving. As soon as we got inside, she brightened visibly, and I thought that whatever it was had been solved.

The school door leads directly to a staircase. From there you open a door and enter the first-floor corridor, on one side of which are classrooms, on the other the cafeteria and the late line. We had fortunately missed the late line, and I led Kathy and the little girl down the long corridor and through the double swinging doors that lead to the center of the school where one corridor continues to the main office and another, at right angles, leads to the opposite wing of the building where the kindergarten classes are located. We had no sooner passed through the swinging doors than we were greeted by a short, bald man in a shapeless gray suit with vest. He was one of the guidance counselors, and he began to scream at the little girl.

"What are you doing here? Don't you know you're not supposed to come till ten o'clock?"

The little girl shrank against me. She looked as though she was about to turn tail and brave the cold again, as the less threatening alternative. I kept my arm around her shoulder, and said that I had found her crying outside, and that I had brought her in because of the cold.

"Well," he said grudgingly, "since you're here, go up to the library for today. But tomorrow make sure you don't come till ten."

The little girl scurried away, and I took Kathy and delivered her to class. Still I did not think too much about it beyond the fact that I felt sorry for the little girl and was appalled at the way she had just been treated.

The next day the temperature dropped some more, and the winds roared around from the park to the river and back in fierce gusts. The radio cheerfully announced that not only was it the coldest day of the year (that wasn't such a big deal; the year had hardly begun), but it was the coldest day in the last fifty-six years, and the lowest for the day since they had begun keeping records back in eighteen something or other. With those words of encouragement, I bundled Kathy into an extra sweater and her snowsuit, wrapped a scarf around what was left of her face, and, feeling like Admiral Byrd, went out to face the polar winds. When we were blown at the school entrance, we almost collided with a little boy, also black, huddled against the slight protection the space between the door and the edge of the building offered. He looked us over, and said to Kathy,

"You in kindergarten?"

She nodded. I think her teeth had frozen together.

"You're lucky," he continued. "I'm in first grade and I have to stay out here till ten."

'The hell you do,' I thought. Aloud I told him to come inside with us, and he willingly allowed me to shepherd him up the few steps and through the door into the corridor. This time I went looking for the guidance counselor. He was at his station, and when he spied the little boy he began screaming at him—a repetition of yesterday's scene, with only a minor change in cast. This time, though, I said I wanted to speak to him and that I would return as soon as I took Kathy to class.

"You shouldn't make the children stay outside in this cold, Mr. Olivieri," I began when I returned.

"They're not supposed to be here," he said. "It's conference time, and they're not due till ten."

"I know that," I said, "but they're here. You can't just let them stay outside and freeze."

"They're not supposed to be here. We sent out notices."

"I know that," I said, "but they're here. You can't just let them stay outside and freeze. It's the coldest day of the year," I added. I was beginning to feel that I wasn't getting through.

"But we sent notices home," he repeated. "Their parents shouldn't send them so early."

"Their parents may not have a choice," I said. "They may work, and they can't change their hours because the school schedules conferences. I don't suppose many of them are bank presidents." He bristled at my sarcasm and what had until then been a friendly conversation (at least on the surface) turned considerably cooler. He drew himself up stiffly and his face tightened.

"That's not our responsibility. We sent a notice home. If they cared about their children, they'd make other arrangements."

"Maybe it's because they care about their children that they're here now," I said.

By this time I was furious and sweating, both because of the many layers of clothing I was wearing in the steam-heated hallways and because of my anger. I opened my coat.

"If they didn't care, they'd let those little children come to school by themselves at ten. But because they do, they bring them at the regular time or send them with an older brother or sister who's on a regular schedule. And the school has a responsibility for those children. You can't just leave them out there in the cold."

"Responsibility," he said. "Of course we do. That's why we notify their parents. Then it's *their* responsibility."

"Don't you understand?" I said. "If the school changes the schedule, it's the school's responsibility to make provisions for these children."

"Oh, we can't do that," he said. "Where would we put them?"

"In the library. In the auditorium. In the lunchroom. There must be someplace they can go where it's warm."

"Oh, we can't do that. We don't have any teachers who are free to supervise them."

"There must be an aide—or a parent—who'd be willing."

"But that's illegal," he said with real horror. "Do you realize what it would mean if something happened? Why, our insurance would be useless. You must have a licensed teacher with children at all times."

"So you'll let them stand out there and freeze because you're worried about insurance?"

"What else can we do? And it really isn't our responsibility. If the parents cared . . . "

I turned and stalked off. We weren't talking the same language. I was talking about children, and he was talking about insurance. Besides, even if you granted him, for the sake of argument, that the children's parents didn't care, then that was all the more reason why the school should. The school functions *in loco parentis;* and if the parent abdicates, then it seems to me that the school must take over. And someone ought to care that those kids were freezing out there, in the shadow of a warm (physically—the emotional temperature rivaled the outside) school building. Besides, I was unwilling to grant that the parents did not care, although it was an easy out for the administration. If the parents didn't care why should the school? That carried over into other areas as well. Parents don't come when they're summoned; obviously they don't care, so why should the school? Children aren't learning; if the parents don't care, why should the school? The school is paid to teach the children; but if the parents don't care, it's not the school's responsibility.

I hardly felt the cold as I stormed home—I was steaming with rage. I kept thinking of those two little children. They were in the library—for the day—but what about all the others whom I hadn't met or who, faced with a bleak hour outside the building chose instead to wander the streets where all sorts of dangers abounded? Columbus Avenue is a busy thoroughfare—a bus and truck route made even more dangerous by the presence of the construction sites and their concomitant traffic. How easily a small child, his head bowed against the winds, could ignore the light and be struck down. But of course that was not the school's responsibiliy. The neighborhood is full of hustlers, addicts, and perverts. There are many abandoned buildings where a small child might seek warmth and find death or terror. But that is not the school's responsibility. The notice said to come at ten, so the school is not responsible. The definition of democracy I had always been taught was that the individual is more important than the institution. Perhaps someone should teach that to the school system!

I reached home twice as angry as when I'd left school. I thought of all sorts of other things I should have said (though I doubt to any greater effect). I felt helpless. It seemed to me that something had to be done, but what and by whom I didn't know. I had a feeling that Mrs. Wachtel would take the same position as her guidance counselor. So I spoke to Anne about it, and she was also outraged. I said I'd be happy to write it up as a formal complaint, and she said to hold off—that she would take it up with the principal. Nothing more came of it. The weather turned warmer, the conference period ended, and we were busy with other things. But it was another lesson for me on the effect of thoughtlessness on the children of the poor.

The conferences, obviously, weren't scheduled to inconvenience or harm the poor children. It only worked out that way in practice. For the middle-class or well-to-do parent the schedule may have been a pain, but the child was assured a safe escort at the proper time. It was only the working parents without maids, and in our neighborhood there are a good many, to whom it presented a problem. And if the school does not have a legal responsibility to recognize this fact, it nevertheless has a moral obligation to do so. Had a child been injured or harmed during this period the school might have been legally blameless, but the sin would have been on its head. Fortunately it did not happen. But even without any catastrophes, how does a child feel toward an institution that lets him stand in the cold for an hour? Is it any wonder that the children and their parents feel the schools don't care?

SIX

Grade Conferences: "There's So
Much Learning That's Not
in Books"

It was a big year for conferences of every description. There were
parent-faculty conferences, where the parents and faculty who
spoke to each other came together to speak to each other, inhibited
by the presence of the principal who would, if she had had her
choice, have spoken to neither group. That segment of the faculty
who never spoke to the parents stayed away. It was comical to watch,
from the hallway outside the library where we waited for the staff
conference to be completed, how, at precisely 3:45, a bloc of teachers arose, picked up their purses, drew on their white gloves, and
marched out en masse. They often left in the middle of someone's
sentence (these molders of our children's manners); but a contract
was a contract, and they could not be kept beyond their required
time. And who could blame them? For years they had been punching a time clock, and every minute's lateness was circled in red ink
and totaled monthly to become a subject of a memo that was included in their file. It was of no consequence that they might at one
time have spent hours above what was required helping a child with
his work or talking to a parent who could not come during school
hours. A minute late is a minute late. Be that as it may, this group
had become time servers; and anyway, they were not interested in
what parents had to say, so they left. The system doesn't only kill
children.

In addition to the parent-faculty conferences, there were the
teacher-parent conferences where a parent might or might not find

out how his child was progressing. I had discovered at mine that Kathy was a "lovely child"; and since I did not wish to probe, I never asked for a definition. A good thing, too, because a friend of mine, on another occasion, after having been told that her kindergarten daughter was a lovely child, asked *her* teacher how the child was doing, and lo and behold, a torrent poured forth detailing all of the child's high crimes and misdemeanors and ending with the thought that the child was seriously disturbed and ought, perhaps, not to be in school—or should at least be under sedation. Which goes to show that one should let lovely children lie.

Finally, there were the grade conferences. The idea behind them was sound: the parents of children in each grade should get together with the teachers for that grade and discuss curriculum, child development, problems, and whatever else each group felt important. The idea for such conferences came, I believe, from the Parent's Association, which is probably the reason it took some time to implement (Mrs. Wachtel did not respond with alacrity to PA ideas), so that by the time these conferences came about it was March and the term was going downhill. The conference, therefore, had lost something of its relevance. I, for example, was no longer very much interested in the kindergarten curriculum. Alas, I knew, first-hand, what it was. Nor was I waiting with baited breath to know what to expect from a five year old about to embark on his first public-school venture or what was typical five-year-old behavior. At that point I was more concerned about the curriculum of the first grade and what six year olds were all about. Still, as a kindergarten mother I was invited to the kindergarten grade conference, there to learn about the joys of coloring turkeys.

The kindergarten grade conference took place in one of the kindergarten rooms (to give us the feel of the place, perhaps). Baby-sitting was thoughtfully provided by the school in the persons of the paraprofessionals who, unfortunately, were not asked in advance whether they wished to volunteer their free time for that purpose and consequently (and rightly) grumbled about it for days afterwards.

The room was filled to capacity with parents, and while we waited for the meeting to begin, we had a chance to observe the children's work. It was amazing how such diverse children as evidenced by their diverse parents here gathered together could produce such identical work. This was not Kathy's classroom, and yet I could have sworn that at least half of the flowers on the walls were hers. Though each classroom was equipped with Creative Playthings hand puppets and dolls, which come in a variety of races, the children's drawings on the walls all depicted white figures. Small wonder, when even on the door of one of the junior-guidance rooms, (where all the children are black and Spanish and the teacher is black) there was a picture cut from a magazine of a white family, under which was hand lettered WE WELCOME OUR FAMILIES.

Mrs. Wachtel wore her usual uniform of a double-knit suit, adorned by the glasses on a chain and touched off by her space shoes. Her welcome-the-parent smile was also officially in place, although her hair was less disciplined, looking for all the world as though it mirrored its owner's wish to escape in any and all directions. The room was overheated and stuffy and bore the traces of the smell of children too long confined. Mrs. Wachtel sniffed in an offended fashion, stamped over to the windows, hoisted the window pole like a lance, and opened the windows the regulation three inches from the top, casting an accusing glance at the teacher in whose domain we were gathered. I'm sure her next observation report would contain a sentence about proper ventilation. Since the window shades were all lined up in accurate formation we could now begin, with some words of welcome from our principal.

She then introduced Dr. Hillard, a psychiatrist from the Jewish Board of Guardians who was working in the school. I had heard that JBG was providing psychological services to the children and had thought 'That's good,' since I knew from my own teaching experience how little was forthcoming from the Bureau of Child Guidance. Dr. Hillard outlined for us one aspect of his organization's work at PS 84: the early-identification program. He said that all the kindergarten children were being observed by JBG to help spot learning or emotional difficulties at this early stage of the child's education. This made me very uneasy, because it seemed to me that a child, by being identified as a potential problem, might, in fact, become one by virtue of this identification. The heretical thought also crossed my mind that perhaps they ought to observe the teachers as well, to identify those who *cause* the problems in the children. I did not voice my feelings, but I was thereafter wary of the role of the Jewish Board of Guardians in the school. Dr. Hillard concluded with the hope that parents would feel free to approach him with any problems they had at any time.

Then Mrs. Wachtel spoke again, saying that she felt a major concern of the parents was with the kindergarten curriculum. She said it was very difficult for a parent to determine what a child does in school by asking him, since at that stage of development he can rarely verbalize it, and that a main focus of kindergarten was to get the children to find words to describe what they are doing. I thought of Kathy's classroom, where discussion, except under the most circumscribed conditions, was discouraged. But it sounded good in theory.

She then read, at great length, from the *Early Childhood Manual* to give a picture of a typical kindergarten day. Board of Ed prose is many things—but not brief. In the interests of democracy, Mrs. Wachtel stopped and turned the floor over to Miss Federman, her assistant principal, who continued reading from the manual, in rolling cadences, all the jargon and cant that I vaguely remembered from my courses in education at college (which hadn't impressed me then, either). When she finished, with a smile and a flourish, she threw the ball back to Mrs. Wachtel who told us that there was no formal math or reading instruction in kindergarten.

"What about children who are ready for it?" someone asked.

"Oh, they get reading work. But not with readers. I know you parents lay great stress on textbooks, but there's so much learning that can take place outside of books. Why, look at this neighborhood. Central Park is only a half block away, and there's so much for them to learn there: science, botany, zoology."

That was lovely, and perfectly true, except that Kathy's class had not been to Central Park once during the entire year. And, from what I had heard from those teachers who talked to parents, neither had most of the other classes, for the teachers were discouraged by Mrs. Wachtel from taking their children to the park on the grounds that it might disturb the elderly people who used it. So much for science!

"And mathematics," she went on, warming to her subject. "There's so much mathematics they can learn just by walking around the block and watching the buildings rise. Why, they can count the windows, the floors as they go up—there's a limitless number of things they can learn from the construction in the area. All of that is much better, and more meaningful to children, than having math books."

I looked at Dotty Steinberg, one of my neighbors, whose son was in another of the kindergartens, and smiled. Our kids hadn't taken any walks around the block, either. The furthest they had gotten outside the school (except for the occasional carefully prepared trip) was for recess into the small yard behind the school where the concrete had caved in due to faulty construction. I suppose they could learn a lot of math there, by charting the rate of progressive concavity in the concrete or by counting the rats that lived in the holes; but the construction sites, as well as the park, might have been on the moon for all the contact the children had with them in the course of the school day. Still, it was an indisputable fact that they offered a rich alternative to the Dick-and-Jane books that they didn't get either.

Finally, we were told that education did not end with the school day, and we were urged to take walks with our children around the neighborhood and to take them to the park after school and on weekends. Then time ran out and so did the principal and her assistant before any parent with an unanswered question could engage them further. Dotty, Millie Miller, and I walked home together —uplifted by the thought that we were living in such an educationally rich environment and voicing the idea that grade conferences might be improved by the absense of the administration.

The first-grade conference, which Dotty, Millie, and I, as well as a number of other kindergarten parents, crashed (after we had tried, unsuccessfully, to get an official invitation from Mrs. Wachtel), had several advantages over the kindergarten conference. In the first place, it took place in a first-grade room where the chairs were, mercifully for my long legs, a bit higher off the ground. Secondly, since first grade was still an untrod path for us, we were less able to contradict, with unpleasant personal knowledge, the rosy picture that might be painted.

The dramatis personae again included the principal, Miss Federman, the guidance counselor, the first-grade coordinator, and a roomful of assorted parents. Mrs. Wachtel welcomed us, the kindergarten parents, enthusiastically. She said she was heartened that parents took such an interest and hoped our interest would not wane as our children advanced as, alas, too often happened. The teachers and some of the parents had brought their lunches and were eating. Mrs. Wachtel and Miss Federman apparently chose to dine only with their friends, or perhaps they lived on loftier stuff than the school lunches or the containers of cottage cheese that the teachers had on their trays.

I looked at the teachers and wondered which of them would be Kathy's for the following year. Since only one of them ever got a chance to say anything other than her name, I could only judge them by their appearances—hardly a rational basis for an evaluation. Three of them were very young and eager-looking; the other two, with pinched lips and bleached hair, were somewhere in that great span between forty and sixty. I had never seen either of them at a parent-faculty conference (they were part of the 3:45 exodus), and though they may both have been crackerjack teachers, they reminded me too much of the days of my youth to inspire me with any great confidence in their ability to deal gently with my daughter.

The host teacher on this occasion either was a better housekeeper than her kindergarten counterpart or else had been forewarned by her unfortunate sister. She had the windows properly opened so we were able to dispense with that small bit of stage business and get on with the meeting, which was chaired by Elizabeth O'Shea, a tall, pretty, pale blonde woman who was a member of the PA Executive Board. She tried, valiantly, to make of the meeting a conference— as it was advertised—instead of a lecture; but she is a gentle woman most of the time and it was a losing battle.

The first-grade conference, then, proved no more enlightening than the kindergarten one had been; and aside from being again less than enchanted by our principal, the only feeling I came away with was the hope, alas, unrealized, that Kathy would not be placed in the class of either of the two pinch-lipped teachers.

That was the last grade conference I attended that year, but from talking to parents of children in other grades, I gathered that that was about par for the course. In no case, so far as I heard, did they live up to the promise of parents and teachers really talking to each other for the sake of the education of the children.

SEVEN

The Birth of the Profile

My feeling about the school, by this time, was not so much a negative one as one of deep frustration. Every encounter there—official
or unofficial—had left me with a sense that this was not what a
school was supposed to be. And yet there were so many positive
things about the place. The building was new; many of the teachers
were truly good and dedicated; the parent body was active and had
many skills to offer the school if it chose to avail itself of them.
Moreover, the student population was ideally balanced with the
kind of integration that can be achieved only by a truly integrated
pattern of housing. The school and the district were in the forefront
of various efforts to improve education. At PS 84 the parents—
black, white, and Spanish-speaking—had fought to eliminate tracking, and when Kathy entered the school there were (in theory, at
least) no longer top and bottom classes. The IGC class (for intellectually gifted children) was being phased out so that once the remaining class of that kind graduated from the school, this vestige of
tracking would also cease to exist.

In addition to the abolition of the tracking system, the district had
acquired state funds for the eight-school balanced-class project.
This had been implemented only in those schools in the district
where the student population was diverse enough to make it feasi-
ble, and what it meant was that children were placed in classes that
reflected the ethnic composition of the school. At PS 84 this was
about 40 percent Spanish-speaking, 30 percent black, and 30 percent other, and classes were formed in keeping with this ratio.
Furthermore, the classes were to be of mixed ability levels, so that
there would be no "creaming" (placing all the highest achievers—

49

regardless of ethnic makeup—in the top class, and so on down to the bottom), which would have resulted merely in a colorful class, but with no true balance. The balanced-class project had been conceived because of the *Coleman Report*—and other similar studies—which had found that *all* children learn better when they are not segregated (either by race, economics, or ability). The study had proved that not only the slow children (or the black and Spanish and poor), but the others as well, benefited from such a mixture. For children learn from each other as much as, if not more than, from their teachers. Furthermore, children are not all of a piece, and a slow reader may be a brilliant mathematician, or vice versa. A child who is academically retarded may have other compensating skills which, if shared with his peers, may both benefit them and simultaneously increase his self-esteem so that his academic progress is enhanced.

Because of the balanced-class funds—which at that time extended only from first through third grade—the classes in those grades were smaller and were provided with additional paraprofessionals, since it was felt that a teacher instructing such a diverse group of children must, to reach them all, have more time to spend with them individually. For this reason, too, Mike Abraham, the director of the project in our district, was very much interested in teacher-training (or retraining) to enable them to cope with what was, for most of them, a very new ball game.

Most parents in the school were in favor of the balanced classes and of the elimination of tracking. Those who were not (and they were generally the upper- and middle-class parents who felt, all evidence to the contrary notwithstanding, that their children would suffer if placed with the others willy-nilly) tended to withdraw their children and put them into private schools—which most of them were prepared to do anyway when their children were ready for junior high. The rest of us, who had ourselves been victims of the tracking system when we went to school, applauded its demise. We did feel, however, that achieving balance was only the beginning and that once the children were in these balanced classes they must all be taught. That, alas, was not happening at PS 84.

And that is why I felt so frustrated by the school. Despite all the things it had going for it, it was a mess; and if the mess was less apparent than elsewhere in the inner city, it was only because there were still enough middle-class children there that the school made some effort to teach (or to train, which is something quite different). What made the situation so frustrating was that there seemed no hope of improving it. Mrs. Wachtel seemed quite satisfied with things the way they were. If she hoped for improvement it was only in the "quality" of the children who would be coming into the school as a result of the urban renewal then in progress. (One teacher happily confided in me that the school was already getting a much better grade of children—like eggs?—than only a few years back.) That there was something lacking in the quality of the education rather than in the quality of the children at the school seemed not to occur to its administration or to much of its staff; and since for change to be possible there must first exist a realization of the problem and a willingness to attack it, the likelihood of change coming from the administration seemed dim.

The Parents' Association tried. They had started a program of parents in the classroom—to give individual instruction to children under the guidance of the classroom teacher—in the hopes of improving the reading levels of some of the most seriously retarded readers. But the program was hamstrung by the fact that it was purely voluntary on the part of the teachers, and the very teachers who most feared a parent in the class were the ones whose children would have benefited most from having them there. In addition, Mrs. Wachtel would not allow any parent in the class who had not first undergone a training (screening?) session of several consecutive hours; and while many parents might have had an hour a day to give to the school, very few of them had a large chunk of time to undergo the training (which, in any case, was more of the pep talk previously described). So very few parents actually ever got into the classrooms, and they could not, obviously, make a dent in the existing problems.

The PA had also tried to improve the tone of the school by trying to persuade Mrs. Wachtel to do away with the daily lineup, which did not so much improve the children's behavior as make many of them hysterical. I don't know precisely how intimidated the "problem" children were by all the shouting and whistle-blowing, though I suspect they were immune to it and simply tuned it out. But for the children who were used to being more gently dealt with, it was a frightening experience, and many of the children of my friends suffered from daily stomachaches that disappeared as soon as they were late enough to escape the lineup and could safely go to school with a note from home explaining their lateness. In spite of the pleadings of the PA, Mrs. Wachtel refused to change the morning routine, as she could envision no other way to start the day.

My feeling of frustration about the school was not leading to anything constructive. I did a lot of grumbling and a lot of wishing that Kathy would be lucky enough to get a less sterile teacher in first grade; but as there seemed very little I could do about that, or about the school as a whole, I simply stayed away as much as possible.

One day Anne Best called me.

"Listen," she said, "I've been thinking. We really have to do something about PS 84. There are so many good things there, but the place is in a mess. Ronnie Rubin suggested that we do some kind of report on the school's strengths and all its weaknesses. And then we'd take it to the local school board and ask them to do something about it. Maybe get the Center for Urban Education, or MARC*, to come in and do the kind of objective study that we can't do and show us how we can solve our problems."

"That sounds like a good idea," I said. "I've had the feeling for quite a while now that somebody ought to do something. I just didn't know what."

"Good. Well, listen. We're going to propose the idea at the next general PA meeting, and I'm going to ask for volunteers to work on it. I'd like you to volunteer."

"But I don't know that much about the school," I protested. "This is my first year here."

"That doesn't matter. You've got a clear head, and you're pretty objective, and we need someone like you to work on it. There'll be other people who have more specific information, but we can use your thinking, and you can help us with the writing. The stuff you wrote for the co-op paper was very good."

Having thus tickled my vanity, she got her volunteer. It was more than that, really. Her idea offered a chance to take my sense of frustration and turn it into something that could be meaningful for the school.

"There's one thing, though," Anne went on. "Ronnie broached the idea with the Executive Board, and they voted it down. The constitution says that if the general membership votes for something, the Executive Board has to go along. There'll be opposition.

*Kenneth Clark's Metropolitan Applied Research Council.

But I've talked to quite a few parents who think it's a good idea, so I think we may be able to swing the votes. Anyway, don't mention to anyone that I've asked you to work on it till after the discussion and the vote. Then, if it's passed and I ask for volunteers, volunteer."

"Why did the Executive Board vote against it? It seems like such a good idea."

"Oh, different people had different reasons. Some of them are scared of Mrs. Wachtel. They think she'll take it out on their kids or on the parents-in-the-classroom program. Some of them are very busy with the governing-board election and don't think we should get sidetracked now. And they don't have any faith in the local school board, anyway."

"And you?" I asked.

"I think it's worth a try."

"OK," I said. It seemed to me to be a constructive thing to do, but—"What's the local school board like? Aren't they just an honorary sort of thing? I know that when I was teaching, all the local school board did was send its chairman around at graduation time to hand out a couple of the awards."

"Oh, they're not a bad group. The chairman, Jessica Malamud, is a very bright woman. I've spoken to her about the idea, and she said that if we do it, she's sure the school board will look into the school."

"But can they actually do anything?"

"They could commission someone to do a study."

Although it didn't seem like a great deal, it was possible that such a study could point up the problems we'd been concerned about. And it seemed likely that the administration, which would not take seriously the complaints of mere parents, would try to correct these same problems if someone with some authority said they were problems. At any rate, as Anne said, it was worth a try.

The night of the meeting, feeling somewhat conspiratorial, I went to the school with Millie Miller. I had not mentioned my conversation with Anne to Millie or to anyone else, but I hoped that if Anne were able to convince the general parent body to give us the go-ahead, Millie would volunteer, too. Millie is one of the most decent, principled people I know; and she thinks things through carefully and acts on her convictions, regardless of what anybody else thinks. She's one of the people I trust completely—with my children and in every other way. And because I value her judgment and her feelings, I hoped that if we did the profile she'd be willing to work on it.

The meeting was supposed to be in the auditorium. The fifteen or so parents who had weathered the cold March night rattled around in it so pitifully that Anne suggested we move into the cafeteria, which, though not smaller, offered a more flexible seating arrangement which would make for a more congenial atmosphere. Besides, smoking was not illegal there. So we took our coats and rearranged ourselves in the cafeteria. I had been there only twice before, once on the first day of school after the strike when it had been a bedlam. The other time I'd been there had been to vote in the fall election, when it was decorated with voting booths and other election paraphernalia. So in a way I was seeing it for the first time in all its stark reality.

It was a huge room, with high windows at its furthest end that faced the school playground and consequently wore a protective covering of heavy-duty steel mesh, in spite of which several windows had cracks. The ceiling lights were also guarded by wire coverings, and they cast a dim reflection off the green tiled walls on either side. The heavy swinging doors leading to the kitchen were a dull green steel. The eight-foot tables and benches were lined up in exact rows. The place was spotless, sterile, and cheerless. It lacked even the smells I'd always associated with school lunchrooms, of peanut butter and tomato soup, that might have indicated that something living passed through here. No pictures or other decorations adorned the walls, and it reminded me not so much of a school cafeteria as of the prison diningrooms of movie fame.

We settled down, and Anne called the meeting to order. Announcements were made, and it was time for the items on the agenda. All this time people were wandering in, so that by then there were perhaps thirty to forty people there. At several points during the discussion Anne answered parents who spoke with what must have appeared to them the puzzling comment:

"Later in the meeting I want to make a suggestion that I think will take care of that."

I, of course, knew she was talking about the idea for the profile of the school; but to anyone with whom whe had not discussed it, it must have seemed strange. At one point the subject was the safety of children in the school. A thin, small lady at the back of the room whom I'd never seen before at any of the meetings I'd attended rose and began to tell, in a highly emotional fashion, about an incident in one of the bathrooms where her daughter had been molested. She spoke so softly at times, and so ramblingly at others, that I couldn't make out who—student or outsider, male or female—had accosted the child. But she was visibly and understandably upset and complained that the school had done nothing about the incident. She, too, was told by Anne that her problem would be dealt with later; and though various people rose to argue that it should be dealt with now (I thought so, too), Anne overrode their objections and continued with the agenda. I can understand that she wanted to get to the proposal. It was after ten, and time would run out at eleven when Pete, one of the custodians, always came in and stared pointedly at the clock. Nevertheless, had I been that woman I would not have been satisfied to wait. But she was black, and black people are always being told by white people in authority, "Not now, later," so I guess she resigned herself to what she considered the inevitable rebuff. She had probably come to the PA as her last resort; and feeling that it was just another face of the school administration, she put on her coat shortly afterwards and left.

What Anne had intended, of course, was that her complaint was typical of an uncaring adminstration and, as such, should be included in the profile. And she truly did mean to deal with it as a problem needing a solution. But she missed the boat and turned another parent off. I spent the next few months trying to track that lady down, to tell her that somebody had heard her plea and that I was ready to do whatever was necessary to see that some action was taken, not only for her child's safety, but for the safety of all our children. But I never found her. No one seemed to know who she was. About two years later I was at a Head Start meeting in the community and saw her again with a shock of recognition. By then, though, the school had changed, and it was too late in any case, but I did tell her that we had been trying to locate her after that meeting.

The agenda droned on, and I only half listened. I was thinking of that lady, and wondering whether the profile really would be a solution for her, and for the school. Or would we just be doing a lot of work that would, in the end, lead nowhere? Suppose some outfit did come in and do an in-depth study of the school? Committees are always being formed and studies made of schools and other institutions. In the end most of them either justify existing conditions or come to conclusions and make recommendations that no one follows anyway. But then I thought, 'What's the alternative?' and since I couldn't think of any, I thought it would be worth any effort we made. If the parents agreed to the idea. It was by now ten to eleven, and Anne was outlining to the parents her reasons for wanting to do the thing, in much the same way she had to me.

"What I'd like to see," she said, "is a report that would show some of the serious problems in the school. . . . For example, the fact that classes are reorganized after the children have gotten used to being where they are. Or that teachers are pulled out in the middle of the year and given new assignments. That's a big problem. Or the whole question of book shortages and lack of supplies. The third grade still hasn't gotten its math textbooks, and it's now March. And the whole business of the lineup, and the terrible atmosphere in the school. I could go on, but I think you know the problems as well as I do.

"I'd also like to show the strengths of the school, because I really don't want this to be a negative report. But I think there are such serious problems here that someone has to deal with them."

Irene Martins was up and yelling.

"The local school board isn't going to do anything. You're wasting your time."

Stephanie Hale, with her clipped British accent: "We're in the middle of an election campaign for the Joan of Arc governing board. Don't dissipate our energies with this. If you want to do it wait till after the election, and then take it to the governing board. At least you know they'll listen and do something. The local school board has no power anyway. And even if you get rid of the principal you'll get the next one on the list. That's just more of the same. Once we're a demonstration district we can go off the list."

To all of which Anne said that she thought it was worth a try.

"And if the school board doesn't do anything, we can still go to the governing board once they're elected.

A few worried voices asked how the principal would react to such a study, and Anne said she thought she ought to be glad that the parents wanted to make it a better school—which was, I suppose, rather naive. At any rate, since it was by then eleven, and Pete was, true to form, lounging in the doorway, she called for a vote and the parents upheld her. She then asked anyone who was interested in working on the project to come up and sign up, and I was pleased that Millie was one of the volunteers. As we went to sign up, Irene, Stephanie, and several of the other members of the Executive Board were shouting at Anne.

"You railroaded that through." "You shouldn't have cut off discussion." "You'll make the school even more of a mess." "You'll split the school in half." "She'll lock us all out of the school again." And so forth. Anne held her ground. She had her vote and could proceed. As we were signing up, one man came up and asked, "Can I volunteer my wife?"

And so the profile committee was born. We were to spend the next two months in intensive work, with almost nightly meetings, writing, arguing, rewriting—and I found that in spite of myself I had become deeply involved with PS 84 and its problems.

EIGHT

"We Have to Be Objective"

We sat in Anne's living room and faced each other nervously. We were now the Profile Committee and didn't quite know what to do with it.

"Where do we begin?" someone asked, "And how?"I looked around the room—which was a duplicate of ours, except in mirror image, and it produced the odd sensation of something familiar but not quite right that I always got when I visited someone in our co-op. The room was rather bare, with a low wicker chair and a butterfly chair providing the only items that could be officially defined as furniture. A slab of wood extended under the length of the windows, and on this several corduroy cushions of red, black, and gold were scattered. Similiar cushions were strewn on the floor to provide additional seats. In the dining room there was a large round wooden table, and behind it, on the wall, a solid sheet of cork covered with paintings done by children at various stages of development. There were plants on the window sills, and along the wall of the living room two huge fish tanks gurgled steadily next to an upright piano. On the other side of the fish tanks stood a gerbil cage —empty. Its resident scampered around the floor, appearing now and then from beneath a chair to stare at the unaccustomed crowd.

There were, in addition to Anne, Millie, and me, seven other women. We were all middleclass, and with the exception of Adalia Romero, another co-op resident who hailed from Venezuela and who, in the ethnic surveys done by the Board of Education, was classified as Spanish-speaking even though her English is fluent, we were all white. This lack of ethnic balance was one of the things that was to plague us during this period and afterwards, for it led to

58

considerable criticism that we were unrepresentative of the school population and that, therefore, what we had to say somehow lacked validity. In spite of our ethnic homogeneity we were a disparate bunch, and from the beginning we disagreed on many things. This had as much to do with our different styles as with our varying outlooks. But the one thing on which we all agreed, and which held us together throughout this period, was that the school was in serious trouble; and, in fact, the longer we worked and the more we learned from each other, the more that became apparent. For each of us brought to the work her own experiences and perspectives, and each was a part of the jigsaw which, when finally put together (even though pieces remained to be fitted in), was a picture of a school that was appalling.

That first night at Anne's house we did not attempt to do any writing. We just talked—about our feelings about the school, about what we had personally experienced, what we would like to see happen, and so forth. Of all the people there, I was the one with the shortest contact with the school. Though Jonathan, Millie's boy, was also only in kindergarten he had attended prekindergarten at PS 84, so that this was her second year. Anne's son was in the fourth grade, Adalia's in the first. Beth Barron and Eileen Ghiozzi had first-graders, Inge Havessy and Ronnie Rubin had third-graders. And each year's experience in the school, apparently, added its share of horror stories, some of which I had heard before from parents at other meetings, others of which I was hearing for the first time.

"What I'd like to do," said Anne over our fifth cup of coffee, "is start with a list of the strengths and weaknesses of the school. After that we can go into details about them. How does that sound to you?"

That seemed to all of us to be a sensible approach, and the rest of the evening was spent compiling such a list. What emerged was somewhat lopsided:

GOOD POINTS	BAD POINTS
New building	Low teacher morale
Optimum ethnic balance	Divided faculty
Many good teachers	Frequent shifts in personnel and children during school year

GOOD POINTS	BAD POINTS
Balanced-class project	Low reading scores
Parent involvement and interest	Bad general atmosphere
No tracking	Lack of textbooks and supplies
Jewish Board of Guardians	After-school study center
	Racism on part of many teachers
	Sterile curriculum
	Lack of communication between parents and staff
	Lack of communication between staff and administration
	The third grade
	Mrs. Young (assistant principal for the upper grades)

Having drawn up our list—which took some time and a good deal of talking—we decided to call it a night.

"Next time," said Anne, "we'll decide who should work on which sections, and then maybe we can start to write. I'd like to finish by next month so that we can take it to the school board for their April meeting."

Her estimate of how long it would take proved overly optimistic, because once we got started we found that it was quite time-consuming, and it was two months before we were even partially satisfied with our efforts. But we left her home that night feeling, for the first time in a long while, optimistic. It was a clear cold night, and the air was refreshing after all the coffee and cigarettes. As Millie, Adalia, and I walked the half block to our building we all felt good that at last we were doing something. We were all very much excited by the possibilities that the profile presented.

Two nights later we met at the home of Ronnie Rubin. Ronnie and Anne are completely opposite types, which was immediately apparent from their apartments. Ronnie's, in an old, high-ceilinged building off Riverside Drive, had a quiet formality. The wood gleamed, the floor shone. Everything was in place—even the sheet music on the grand piano sat properly—and even though I knew that three children shared the apartment with their parents, no signs of them were visible in those quarters. It was an adult's room, neat, well-ordered, and cared for. Ronnie herself is like that—though there's nothing formal about her. But she's a quiet person, who sits and listens and two days later, when she's thought it all through, comes back with the next set of questions which she then goes home and thinks about.

Ronnie had been involved in the school longer than any of us. David had started kindergarten there and had had one awful year after another. He was now in the third grade—which was a disaster area unto itself. Ronnie had been one of the parents most active in the fight to eliminate tracking. She was, at this time, very active in the preparations for the impending governing-board election and deeply committed to the idea of community control. The idea for the profile had come to her late one night and she did not feel, as other members of the Executive Board did, that the work on the profile was an act of disloyalty to the community-control idea. And certainly her credentials were beyond reproach.

We settled down with coffee and began to apportion the work. We decided that the form the profile should take would be a general introduction, with facts about the school such as the number of pupils, their ethnic composition, the number of teachers in the school, whether they were regulars or subsitutes, how many actual teaching positions there were, reading scores for each grade, and so forth. After the general introduction there would be sections on each of the points we had outlined at our last meeting, with corroborating statements wherever we could get them. Finally, we would write a conclusion based upon what we came up with in the various sections. And I must say at this point that we had no idea, then, what our ultimate conclusion would be beyond that the school needed help. We really did not go into the project with any preconceived ideas as to where the blame lay, and, in fact, for a long time we fought the conclusion that began to emerge: that a good part of the blame lay with the principal. And even when we were finished and that conclusion stared us in the face, we were reluctant to admit it.

We began to divide up the sections, giving to each person those parts with which she was most familiar. Since Millie and I were the newest in the school we decided that we would work on the kindergartens, and, where possible, add our experiences to the sections on the general atmosphere, racism on the part of teachers, and lack of communication between parents and staff. Ronnie and Inge would concentrate on the third grade which, from its entry into the school in kindergarten, had been subjected to a series of incredible messes, involving—during one year—frequent shifts of teachers, incompetent teachers and teaching, experiments that were begun and dropped in midstream, and the like. That grade exemplified all the ills of the school, and its experiences spilled over into all the other areas we had cited.

Anne would work on the good points of the school. Eileen, Beth, and Adalia would fill in wherever they could. And we would all work together to get the report into its final form, as well as on the introduction and conclusion.

"For the general introduction we'll have to get some facts from Mrs. Wachtel," Anne said.

"Will she give them to us?" Beth asked.

"I think so," said Anne. "I'll go and ask her. Who wants to come with me?"

"I'll come," Ronnie said.

"Good," said Anne, "but I think we ought to take someone else. How about you, Hannah?"

"Sure, if you think I'll be useful."

"Well, you're a neutral person. Ronnie and I have both had so many fights with her that she may be more likely to give us the figures if you come along. I'll go in tomorrow and set up an appointment. Now what I think we ought to do is start working on our sections and see how it goes."

Since I'm not very good at joint writing I said to Millie, "Why don't we each write our general impressions of the kindergartens and then compare notes. Then we can put them together." So we began and the others did likewise. I thought about the kindergarten. I certainly had many impressions and opinions on the subject, but I wanted to be as objective as possible, and also as general. For one thing, I had no desire to pillory the particular teacher. Whatever I felt about her personally was not relevant. What was relevant was the educational climate of the class and how this affected the children in it. Furthermore, I felt from talking to other parents that this climate transcended that particular class and was equally present in the others. And yet, as I began to write, I realized that I was, in trying to generalize the situation, coming up with accusations that I could not prove because I had no firsthand knowledge of anything but Kathy's particular class. And whereas I could say, in all honesty, that Kathy's class had never experimented with any media but crayon, I could not, with the same certainty, say it about the other kindergarten classes. And so on for other criticisms. But if I wrote only about one particular class it became an indictment of only one teacher, which, however valid, would just prove to be a bit of bad luck for those children—but nothing to warrant an investigation by some outside body. In short, unless I could generalize, what I was saying added up to nothing more than a gripe (however justified), and if I generalized I could no longer be sure of the integrity of what I was saying.

When I voiced my dilemma to Millie I discovered that she had been encountering the same difficulty; and though between us we represented two classes and two teachers that only comprised 50 percent of the kindergarten experience.

"Well," said Millie, "let's try writing a general statement about the kindergartens and see how it works out. If it doesn't we'll just have to scrap it and find another way."

So we began—together, this time.

"The kindergartens at PS 84 provide, on the whole, a completely sterile experience for the children in them."

We stopped and looked at each other. "How do we know that?" we said in unison. And so it went. Every categorical statement we made we scratched as soon as it was finished. What emerged was such a hodge podge of qualifications and modifications that it sounded like a liberal's nightmare. ". . . on the one hand . . . but it must be remembered that . . . and you must also consider . . . as far as can be ascertained . . . in most cases . . . that the kindergartens are probably, for most children, a sterile experience. But on the other hand . . ." It was ludicrous.

"Oh, it's hopeless," Millie said. "We can't do it this way." When we interrupted the others to tell them of our difficulties we found that some of the same doubts were plaguing them. There just weren't enough of us, and our experiences simply did not cover the entire spectrum of possibilities, for a total picture to emerge. We could fake it, of course, with generalizations, but we truly wanted to depict the school accurately, and even had we not decided at the outset that we had nothing to hide and would, therefore, sign our names to the finished report, we did not want to hide behind generalizations.

"Well, then," asked Ronnie, "what do we do instead?"

"I don't see what else we can do but write individual statements about what we know," said Millie. "I really can't sign my name to something that I don't know firsthand."

"That's right," I said. "Even if I've heard from someone that Miss So and So hits the kids, if I haven't seeen it how can I say it's true? I think Millie has the right idea."

"But then how do we get a total picture of the school? There are only ten of us," said Eileen.

"We'll just have to get other parents to write of their experiences, and maybe the cumulative effect will be what we want," answered Millie.

"Fine," said Anne. "We'll get out a flier asking parents to submit their experiences in the school—good and bad—to us. And then we'll put them all together. In the meantime, why don't we all write statements about things we know personally?"

"Naming names?" someone asked.

"Why not," someone else said. "We'll sign our statements, so why shouldn't we name the people we're talking about?"

So it was agreed, but in the end we decided to delete the names of the people in the school, with the exception of Mrs. Wachtel and her assistants, on the grounds that they bore the major responsibility and, further, could not be protected in any case since the description of the events would reveal their identities. And in the case of Mrs. Young, the assistant principal for the upper grades—who warranted a section for herself—she was such a sore point in the school that not naming her would have been silly. It was she who blew the whistle during the morning lineup, and who was the grand inquisitor of the infamous late line. Furthermore, it was she who, when the school had needed ethnic breakdowns for the Board of Education survey (which is supposed to be done as a sight census), had descended on one class and, to the horror of the teacher, had demanded: "All Negro children stand." Then, "All Puerto Rican children stand," and when some, in confusion, stood twice, or not at all, she had berated them for not knowing what they were and had begun again, this time saying, "Come on. Stand up. You know who you are." Some of the children, the products of mixed marriages, were particularly at a loss as to which category they fitted ("human" being one the Board apparently doesn't consider), and they went home visibly shaken. Mrs. Wachtel was visited by a delegation of their angry parents, and when Mrs. Young was confronted by them, she apologized for any discomfort she might have caused, but justified herself by saying "We needed the figures by Monday." So we could not grant Mrs. Young anonymity; but for the rest of the statements we deleted all names and identifying traits, though we did sign our names to our own statements.

After deciding on this procedure we broke up and went home to say our piece. I wrote about my experience with Kathy's kindergarten class, using only those details that I had myself observed. And it was quite an indictment. I don't know whether Mrs. Winter ever read the profile. If so she must have recognized herself in my account (how could she fail to since I signed my name to it?) but if she was aware of its existence she never let on, remaining till the last day of the term her same effusive self. The other statement I wrote concerned my encounter with Mr. Olivieri over the conference schedule. Again, the gentleman in question could not have failed to recognize himself—and he, I know, did read it—but he did not acknowledge his portrayal till several years later when he denied my version of the incident.

The other statements that emerged at our meeting were all equally damning. Since they all dealt with specific incidents—witnessed or experienced by their authors—they were pretty strong stuff; and we realized, when next we met, that we had something going. As I sat and read what Ronnie had written about the experiences of David's class from kindergarten to the present, I was moved by how badly they had been treated. And the same was true for the other accounts. No one, it seemed to me, could read what these parents had to say and not see that the school was in need of help.

At the same time we all realized that what we had was too limited, and it was at this point that we began to solicit the experiences of other parents. At first we did this by word of mouth. Anytime someone stopped us on the street to gripe about something, we said, "Write it down," and then hounded them till they gave us a statement. At this point we also began to realize—from the hemming and hawing we encountered when we asked parents to translate their gripes into documents—that we had to deal with the fears, justified or not, of some people about signing their names to what they said. After all, they had children in the school, and some of them were not, perhaps, so cavalier about putting those children on the line. And certainly we could not guarantee to anyone (not even to ourselves) that there would be no reprisals. We hoped there wouldn't be, but how could we guarantee that a teacher about whom some parent wrote a complaint would not make life miserable for the child of that parent. Nor could we look to the principal for protection under those circumstances. As a result we changed our position, and decided that we would ask the people to sign their statements, but that we would retain those signed statements only for our own use, and on the finished product we would delete the signature unless the person specifically authorized its use. In that way the parents and their children would be protected, and at the same time, should a suit ever be brought, we would have some measure of protection against the charge that we had fabricated the statements. And with the assurance that their names would not be used, more parents became willing to air their grievances.

During this time Anne arranged a meeting with Mrs. Wachtel to get the hard data about the school. On the appointed morning I met Anne and Ronnie, and I entered, for the first time, the principal's office. Her desk, under the window, was cluttered with papers. Other papers were scattered over the long conference table at which she seated us. Next to her desk stood a microphone and a wastebasket, as well as an additional chair, presumably used when she was conferring with an individual visitor. On the wall of the office were several pictures done by children, as well as a large American flag. Toward the other end of the office, near the door that led directly to the outside corridor and which was always kept closed and curtained, stood a glass-enclosed bookcase with various textbooks, readers, and curriculum manuals. The top of this was also strewn with papers and manuals of various sorts.

Since I had never met her before, except at group meetings, I introduced myself and we exchanged a few platitudes. Then Anne told her that we were doing a profile of the school (she did not mention to what end, and Mrs. Wachtel did not inquire) and that, consequently, we needed certain statistics from her. At the mention of statistics she brightened visibly and said that she would be happy to give us whatever information she had available that was not private. She thereupon gathered together the relevant material, and we got from her the following statistical picture for the 1967–1968 school year:

I. FACULTY

There are fifty-three teachers at PS 84. Thirty-nine are regulars, fourteen substitutes.

A. YEARS IN SERVICE

	1 - 5	6 – 10	11 plus
Regular	28	7	4
Substitute	14		

Eleven teachers walk to work; a few come from the Bronx, Queens, and New Jersey, and the rest come from Manhattan.

B. TURNOVER

There have been three new teaching positions in PS 84 this year. These positions were created by the formation of two new classes (one in third grade, one in fourth). A new cluster teacher* joined the staff in February. Eight teachers have left the school this year.

REASONS

Sabbatical 2	Maternity 2	Study 2	Personal 2

This teacher turnover has resulted in changes affecting children in the following classes:

1st grade	1–1	3 teachers
	1–6	2 teachers
3rd grade	3–3	2 teachers
		1 reorganization to form a new class
4th grade	4–3	3 teachers
	4–5	2 teachers
		1 reorganization to form a new class
6th grade	6–3	2 teachers
TMR (The Mentally Retarded)		3 teachers
Junior Guidance		2 teachers

C. ABSENCES   *566 man days lost (after strike to April 1, 1968)*

D. NUMBER OF PER DIEM SUBSTITUTES HIRED *(Figures not available)*

II. PUPILS

A. READING SCORES   *(Will be forthcoming)*

B. NUMBER OF PUPILS AS OF APRIL 1, 1968   *892*

C. ETHNIC BREAKDOWN OF PUPILS

Black	Puerto Rican	Other
30%	40%	40%

*A cluster teacher is one who does not have a regular class, but provides coverage for classroom teachers when they have a free period.

We never asked for an ethnic breakdown of the faculty. I don't think the Board keeps official records on that; but at that time there were, as far as I know, three black teachers (all women) and no Spanish-speaking teachers on the staff. We did have one position for a bilingual teacher, but his job, as far as I could determine, was not in the classroom, but with the parents—translating, acting as their go-between with the administration and with social agencies, and performing for them whatever services he and they felt necessary.

During this session with Mrs. Wachtel, she was most cordial. I had never seen her so happy as she was while she was counting and adding up the various columns and figures, and it occurred to me that, at that moment, she was doing what she liked best. She literally beamed with satisfaction as her pencil went down the pages and she jotted down her tallies, and I felt saddened. Here was a woman who had spent years in study, years in the school and with children. And she whistled while she worked only when she was working with papers and figures.

As we left her office, I said to Ronnie and Anne, "I felt kind of dishonest. There she was, giving us all that data, and if she had known what we were going to use it for she would have thrown us out."

"Yes," said Ronnie. "But then we wouldn't have gotten the information. And we're entitled to it. And notice that she didn't give us the reading scores."

"She said she didn't have them available," I said.

"They were available at the conference on reading." said Anne.

"That's true," I said. "But she said she'd get them for us."

"Want to bet?" asked Anne. And of course we never did get the figures.

The statistical picture of the school, as presented, was probably better than that of a lot of schools, but we felt it was pretty bad. Although only eight classes had been affected by teacher changes, many of those classes had had not one change but two—with lord knows how many per diem substitutes in between. And eight classes of about thirty pupils meant that about two hundred and forty children, or better than a quarter of the children in the school, had been affected by these changes. In addition to these changes resulting from teachers who left, there had also been various class reorganizations, in several cases affecting these same children, so that the fabric of their education had been torn beyond repair during that year. Of course it could be argued that it was worse in other schools. No doubt that is true, but that particular argument has never moved me. It's not very comforting, when your arm is broken, to hear that someone else has broken a leg in addition. And though the principal cannot be blamed because her teachers get pregnant, the manner in which some of the class shifts had been made was directly attributable to her lack of feeling for the children, as well as to her lack of administrative skill.

One case in particular had come to our attention as we worked on the profile. It concerned a second-grade class in which the parents of certain children had received letters saying that their children would be transferred to another class the following day for their own good. One of the mothers had gone to the school to find out what lay behind this class change; and after being kept waiting by Miss Federman for more than two hours (while the principal, who was in her office, refused to see her) she was told that the change was the result of the school's having secured an additional teacher to relieve overcrowding. This satisfied the mother, but she was curious as to how the children had been selected. She was told that it had been done upon teacher recommendation; and since she knew that many of the transferred children were behavior problems, she wondered whether this had been wise. Still, she held her peace and the children were transferred. Other parents, however, continued to protest this change after the children were already adjusted to their situation; and bowing to protests, after only two days of the new class, Mrs Wachtel disbanded it. As the mother wrote:

"I happened to be in the classroom (on an Open School Week visit) when Mrs. Wachtel entered and asked the children if they all missed their little friends in the old class. 'Well,' she responded to their dutiful chorus, 'you may now go back to your own class and your own teacher.' I helped several of the children carry all their unwieldy second-grade possessions, their plants, their clay creations, down the hall where a warm welcome home awaited. Except that the door was locked and the room empty. When we finally caught up with the class (in the gym), I attempted to make light of an awkward moment. I told the teacher I'd brought the children, and would give her the baby in my arms for the same price. She gave me an odd look, and the ensuing discussion revealed that Mrs. Wachtel had forgotten to tell her she was getting them back. She wasn't very happy, but she certainly was happier than some thrice-rejected children who listened to us. (The children in other classes went back, I hear, to situations where there were no desks for them.)

"The real comedy of errors developed when I learned it wasn't the second grade in the first place which had been overcrowded; it was the third, and that is where the extra teacher finally went."

So it was not only the matter of the changes—but also the manner —which we found disturbing, and which made the statistical analysis just received seem worse to us than it might have to an uninformed observer.

NINE

"We Will Read the Profile.
You Will Be Heard."

Our work on the profile continued, with so many meetings that on many nights we'd all bolt dinner, I'd wash the dishes and dash out, leaving Walter to put the kids to bed. I realized it was getting a bit excessive when I overheard the children playing house and Kathy, who was, as usual, the mother, said to the others, "Okay, goodnight. I'm going to a meeting." Still, duty called, and it was for their sake that I was going, and I went. And we worked. And argued. We agreed that statements that came from other parents had to be accepted without editing, no matter how inflammatory they might be. Our own, on the other hand, were fair targets, and many a night we argued about semantics, with Eileen usually acting as the toner-downer. She was probably right and may have saved us all from libel suits; but at the time, when our passions were high, we did not always see it that way.

One night, when Kate Hulbert had just finished telling us about life in the third grade, where the reading teacher was such a bully that Lisa developed a stomachache daily before the class split up for reading, we were visited by Carole Arnowitz, who was one of the members of the Executive Board who had opposed the idea of the profile. It had been Carole who had organized the parents-in-the-classroom program, and she feared that the profile would put the program in jeopardy. Her own son was in Lisa Hulbert's class, and he had been the almost daily butt of the reading teacher's ridicule. Nevertheless, she was not rocking any boats. She came to read us a statement, signed by six members of the Executive Board, which they intended to send to the local school board. It said:

Many positive events have occurred in the school in spite of rulings that have hamstrung the process of good education. The communications barrier is being broken down slowly, permitting us to achieve, in some part, our goal of educating all of our children. We list some of these events below:

1. The parents have had free entry to the office. Very seldom is it necessary to secure an appointment to speak with the principal. Her door is always open.
2. With the permission of the principal, teachers who wish to experiment in a creative manner may do so.
3. With the cooperation of the principal, the second-grade teachers have been permitted to institute a program of less formalized education known as team teaching. They have pooled their specific abilities for the use of all classes in that grade.
4. The principal has expressed a desire to institute an ungraded program starting at the third year, if the teachers are willing to cooperate.
5. A parent volunteer program which is growing and which we hope can be utilized to help all children reach the goal of reading on or above grade level.
6. Grade-level conferences have been held in the form of luncheon meetings from sixth grade through the kindergarten. Additional ones may be held before the end of the school year.
7. Parent-faculty meetings have been held approximately twice monthly at which time parents and teachers were able to hold dialogues to express concern, discuss problems, and determine methods of alleviating them.
8. The Jewish Board of Guardians have a team of specialists in the school who meet with the principal, teachers, and parents, separately and together. They have been given a free hand to make their investigation, recommendations, and referrals. They are still in the school approximately two days a week.

We believe that the above-mentioned items are positive factors in the school—steps upward toward our mutual goal of good education for all the children.

So spoke the loyal opposition. We sat there for a moment, stunned. We had been gathering and reading statements for weeks —statements which told of the brutalization of children, of racism thinly veiled—if at all—on the part of teachers. We had sat at those meetings and conferences and seen that they made not a bit of difference to the level of education in the school. We had read of teachers who had told white parents their children were associating with unsuitable children (black or Spanish). We had read about the

IGC teacher who plainly admitted that she didn't like teaching bright children, and who didn't—teach them, that is. She covered the bare syllabus and then did review work. And the principal was aware of it and did nothing. We had read of black parents who, by themselves, were never granted an audience with the principal; but when they were accompanied by a white parent, they were given an appointment. And more. And then we listened to this statement by the Executive Board, which said that the school was a pretty good place, and we were stunned.

"You don't believe all that," I finally said to Carole.

"No," she answered, without blinking her baby-blue eyes, "but we're sending it anyway."

"But why?" I asked.

"Because we think the profile is harmful. It will divide the school. Sure there are things that could be improved, but we think the principal can be worked with, and if you go ahead with this you'll ruin whatever chance we have of working with her. We don't want that to happen."

She never budged from that position, though we all argued with her. She left shortly thereafter, and we were left with the bombshell.

"What made them do that?" Inge asked.

"They're scared," Beth answered.

"Stephanie Hale and Carole are busy with the Joan of Arc election. For them it's political," Ronnie said.

"Carole is political—*and* scared," I retorted.

"But what do we do now?" someone asked.

"We go on," Anne said. "We knew that some of the Executive Board was against the profile."

"But we didn't know they'd do this."

"What do we do with it?"

"We'll use it," Anne said. "We always said we'd show the good and the bad aspects of the school. They've just summarized the good aspects."

"Except that they're not true," I said.

"I think the statements we have will show that. But if we include this in the profile I think it will be less harmful."

And so we agreed. Looking back now, I think we should have done more and should have, with our statements, refuted their points one by one. Certainly for every statement the dissenters made, we had several that belied them, or that at least gave them a different construction. The one about teachers being free to experiment should have had appended to it the letters we had from teachers telling what happened when they tried. The open door should have been followed with the statements from all the parents who cooled their heels in front of it. The grand dialogue of the parent-faculty conferences should have been followed by the actual minutes of those conferences. What the Executive Board members had set forth was a lofty ideal—and we should have put reality beside it. But that is retrospect, and it comes now when, several years later, I have just reread the profile and find it not quite so damning as I did when we were writing it. Not that the evidence isn't there, but that to a dispassionate observer it may seem no worse, and perhaps better, than other institutions of learning. Perhaps we should have structured it differently, but we were so deeply involved in it, and so outraged by what was being done to our children in the name of education, that we thought any reader would be equally outraged and react as we did. We thought that all they needed was the facts and that all we had to do was present them.

And so we went on gathering those facts, trying to make the profile as broad-based and as representative of the total school population as possible. We sent out fliers and leafletted the buildings, calling for a meeting at which all segments of the community could have their say. We would have translators available to take down any statements the Spanish-speaking parents wished to make. And we would be there to write down the statements of any parent who did not feel comfortable about writing his own but who nevertheless wanted to go on record.

We had decided to hold the meeting in the cafeteria because it would be easier, with the tables, for people to write. We had set up two tables outside the cafeteria, and some of us who had been working on the profile sat there with pencil and paper so that anyone who wished could dictate his statement to us. Adalia was ready to provide her services to any Spanish person who desired them. And Millie, Kate, Beth, and I were ready to do the same in English.

Since at the outset no one needed us, we went into the cafeteria. It was heartening to see the turnout. Not only were there more people there than I had seen at most of the meetings I had attended (with the exception of the strike speakout), but there were also far more Spanish-speaking parents than I had ever seen at a previous meeting. And they talked. Adalia translated for a while and then

Maria Conrad, a parent active in the Spanish community, took over and translated both from English to Spanish and from Spanish to English. What was said that night was, substantially, the same as what we had been hearing for the past month—with individual variations. The details differed slightly from speaker to speaker, but the picture remained unchanged. If we had had any doubts about what we were doing, they faded that evening. It was impossible to listen to person after person, telling—sometimes in Spanish or in broken English—how the school had failed their children and subjected them to insult, without being convinced that it could not continue. It was also interesting that that night there was not one voice raised in defense of the school.

And we wrote. Some of the parents wrote their own statements. Others preferred to have us do it for them. What was perhaps most moving was that of all the parents who came that night none asked that his name be withheld. It indicated not so much their faith in us (they had no reason to have that) as their despair about the school. It had already done its worst to them and their children. Anonymity was beside the point.

We had hoped to hold another public meeting after that—to give people who had not been heard from a chance to go on record. The press of time—it was by then the middle of April, and we were on the school-board agenda for the beginning of May—prevented it, and we decided to go with what we had. We spent the last two weeks before the school-board meeting mainly on mechanics. The statements had to be typed, the whole had to be put into some kind of order, and we had to write an introduction. We also had to have enough copies made so that each member of the school board could have one, with enough extras for the principal and the district superintendent. And since we had neither an office nor a staff, nor access to any of the equipment that comes with them, it was a rather major undertaking. We would type away, come to a meeting in the evening, and hand the stuff to Anne, who took it off to her husband's office to have it all Xeroxed.

The night before the school-board meeting it was pouring—one of those nights when the rain comes down in sheets and you think it can't keep on like that and will let up in a few minutes but it keeps coming down so that the gutters are streaming, and the pavements, too, and as you look out of your window the whole world seems liquefied. It was a good night to be at home—something that hadn't happened in a long time, anyway. I was tired and was planning to get a good night's sleep in preparation for the meeting the following night.

And then of course the phone rang. It was Beth Barron, and she told me that Ronnie needed help in deleting all the names from the ten or so copies of the profile. No one else was available, and could I go with her? I grabbed my raincoat and boots, said a quick good-night to Walter, and dashed out. Beth was waiting downstairs, and since no cab was anywhere in sight—they had more sense than we —we swam to my garage and headed for Ronnie's house. It was only five blocks away, and ordinarily we would have walked, but the rain continued to stream down, so that the wipers hardly made any inroads into the steady deluge against the windshield and I had a hard time seeing where I was going. I also realized, when we were about three blocks from home, that I had left my wallet, with my license and registration, safely at home. "It'll be just my luck to get stopped tonight," I said. But I wasn't, and we got to Ronnie's house without incident. Of course there wasn't a parking space to be had, and I circled the block, and then spread out in a widening circle. By the time I found a space, we were half way home again and might almost as well have walked in the first place. When we got back to Ronnie's, we were both soaked through our raincoats, and my hair kept dripping down my neck as I worked.

I had thought when we were writing the profile that we had omitted most of the names at the outset. Now, going over each statement carefully, it seemed that everyone had, perversely, named everyone, and as we inked out each offending name ten times I cursed the whole concept of anonymity. Finally, though, it was done, and as we staggered to my car I realized that, for whatever would come of it, it was finished. It was after one, but at least it had stopped raining.

The night of the meeting (May 13) the profile committee met at my corner, and we walked over to PS 75 where the district office was located, and where the local school board held its executive sessions. For open meetings the board moved around from school to school throughout the district, but its executive sessions were always held in the superintendent's office. In addition to those of us who had actually prepared the profile, there were about twenty other parents from the school who joined us to lend their support. We had agreed to let Anne be the spokesman, though we would all fill in if it became necessary. We really had no clear idea of what would happen. We had gotten the copies to the school board that morning, and we weren't even sure whether each member had received his copy—or whether, having received it, he would have read it. Further, we did not know how it would affect them. I had never been to a school-board meeting before and had, before Anne had come to me with the idea for the profile, in fact hardly been aware of their existence. I was therefore curious to see who these people were who held the fate of our school in their hands. Anne thought very highly of Jessica Malamud, so I was hopeful that she, at least, would be sympathetic. Beyond that it was anyone's guess.

PS 75 is a red brick building—prewar, I would guess by its construction—that covers the block from 95th to 96th on West End Avenue and then runs halfway down toward Riverside Drive. We filed in the main entrance on West End, and I followed the group down a flight of stairs, on the wall of which was lettered DISTRICT SUPERINTENDENT'S OFFICE with an arrow pointing down. When we emerged from the stairwell we were in a large hallway, with several locked offices to our left, another hallway stretching endlessly in front of us, and a shorter one to our right. Also in front of us was a short blond man with thick horn-rimmed glasses. (He turned out to be Robert Goodfellow, one of the local school-board members assigned to our school.) He wore shirtsleeves and no tie, and was perspiring rather heavily. He apologized that they would have to keep us waiting in the hallway, but said that the school-board had decided that they wanted to speak to Mrs. Wachtel first and that then they would see us. Equal time, apparently.

"I'm sorry to keep you waiting. Mrs. Wachtel was supposed to be here at seven thirty, and then we would have seen you at eight. But she was late, so you'll have to wait a little while. It shouldn't be too long."

We were annoyed, both at being kept waiting and at having to follow Mrs. Wachtel, but there was nothing we could do but grumble, which we did. Finally a door down the hall opened, and Mrs. Wachtel emerged with Miss Federman. They were leaning on each other. Turning their backs on us, they headed for a stairway down the hall and out of sight. We entered the office.

The school-board members seemed somewhat surprised to see so many of us, and our numbers forced them into a hurried consultation. For a few minutes it seemed as if they would not meet with us at all, and I saw one gentleman begin to stuff his papers into his briefcase angrily. Saner heads prevailed, however, and a tall, slim young woman, with long hair tied back by a large bow into a ponytail, came towards us. She was wearing a Peck and Peck type tweed suit of various shades of blue, which the ribbon in her hair matched. She looked well-scrubbed, feminine, and innocent, like a cub reporter on a college paper.

"Hello, Jessica," Anne said, and I realized she was the chairman of the school board on whom we had pinned all our hopes. She didn't look the part. Somehow I had imagined a solid, middle-aged type in sensible shoes.

"We weren't expecting such a crowd," she said to Anne. "So we won't be able to meet in Dr. Selig's office. But if you'll all find chairs, I think we can manage out here."

Out here was the office of the district's clerical staff, and by moving desks around and out of the way we were able to transform it into an auditorium-type meeting place—with a table and chairs at the front for the members of the school board to sit in judgment.

"We'll only be able to give you about half an hour," Jessica went on. "We have lots of other business on the agenda tonight. But we'll listen to you, and then we'll study your profile, and we'll let you know our decision."

"Only half an hour," Anne said, the disappointment audible. "We can hardly get started in that time."

"You'll have to try. It's the best we can do. There are twenty-two other schools in the district, and they have problems, too. And we will read the profile. You'll be heard. I promise you that."

We took our seats facing the school board. During the time we spent there, more parents from the school kept filing in, putting a further strain on the seating capacity, so that finally there were about fifteen people standing in various parts of the room. I looked around me as I waited for the inquisition to begin. The fluorescent lights on the ceiling bathed the room in a harsh white glare, increasing my feelings of an interrogation that was less than friendly. The windows on my left were high, and before it grew dark outside I could watch feet passing—hurriedly or slowly depending on the inclination of the body to which they were, supposedly, attached. From my viewpoint, though, it was just a steady procession of feet of all descriptions—sneakered, booted, high-heeled, shiny, scruffy, and, occasionally, four-footed. I amused myself by trying to imagine what their possessors looked like, which was a fair game to keep me from thinking and to control my nervousness.

"I think we should begin," Jessica said finally, pulling me away from a running pair of loafers. "First let me introduce the school-board members. And when you speak, would you please state your name. I assume you're all parents at PS 84."

We all nodded. I looked around and saw a few faces I did not recognize, which increased my feeling of nervousness because we had been warned that the opposition might be present. But I was relieved that Carole Arnowitz, Stephanie Hale, Irene Martins, and the other dissident members of the Executive Board had not come. (I learned later that they had asked for equal time with the school board, rather than for sharing the hearing with us. Then I was bitter and felt it was because they could not confront us, knowing that what they were saying was less than the truth. Now I think, though, that they only wanted to prevent an open confrontation in front of an unfriendly board; and whereas it is one thing to present a differing point of view, it is quite another to engage in internecine warfare in front of the enemy, which is how they viewed the school board.)

Jessica then introduced the other school-board members—Robert Goodfellow, Victor Gonzalez-Patron, Moses Patterson, Richard Somers, Arnaldo Torres, Elizabeth Dodge, and herself. Also present were Dr. Herman Selig, the district superintendent, who sat silent throughout with a bemused expression on his face, looking vaguely like a ventriloquist's dummy, and his assistant, Marion Poderof. We had met Robert Goodfellow in the hall. Victor Gonzalez-Patron, I realized with a start, was my upstairs neighbor whose two dogs barked hysterically whenever anyone passed outside their door and, between times, scurried above our heads sounding like rats in the ceiling. He was a short olive-skinned man with black-rimmed glasses and a head of thick, wavy-black hair that was beginning to turn silver. He wore, at all times, gray or black business suits with vests, and I sometimes wondered whether he wore the vests to bed. He had two children in the district's schools.

Mr. Patterson and Mr. Somers were two elderly men, both with white hair (though one had a full head of it and the other had only some remnants around the ears), and in all the time they both served on the school board, I never remembered which was who until Mr. Somers solved my dilemma by resigning. Elizabeth Dodge was a pretty black woman who that evening listened and spoke not at all. Mr. Torres was a social worker. The other member of the board, Matthew Prior, was not present that evening.

Looking at that board I was not inspired by any great feeling of confidence that they would listen and hear us. But we were there and we had to try to convince them. Anne began.

"For a long time we have felt that PS 84 was a school in trouble. The general atmosphere is poor. Children are tense. Reading scores are low. There seems to be very little communication between the administration and the staff, so that parents are constantly put in the role of go-betweens. The teachers complain to us about the principal. The principal complains about the teachers. We don't think that is a healthy condition for the school, but we don't know what to do about it. That's why we've come to you.

"We thought that if we could sketch some of the problems, you might be able to get some outside body—either yourselves, or the Center for Urban Education, or Kenneth Clark's MARC—to come in and take a closer, more objective look and tell us how we can make the school more effective for children, teachers, and the administration."

JESSICA: "Could you tell us, briefly, what you mean by a bad general atmosphere?"

KATE: "Well, there is constant tension. The teachers and the staff treat the children like animals, and the children then act the part. People are always yelling at the kids. Kids go tearing down the halls so that it's worth your life to walk there. No one seems to be able to control them. Whistles are always being blown at them. My daughter comes home daily with stomachaches. She can't stand the way the children are treated. On her first day of school there, she was in the yard crying because she was in a new strange school and missed her old school and friends. Someone went to the teacher in charge and said a girl was crying. The teacher went over to a boy who was near my daughter, but who had in no way been connected with her tears, grabbed him by the arm, and accused him of hitting my daughter, shrieking at him and asking 'Why did you hit her?' I intervened and explained why my daughter was crying, whereupon she let go of his arm, but with no apology. When he left she said to me, 'He's a troublemaker. He's in a junior-guidance class.' That's what I mean by a bad atmosphere."

Other parents then related similar episodes, telling of harsh treatment of the children by the staff and administration.

Gonzalez-Patron interrupted. "I can't see what's so terrible about that. When I went to school in Puerto Rico they rapped us over the knuckles with a ruler if we got out of line. And we didn't have any discipline problems, believe me. That's what those kids need."

Jessica asked, "Would you want the teachers to hit *your* son?"

"Of course not," he replied.

That was one for our side, but there weren't many. The questioning on the whole was, if not hostile, certainly not friendly. Robert Goodfellow asked whether what we were presenting was the whole picture or only the tip of an iceberg? We answered that it was the latter, that we were limited in what we could present, and that was why we wanted the objective investigation.

A slight, blonde woman with a French accent then said that she was a parent in the school, and she saw none of what we saw. She said her son had always had good teachers and that the only thing that threatened his education was the behavior of his classmates. She felt if the school had a fault it was that the discipline was not firm enough. Another woman echoed this sentiment, saying that she was more than satisfied with the quality of instruction in the school. Anne whispered to me that that woman had just transferred both her children to private school.

Somers or Patterson then pointed out that there were only about forty of us out of a parent body of perhaps five hundred, and that we were highly unrepresentative. Why should they believe that we were presenting an accurate picture? We answered again that that was why we wished the investigation. We were only saying that we believed the problems serious enough to warrant their looking for themselves.

JESSICA: "Do you think if you got a new principal it would solve the school's problems?"

We all answered no, that we felt that although the principal shared part of the blame, simply replacing her would be no solution. We changed our mind on that subsequently, but at the time we really believed that.

Jessica then thanked us for coming and dismissed us, repeating that they would give serious consideration to what we had said, as well as to what they had heard from Mrs. Wachtel and from the dissident members of the Executive Board with whom they were meeting the following week. She promised that we would hear from them soon. And so we were dismissed.

We left with a sense of anticlimax. We had worked so long and hard, that we had expected—what? That the school board would say "Okay, ladies, we'll take a look." Or maybe, even, "You're all crazy. What do you think public schools are? Of course you have to beat them into submission. How could our system operate if we really educated everyone? Who, to quote the esteemed Congressman Celler, would run our service industries? What's the matter with you, taking that education-for-all business at face value?"

What we had not expected was the vague hostility, the almost querulous feeling of annoyance that several of the board members had evidenced towards us. It was as though they really did not want to know of the school's trouble. We were forcing them to act, to make a decision that they were reluctant to make. What I sensed from their reaction was that they wished, if we were in trouble, that we would solve it ourselves or die quietly in a corner. Of course none of that was stated, and not every member of the board showed that reaction, but the feeling was there. And though as we walked home we tried to convince ourselves that obviously they could not act precipitously and that they had said we would hear from them soon, deep down I think we all sensed what they would say. Perhaps Irene Martins and Stephanie Hale had been correct in saying we were wasting our time with the local school board.

So it was over, and now we would have to wait till we heard from the school board, whenever that would be. And in the meantime things would continue as they had been—or almost, since now Mrs. Wachtel was quite aware of the profile and its contents (we had given her a copy when we presented the school board with theirs) and could be counted on to react in some way. We half expected the school doors to be barred the following morning.

Nothing of the sort happened, except to Ronnie, who was the first of us to run into Mrs. Wachtel post profile. The luckless Ronnie was subjected to a lengthy tongue-lashing, beginning with a catalog of her sins—from ingratitude to dishonesty to lord knows what all. Ronnie just stood and took it all to its conclusion, which was "I don't know whether to ignore it or to sue for libel." Upon sober reflection (or perhaps after consultation with an attorney—I don't know which) she chose the former course. And if anything further were needed to convince me that she was a woefully inadequate administrator, that reaction clinched it. It seemed to me there might have been other alternatives she could have considered—like calling us in and saying "Hey, those are pretty serious charges you make. Let's examine them together and see which are accurate and which distorted. And let's see what we can do about the charges that are accurate, to improve the school." I would hope that that's what I would have done.

After that harangue at Ronnie, nothing further happened. When I met Mrs. Wachtel in the hall, she was as friendly as ever. It gave me the creeps. And we waited for the school board's reply.

TEN

A Teachers' Proposal for an Alternative School—The Birth of the Infant-School Idea

During the last hectic weeks of our work on the profile, Anne had asked me to go in her place to a meeting she could not attend since she was on her way downtown with that day's pile of papers to be Xeroxed.

"A group of parents in the district want to start an infant school. Toni Diamond, Nancy Calvert, and Marion Rich (another of the PS 84 teachers who had taught in last year's Freedom school) will be there. I think they have some kind of proposal for starting it here. Can you go and report back to me?"

At that point I had only the vaguest idea of what an infant school was. I'd heard from the teachers about the kind of thing they'd done in the Freedom School and had seen the excitement and enthusiasm of the children during that time. But when the strike had ended, I really hadn't thought too much about it any more. However, I agreed to go, as much as a favor to Anne as for any other reason. I asked Millie whether she'd like to come along and she agreed, so on one bright afternoon the two of us made our way down Columbus Avenue to 87th Street where the meeting was being held.

It was a glorious spring day. The sun shone bright but not too hot, and a clean breeze blew from the river. Even Columbus Avenue, which on those blocks had not been entirely bulldozed into rubble and which still retained its original flavor—complete with the smell of cats and decay emanating from the tinned-up tenements—looked almost cheerful. In contrast to the empty lots and the abandoned

84

buildings, there was the two-story structure housing the office of the field representative of HDA, the outfit in charge of the whole urban renewal area. Its outer walls contained a multicolored mural that shone in the afternoon sun. We walked on past it to 87th Street, and turned east toward the park, looking for the house where the meeting was to take place. It was a renovated brownstone that we entered, and we introduced ourselves to the hostess, Sue Raskin, whom I had never met before but who greeted us warmly. She offered us our choice of iced tea or coffee and then directed us outside to the garden where, because of the beauty of the day, we would meet. We went outside and found about ten people already there. With the exception of our three teachers, none of them was familiar to me. We sat down on a bench, leaning against the wood fence that enclosed the garden from the surrounding houses and yards.

Most of the people there knew each other and talked of people and events strange to us. They also spoke with familiarity of the free day, dienes blocks, cuisenaire rods, Holt, Featherstone, Weber, and the Plowden Report. Millie and I felt as though we'd stumbled onto the wrong set of a movie lot. I felt out of my depth, so I listened a lot and discovered that a great deal had been written in the past few years about the type of education that our teachers had independently stumbled on in the Freedom School.

Nancy Calvert and Toni Diamond had put their thoughts about their Freedom School experience on tape, and excerpts of this had been published in *The Center Forum*.* While I waited for the formal meeting to begin, I glanced at the article, which described their feelings about the conventional school and classroom:

" . . . I slowly died within the public school system. I was not giving anything of myself. I was giving things that I felt had to be given, and I was becoming dull. I was becoming more concerned with the impression I was making generally rather than with what I was doing with the children, and I had gradually begun to feel more and more helpless and hopeless. If I was doing anything, I was maintaining a kind of hell, really, particularly since I've been teaching for three years children who've been two years behind grade level in reading. So I have basically been doing—or trying to do—

*Vol. 2, No. 4, October 5, 1967. *The Center Forum* is a publication of the Center for Urban Education.

and I'm not trained to do it—remedial reading and remedial math, and I have been making very little progress. And if somebody said to me, 'Well, there must have been one child you helped,' I'd have to say honestly and frankly that there was more than one. Probably in the three classes I've had, I could pick four or five to whom I felt I really gave a spur—you know, a reason for going to school, a love of learning, encouragement, that it's not so hard, you know, it's possible. They can learn to read better, they've got a brain that works—something like that. I've given this to these four or five children."

An incident that had made them conscious of what the school system was doing to them and to the children occurred on the Friday before the fall 1967 term began, when they had met with the principal and staff for the opening conference.

" . . . several of us were sort of dismayed when we were told by our principal that on the first day of school, we should be sure that we taught the children at least one new thing. Somebody nudged me and said 'That's for the parents' benefit.' Well, we were kind of involved in what we would be doing over the weekend and whether we would be coming back to school on Monday or not [the threat of the strike loomed], so that this statement the principal had made sort of went through us rather quickly, but it's been catching up with us since then, because we suddenly realized that to go in with an attitude where you spend the whole day with a kid, and all you have to be sure of is that you teach one new thing, when the kid is with you for six hours and twenty minutes—this is the standard that was being set for us."

But beyond a recitation of the shortcomings of the conventional school, of which by this time I was well aware, the two teachers had sketched a picture of what a school could be like, where education flowed out of the experiences of the children and the teacher, and subjects were learned (which is quite different from subjects being taught) as the need for them arose, so that from the reading of a book which one child had with him,

" . . . we got into a discussion of the Yiddish language, and a discussion of Central Europe, and how language sounds funny to some people, what kind of language Yiddish was. . . . They began to, you know, discuss with each other. As a matter of fact, I was no longer in the class. I was listening to them, but they were also absolutely unaware that I was there, except for a few questions that

I might have thrown after them, to keep them talking with each other, and they kept saying, 'No, you're wrong, listen,' and they were really trying to convince each other, and you don't see that in Board of Education rooms. You just don't see it. And there was no chaos. There was no chaos at all. The kids waited to be heard, and they waited to give each other a chance."

And further . . . "I even had a boy whom you might call a disruptive child—who, you know, in a regular classroom would be [considered disruptive]—and I said 'Wouldn't you like to sit here?' He said 'No, I'd rather sit here.' And I said, 'Well, if we're going to do some taking down of names of the people in this story, you won't be able to write.' He said, 'Oh, I can write.' And you know, he wasn't sitting. He was lying on the table that we were working around. And, you know, the thought occurred to me: 'What if somebody comes by and sees this?'

"Then I thought: 'Where the hell do you think you are? There's no principal who's going to walk by, there's no supervisor who's going to walk by—and why can't the kid, if he's more comfortable, if this is the way he wants to do it—we're not doing tremendously beautiful manuscript work that has to be presented to somebody or put on the wall for esthetic value—why not lie on the table and write that way?'

"And that's the way he did it. That's the way he worked. You know, from that point on, I realized that I was sort of breaking away or breaking through this kind of prison we seemed to have been working in."

What emerged from their account was a picture of a school without compulsion, a place where children learned because they needed to know, and consequently the problem of discipline, so prevalent in the traditional classroom, was all but nonexistent. When visitors came, as they frequently did, the children did not, as in the normal class, take it as a cue for bedlam, but went about their pursuits. They were too absorbed to be disruptive. And where a child did act up, since his classmates were by and large occupied with other things, the teacher could turn him around without a showdown, without his losing face as he would if all eyes were on him as in the traditional setup where the teacher is the focal point and all the children sit glued in their seats with their eyes front (though their minds may be elsewhere).

This glimpse of what a classroom could be was an exciting contrast to the reality I had come to know in the past half year at PS 84, and I was eager to learn more about this kind of education and what had prompted all these people—by then there were close to twenty—to come here of an afternoon to find an alternative to the conventional classroom.

In England, in early 1967, a government commission had made a study of the state schools and had issued a report of its findings. This Plowden Report (named for the commission's chairman, Lady Plowden) became the basis for many subsequent articles*, for it outlined an approach to teaching that was quite different from the traditional methods used in most schools in America. Whereas in the traditional classroom, with its fixed desks and seats, the teacher was the central focus of attention (when it worked) and the source of all knowledge, in the open classroom, or child-centered school (or any of a number of other names by which it is known in England and here), the child became a participant in his education. He ceased to be an empty vessel into which information was—hopefully —poured by the teacher, but rather, he became an agent, seeking out knowledge from many sources: books, classmates, tools, his world, the teacher—in short, from his total environment. As the teacher was no longer the only source of education, her constant presence at the front of the room became unnecessary, and she was freed both from the need to remain apart from her class (and to pretend to be omniscient) and from the attempt to force-feed forty children at once. She, and the children, moved about the room, partners in the pursuit of learning. And whereas in the traditional classroom the teacher is forced to aim at some middle, mythical child—thereby ignoring both the accelerated and the retarded learner—and producing some middle pablum that excites no one, including herself, here each child worked individually or in small groups devoted to a common goal, and each child got what he needed at the moment. This method made it possible for the teacher to work individually with each child at some time during the day, and though this time may have been no more than five or ten minutes, it would be a period in which the child would have the teacher's whole attention, geared to *his,* and not the entire class's, needs. And this would not be achieved at the cost of the boredom

*Among them Joseph Featherstone's in *The New Republic,* August 19, 1967, September 2, 1967, and September 9, 1967.

or irritation of the rest of the class, for they would be engaged in fruitful work of their own*. And this in a class of forty children in state schools in an urban industrial society not too different from New York City. This method of education, in some form, had been in use in various American private schools for some time. What caught the excitement of educators (and mine) was that it was being done successfully in public schools in England. And if it could work there, then why not here? It was to this question that we had come to address ourselves.

What emerged as the meeting progressed were two divergent strains. On the one hand, there were the teachers who were still not quite ready to give up on public education. On the other hand, there were the parents who had been gathered by Sue Raskin and who were, apparently, eager to set up an alternative school along the lines suggested by the Plowden Report, the Featherstone articles, and the writings of John Holt, Herbert Kohl, *et al.* And then there were Millie and I who at this point were observers—but learning fast.

Our teachers had written a tentative proposal of how a child-centered school could be set up within the framework of a public school in the district. They had, throughout the fall and winter, been trying to get the Ford Foundation or Columbia Teachers' College to provide funds to set up a pilot project within one of the public schools in our district. They had received encouragement (but, to date, no funds), and so they had shown it to Jessica Mala-mud, who had turned it over to Matthew Prior, the chairman of the Education Committee of the local school board, and they had just heard from Matt Prior that he found the idea interesting and wanted them to present it to the entire school board on May 20. The teachers were therefore hopeful that the school board might be

*Learning, with this approach, was an opening up of the child to unlimited possibilities. He or she could go as far as his or her interests and abilities allowed. Whereas traditional education is frequently the learning of limits (behavioral, intellectual, sexual), in the child-centered class the child was limited only by his own capacity. This means, among other things, that boys are not required to be quiet, conforming, passive, and that girls are not required to be interested only in things feminine. The materials are there for all the children, and a boy may knit, and a girl build a table, without the stereotyping so common in traditional schools.

willing to let them go ahead with plans to begin such a school in the fall. Sue Raskin and her friends, on the other hand, hoped to get foundation support for such a school, and to set it up in the community as a free community school—drawing children from the neighborhood on a first-come-first-served basis, but, by filling openings according to the ethnic composition of the neighborhood, making sure that they did not create another private school. Thus, if there were one hundred seats available, forty would be Spanish-speaking, thirty would be white, and thirty would be black, but within that framework it would simply be a matter of who applied first. Ability to pay would not be a factor since they were emphatic that the school must be tuition free and that its financing must come from foundations and from whatever fund-raising activities the involved parents could supply. What these parents wanted from our teachers was both their educational expertise—they had seen a copy of their proposal for an alternative school system—and, hopefully, their services as teachers in the school they were planning.

I listened to their plans for a while, then picked up a copy of the teachers' proposal and began to read and completely tuned out the conversation around me. The first part of the proposal dealt with the premises upon which it was based:

that the education of children could best be realized in an ungraded school where each child could develop to his maximum potential; that both free expression and self-discipline can best be developed in an environment of mutual respect; that schools *can* educate all children when such an environment is created; that children need a continuity of educational style in the early years; that the physical and personal arrangements of a school can be so structured as to enable the children to acquire the skills that are required of them in the early years.

The next part dealt with three broad areas—personnel (students, teachers, and administrators), materials and supplies, and the physical plant—and then went on to describe these three areas as they existed at PS 84. What they proposed was to take the school's approximately nine hundred children and fifty staff members, and break them down into three or four units, each reflecting the ethnic distribution of the current kindergarten through sixth grade populations. Each unit would group its children family style, with groups of five to seven year olds, seven to nine year olds, and nine to twelve year olds. Each unit would occupy one part of the school building, and be more or less self-contained except for a few schoolwide activities (such as fire drills or special assemblies). This would have the effect of breaking down a large, anonymous school into a series of more personal schools, which, in turn, would give each child more of a sense of identity with his school, his classmates, and his teachers. Each unit would have its own supply center, its own administrator, and its own library. What it would not have would be the old concept of closed, self-contained classrooms where every teacher did his own thing (good or bad) cut off completely from the rest of the school. Though teachers would be assigned to specific groups of children, there would be a great deal of interchange, both of children and of teachers, so that a child engaged in one activity might go to the teacher who was expert in that area. This would do away with the need for a teacher to be seemingly omniscient, or expert in all areas (clearly a human impossibility, though it is one our educational system tries to foist on our children, thus adding to the general dishonesty of the whole) and would provide everyone the freedom to learn—teachers as well as children. It would also provide children with the opportunity to go back to solve a problem that they had missed in an earlier stage of development, or to move ahead at their own pace even though, in the present scheme of things, they were not yet deemed chronologically "ready."

Since not all children would be engaged in the same pursuit simultaneously, the whole aspect of books and supplies would be altered. There would no longer be a need for a complete set of basal readers—a few copies per room would suffice—and therefore the variety of materials available could be increased at no additional cost. The same would apply for math and science materials, which, again, because the need for whole sets would be eliminated, could be enriched and varied with no greater expenditure of money. And thus the children would get, for the same price, increased value in the number of experiences available to them within the school setting.

The teachers' proposal then went on to draw a picture of a typical school day for one of the units. Looking at it now, I do not find it revolutionary; and when I consider that its architects were the very teachers who were almost brought up on charges by Mrs. Wachtel for refusing to salute the flag each morning (only the intercession of the PA prevented it), I am struck by how unrevolutionary the plan appears. And yet, as I was reading the proposal for the first time,

I felt it was most visionary and radical (which says something about the condition the school was in then and also something about how it has since changed.)

I finished reading the proposal (which included a bibliography of works written about this type of education) with a sense of excitement I had not felt about education for years. I wanted to know more, to read more, but at the same time I was already convinced that this approach to children and to learning made sense. Up until now I had known what was wrong with education as I saw it daily at PS 84. I had seen it in my contacts with Kathy's class, and I had seen it in the documents we were compiling for the profile. But all that was a document of what should not be. Here for the first time was an alternative—a positive, constructive proposal of what a school could be. And the feeling of frustration that had plagued me for so long, and that had been only partly dissipated by our work on the profile (which seemed a constructive step towards solving the school's problems, but which was not a solution in itself) was lifted. I said to myself, 'Yes, that's what a school should be like.'

I looked at Toni Diamond, Nancy Calvert, and Marion Rich with new respect. I had known that they were among the best, most creative, most concerned teachers in the school. I knew that their students, as well as their students' parents, loved and respected them. But now I saw them as the people who could lead our children out of the prison that was PS 84—and it all seemed so simple and so sensible. If only the school board would see it that way.

Millie and I walked home, clutching the copies of *The New Republic* containing the Featherstone articles, and bubbling over with visions. We were agreed on two things: that this was what we wanted for our kids, and that we did not want it outside of the public school. The type of community school that Sue Raskin and her friends envisaged, although free, would still be, in essence, a private school. By drawing off the most active teachers, parents, and children from the public school, it would weaken that still further. And though it might be grand for the hundred or so children thus creamed off, what would become of the rest? Besides, this sort of thing had been tried in private schools—with success—for years. Another experiment of this type would prove nothing. But if it could be introduced into a public school with all its problems, and if it could work there, then that would be proving something that could revolutionize public education. So we felt we had to make the push to make this happen in a public school (preferably ours, since we already had a nucleus of teachers committed to this philosophy), and as we walked home we resolved to do several things: first, to go with the teachers to the local school-board meeting scheduled for May 20th to support their proposal; second, to mobilize parents in our school community to come along to the school-board meeting; third, to press the candidates running for the Joan of Arc governing board for a commitment to this philosophy, and to vote for those candidates who shared this commitment. During that six-block walk we outlined a series of meetings throughout the community to let parents see the proposal, talk to the teachers, and ask questions. We had also learned at the meeting that Lillian Weber had made a film about the infant schools in Britain, and we thought that perhaps we could show this film, as well as one made about the Nova School in Florida, so that parents could actually see this type of education in operation.

That afternoon marked a turning point for me. From that point on my activities had a focus. I was so longer merely criticizing those aspects of the school that I had felt, all along, were damaging, but I was now working toward something positive. And for the first time I understood what Stephanie Hale meant about principals on the Board of Examiners' lists being interchangeable parts—that to get rid of one and replace her with her twin sister would not help the school. She was right, and from then on the only principal I would be interested in would be one who viewed education as it was being practiced as the same disaster we did, and who would work with us to transform it into the kind of exciting experience it should be. So that when Jessica Malamud asked us at the school-board meeting where we presented the profile whether a new principal would solve the problems, we answered no, and we did so for several reasons. On the one hand, the dissenting members of the Executive Board had accused us of using the profile as a subterfuge to get rid of Mrs. Wachtel, and we wanted to disprove that. On the other, we felt that only if the whole structure of the school could be changed would it be meaningful to have a new principal. It wasn't till things got so bad at the school that we realized we couldn't wait and that we needed a new principal even while the school was still in a transitional stage—but at that moment we still believed that the structural changes must come first.

ELEVEN

"The Problems at PS 84 Seem to
Us Capable of Solution"

The profile was hardly dead and buried (we hadn't even gotten the death certificate from the local school board yet) when we began to organize a series of meetings around the community to discuss the teachers' proposal. One of these was held in our co-op community room, and in addition to about fifty parents from our co-op (only some of whom had children at PS 84) there were present Nancy Calvert, Toni Diamond, Marion Rich, and a few other teachers from PS 84. When we first moved into the co-op, many parents had put their children into public school. I don't know on what basis they had decided. I do know that when Walter had asked a member of our Board of Directors about PS 84, she had answered that it *had* been awful, but that now, under the aegis of the new principal (Mrs. Wachtel), who was marvelous, things were looking up. Well, if Mrs. Wachtel was marvelous, I shudder to think what her predecessor was like. At any rate, whether on that recommendation or on faith, many Stryckers Bay children started at PS 84. Many of those did not stay long. One or two experiences with the school sent the applications flying to private schools, so that by this time perhaps half of our co-op's children were no longer in the public school system. The fact that their parents came to our meeting on the teachers' proposal indicated, I think, that they had left in desperation and that given a viable alternative they would consider giving the public school another try.

We showed two films that evening, first Lillian Weber's and then the film on the Nova School. Mrs. Weber's film was in black and white—not a slick production, almost candid-camera style. It

94

seemed practically unedited, as though the camera had been set up and left to record. And what it recorded was a scene of teachers and children coming together with joy—busy, active, lively—noisy at times, seemingly unstructured at others, but without that element of chaos and repression that was the essence of public education in New York City. The feeling that emerged from the teachers and children was one of interest and excitement in what they were doing. And what was fascinating was that they seemed oblivious to the presence of the camera. I can picture a movie crew in a Board of Education classroom (and I have seen films taken in the New York City schools). Either the children ham it up for the camera, or they studiously avoid it by keeping their eyes glued to the front of the room, their backs rigid with the effort of ignoring the photographic eye. But in neither instance do they move with complete lack of self-consciousness because they are not absorbed by what the classroom has to offer. This was obviously not the case in the school Mrs. Weber portrayed, and it was beautiful.

The film on the Nova School was slicker. First of all it was in color. Secondly the school itself was physically more impressive. The British school was housed in an old building, lacking in all the *things* from which Americans derive such joy. The Nova School was shiny, new, chock full of the latest educational gadgetry—electric typewriters, teaching machines with individual headphones, well-equipped labs, closed-circuit television—a cornucopia of books, supplies, games—you name it. The children themselves, though colorful, seemed sleeker, better fed, more middle class than their British counterparts. But what was as evident in the children in the Nova School as in the British schoolchildren was their joy in learning. The camera here, it is true, seemed more selective, but even granted that, it was awe-inspiring that they had such material to select from. Here were children discussing—with thought—current events and the democratic process. The point, over and over again, was that their minds and their hearts were engaged. They were thinking. They were feeling. They were learning. They helped each other, taught each other, argued and disagreed with each other—and respected each other. And I thought of Kathy in her kindergarten, endlessly coloring, coming home to tell me that Jose wouldn't be promoted to first grade if he didn't learn to sit still, and I wanted to cry.

The response to the films, and to the teachers' proposal, was

enthusiastic. There were many questions, of course, largely centering about two general areas: 1) What happens to a child who only
wants to play (or who goes on for weeks pursuing only one thing)?
and 2) Will they really learn as much this way as the other way?
These questions would crop up again and again at subsequent
meetings, and the answers to them were not simplistic. The point
is that few children, given the opportunity to explore many exciting,
educationally constructive areas, will, for any length of time "just
play." Of course, what may seem like play to an outsider may be
serious learning to a child. For example, a child pouring water
endlessly from one container to another may appear to be just
splashing when, in reality, he is testing and mastering the concept
that a half ounce remains a half ounce whether it is in a large
container or a small one. Furthermore, where a child does persist
in fooling around over a long period of time—because he has already been so conditioned that he is incapable of moving without
firm direction—the teacher, freed from her obligation to assume
that everyone is at the same stage of development, will see the
child's floundering, and will be there to direct him and to encourage
him, slowly, to develop the kind of inner direction which should be
the aim of all education.

As for the second question, we have assumed for too long that
because certain curricular material was "covered" by the teacher in
a certain grade it was learned by the children. A look at the scores
on achievement tests should be enough to convince anyone that
nothing could be further from the truth, so that an answer to this
question might be another question: how much are they learning
now? And, more important, what are they learning now? Those of
us who had been working on the profile could answer that—not very
much besides how to judge their peers, how to sit still and conform,
and how to still the questioning voice inside of them. If they learned
at all, it was that there were "right" answers to complex questions
and that thinking was less important than spitting back those right
answers. If the definition of a liberal is that he sees both sides of an
issue, then our children were certainly not being given a liberal
education in New York City schools.

The point of the films, and of our discussion with the teachers,
was that education could free the children to learn and that, once
freed, they would learn more than they were presently doing. I think
anyone who looks back honestly at his own education will recall all

the occasions when he sat in a room, seemingly rapt by the wisdom the teacher was imparting, but actually miles away in another world. It is easy to fake attention. It is impossible to fake life!

We took our traveling road show of films and teachers to various other co-ops and buildings in the community. In each case the response was equally enthusiastic. We began to talk of setting up such meetings for the Spanish-speaking residents of the neighborhood, and arranged one for the Centro D'Accion. It was all set, fliers had gone out, Spanish-speaking parents had agreed to accompany the teachers and act as interpreters, when Martin Luther King was assassinated. And so the meeting never took place.

In the meantime we went with the teachers to the local school board and Dr. Selig to present their proposal. It was a replay of the profile meeting. The characters were beginning to speak predictable lines. Jessica was sympathetic. Gonzalez-Patron recounted his happy school life with rules and rulers. Somers and/or Patterson asked hard, practical questions. Goodfellow exuded charm and not too much comprehension. Elizabeth Dodge listened. And Dr. Selig sat impassive. He came to life only once, to ask the teachers whether they had shown their proposal to Mrs. Wachtel. When they answered in the negative, he asked why not. (I was interested to see that he had a voice.) The teachers answered that they felt she would not be receptive, since she had, in the past, vetoed any innovative ideas they had approached her with and that, further, she must have been aware of their article in *The Center Forum*, yet she had never discussed its ideas with them. They therefore concluded that she was not interested in their ideas. And since they did nót wish to waste anyone's time—if this program were to be implemented in time for the fall opening of school, time was of the essence—they had written their proposal, bypassed Mrs. Wachtel, and come directly to the school board and the district superintendent. This social blunder on their part produced, in due course, a letter from Dr. Selig to Mrs. Diamond. Dated June 10, 1968, the letter thanked the teachers for sharing their proposal with him. He went on to say that though he found the proposal interesting he would, in the end, find it unacceptable unless the final plan was the result of direct and close participation between the teachers and Mrs. Wachtel.

He then took them to task for sending the plan to him without their principal's permission. He informed them that Mrs. Wachtel wished to work in close partnership with them, other interested teachers, and representative parents in producing the final plan that could then be submitted to him.

He said he had a number of questions about their tentative plan, but that he preferred to hold these questions until he saw a final, cooperative work. He warned that any experiment would be limited, at the outset, to no more than two or three classes, in order to be able to assess its validity. And finally he pointed out that the implementation of any plan could not take place before a period of at least six months to a year.

June 10 must have been an auspicious day for letter writing, for the same day produced an answer to the profile committee from the local school board. To wit:

RESOLUTION OF LOCAL SCHOOL BOARD 5
CONCERNING PS 84 ADOPTED AT
EXECUTIVE MEETING OF JUNE 10, 1968

The local school board has studied the material concerning PS 84 submitted by a group of parents, and has met and spoken with a variety of parents, teachers, and administrators.

1. The problems at PS 84 seem to us capable of resolution if each element in the system would do its share and if all pulled together. The principal has demonstrated a willingness to make changes and to innovate. To assist in the resolution of specific problems, and thereby to improve the entire school atmosphere, we recommend that a parent-principal complaint committee be created, the parents to be elected by the PA, and to consist of parents who can work constructively and vigorously with the principal. The committee should meet frequently, and regularly, and must have the whole-hearted cooperation of the principal. It should be a channel for the prompt consideration of complaints and implementation of remedies.

2. Moreover, the District Superintendent and his staff should visit PS 84 more frequently in order to provide more direct leadership and to assist and supervise the principal and to help improve teachers and teaching.

3. In addition, a teacher trainer should be assigned to PS 84 with a skill and sensitivity suitable to the needs of that school.

4. The Board of Education has directed that complaints of parents and others concerning the operation of the school, when they cannot be resolved at the school level, should be referred to the local school board. Our board has reviewed, and will continue to review, such complaints in order to provide remedies where we can, or to fix professional responsibility, so that appropriate steps can be taken against the teacher or supervisor responsible. With decentralization imminent, we hope, we shall continue to

work with parents, teachers, and administrators to improve schools. Where principals or teachers function below appropriate professional standards, we shall insist that administrative machinery for rating professional personnel be more stringently adhered to, even if transfer from this district or separation from the service may be the ultimate outcome.
We invite the members of the PS 84 community to remain in contact with us.

So there we had it—two communications from up the bureaucratic ladder, telling us, in each case, to be good little boys and girls and cooperate with our principal, who waited eagerly, arms open, to welcome us (sinners though we might be, and unrepentant at that) back to her ample and forgiving bosom and to work with us cooperatively for the greater good and glory of PS 84. The teachers had been working on their proposal for close to a year. We had been working on our profile for two months. Now we were told that nothing could be done except jointly with the principal, whose indifference to our pleas for help had sent us to the school board and Dr. Selig in the first place! Dr. Selig's letter was particularly offensive because it implied that whatever the merits of the teachers' proposal might be, they could not be considered until and unless the principal put her stamp on it by making it a "final, cooperative document." And if a camel is a horse designed by a committee, I could imagine what that final cooperative plan would look like!

Still, we were good little boys and girls, and if committees were what they needed, then committees they should have. Thus, one bright morning, Anne, Millie, Dotty Steinberg, Beth Barron, Walter, and I went to see Mrs. Wachtel to set up a parent-principal committee. So here we were again in Mrs. Wachtel's office (throughout this whole time the events took on more and more of a feeling of déja vu), and she was as cordial and smiling as though the profile had never been comtemplated, much less written, and as though there were not four of us present who had been its creators. There were two areas of confusion on Mrs. Wachtel's part—the first minor and quickly cleared up, the second apparently insoluble. The first concerned the presence of Walter. She wanted to know, first, who he was, and second what he did (I guess it was unthinkable that a father would take time off from work unless summoned because of a serious infraction perpetrated by his child). On this question we were able to enlighten her easily: he is my husband, and he is a freelance film editor. The other area of confusion, though, she never did resolve, and that was her belief that we *were* the committee requested by Dr. Selig, rather than that we had come to set up the mechanics for forming such a committee. And try as we might to make that distinction, she never did grasp it, so that when we finally managed to set up a meeting of parents, teachers, and administration to discuss a child-centered program at PS 84, no committee of parents was formed, and Millie and Dotty became, largely as a result of their efforts to make that meeting happen, the heads of the committee.

And effort is what it took to get that meeting. Mrs. Wachtel agreed to it, and even set a date—Thursday, June 20—but from that point on Millie and Dotty were on their own. They wrote the flier to the parents. They saw that it got translated. They nursed it through the stencil-typing and mimeographing. They stuffed and addressed the envelopes to the parents, licked the stamps, and took the finished mailing to the post office. And this was the lady who, in the words of Dr. Selig, wished to be "a close partner" with us. Well, we were pulling together, as the local school board had directed, but we had not bargained for the fact that while pulling together we would have to pull her along.

The one thing we asked for that Mrs. Wachtel agreed to without resistance was that she arrange a time for a showing of the Nova School film for her teachers. Many of them had seen Lillian Weber's film when she had spoken at PS 87, but we felt it would be useful if they could see the program at work in an American school. Since Walter had a print of the film, and was willing to act as projectionist, Mrs. Wachtel had only to provide the time, the space, and the teachers. And she did—but in her efficient fashion she chose a forty-five minute lunch period to show a one-hour film. The result was that as the film ran on, the teachers trickled out (they had to get back to their classes), and so the visions of educational change were displayed, finally, to Mrs. Wachtel, Miss Federman, and Walter, surrounded by the grandeur of the empty auditorium.

"June 20th, at 3 PM in the school auditorium—Come and Help Plan an exciting new educational program for PS 84" promised the fliers, under the imprimatur of Mrs. Wachtel and the PA of the school. Those of us who had been living with the idea of a child-centered school for the past few weeks had high hopes and grand plans. True, we had met a verbal barrage from Mrs. Wachtel in her office. True, Dr. Selig's warning that "its application will be limited at first to two or three classes" and not for a period of "at least six months to a year" was on our minds, but we were eager to discuss specifics with the teachers and with Mrs. Wachtel. Furthermore, in our own conversations we had agreed that though we obviously could not convert the entire school overnight, we felt it not unreasonable to ask (and be granted) that one class on each grade be designated a child-centered class and that these classes be given one wing of the school, thereby creating a minischool, a school within a school, where the efficacy of this type of education could be proved—or disproved. One of the reasons for asking this was that time after time in our school (and, no doubt, in others, too) noble experiments were begun in the first grade with a small group of children, and by the time those children got to third grade the experiment had been dropped and the kids left hanging, while a new one was begun with the next crop of first graders. This had happened to our present third grade—one of the sources of complaint in the profile—and those parents in particular were determined that this would not happen again and that anything that was begun should have some kind of continuity. And further, since our present third-graders had already had a series of educational fiascos, we felt the school had an obligation to include them in a program which held such promise of success. And so we went into the meeting agreed that we would accept no less than one class per grade.

The auditorium, even in winter, is airless. On this June afternoon it was stifling, and the hundred or more parents and teachers who sat cheek by jowl fanned themselves absent-mindedly with whatever papers they had on hand. Dotty, who had nursed the meeting into being (and who was reeling with a high fever), opened with a brief speech outlining the history of our interest, and the teachers' efforts. She concluded with our demand: at least one child-centered class per grade, and a commitment that every parent who requested that his child be in the program have the request honored, so that, if need be, in some instances there would be more than one such class for a grade.

Dotty had spoken from the front of the auditorium, from the floor. Now Mrs. Wachtel climbed the three steps onto the stage and, tight-lipped, began to talk. She said she was sorry that not all the teachers who were interested in the program could be there, but she had sent several of them to Queens to look at Reba Mayer's school in the round, where such a program was already in effect; and since these teachers were the ones who would be staffing our classes in the fall she wanted them to have an opportunity to see this program in action.

"Why today?" someone called out. "Shouldn't they be here with us?"

"There was a conflict in time. I'm sorry," said Mrs. Wachtel. We were furious. She had known of this meeting for over a week. It seemed more than coincidence that she had sent the teachers off at the very time our meeting was scheduled.

"Who are the teachers?" someone else called.

"We're getting ahead of ourselves," said Mrs. Wachtel. "Let me tell you what I have planned." That "I have planned" set the tone of the meeting. If we had imagined that this would be a joint venture that phrase disabused us. Now a tall, pretty young woman rose. I recognized her as Wilma Austin, one of the first-grade teachers.

"I was supposed to go to Queens," she said, "but I feel torn. I'd really like to stay and hear what the parents have to say. But if I stay does it mean I can't participate in the program?"

Mrs. Wachtel smiled and said, "It might."

We gasped. Wilma sat down and stayed—a small and uncharacteristic act of definace on her part. She was, from all accounts, a good teacher, and she was interested in the program, but she was unpolitical. She did her job and fought when it came to principle, but she was not engaged in the intrigues and in-fighting that were so characteristic of the school at that time. But now she sat and did not give in to the thinly veiled threat and I cheered her silently.

Mrs. Wachtel then continued, again with a small tight smile. She had, she told us, gotten from Dr. Selig (here it came, out of a hat) funds to set up four ungraded classes in the school. These would be two kindergarten and two first grade classes, and they would carry with them an additional position of a coordinator. She spoke at length, using the term ungraded classes interchangeably with the child-centered school. At this point we got even more uneasy. Ungraded classes are quite different from the infant school. The former is simply another means of structuring classes; and though within it there *can* be a child-centered approach (and in England the infant schools do group various ages together), the two are by no means synonymous. It seemed inconceivable to us that Mrs. Wachtel could confuse—or equate—the two. Either she thought she could deflect us by dangling the carrot of ungraded classes because she was philosophically opposed to the infant school, or else she truly did not see the difference. In either case she was hardly the person who could implement our program.

Someone asked how the teachers' proposal fitted into this setup. Mrs. Wachtel bristled and seemed to have little knowledge of any teachers' proposal. This idea was hers, had been germinating for years; and when the district office had sent a circular to the school asking whether they would like to set up such classes, she had naturally jumped at the chance, and presto, here we were. What were ungraded classes? Well, the kindergarten and first grades would be combined, so that each class would have both five and six year olds. The children would be selected by her on the basis of their maturity or lack of maturity, so that mature kindergartners would be grouped with less mature first graders. We asked how she could judge the maturity of incoming kindergartners who had never been in the school before.

"I will make that judgment," she answered. In addition to the maturity mixture, the classes would, of course, be ethnically balanced.

"Will you honor parents' requests to have their children in the program?" I asked.

"I'll take it into consideration."

"But will you honor them?"

"I'll take it into consideration. I must make the final judgment. That's my job."

"How will you choose the teachers?" someone asked.

"I'll choose them."

"Will you honor teachers' requests?"

"I'll consider them."

"What about the teachers who made the original proposal? Will they be considered?"

"They'll be considered."

"Will they be selected?"

"They'll be considered."

"Suppose," asked Mrs. Sumner, a teacher who had been coming to our meetings on the child-centered school, "we're not one of the teachers selected? Can we work outside of those classes and pool our skills with other teachers in the grade who want to try?"

"NO!"

Nancy Calvert shot up as if she'd been jabbed by a pin.

"Why can't we work on our own with another teacher in our grade or in the next grade?"

"Because, Mrs. Calvert, there's a Board of Education curriculum and it has to be covered."

"I know that, Mrs. Wachtel. But if we cover the curriculum, but want to do it in a different way, can't we do it? As long as we cover the basic curriculum?"

"No!"

"Why not?"

"Because this is a small experiment. We have to proceed slowly. We don't have the proper supervision. And even *good* teachers need supervision, Mrs. Calvert."

"You mean you won't let us work on our own program?"

"It's not your program. You may have written some plan, but this is *not* your program. It's my program, and I'll decide who teaches in it."

"Suppose more parents express interest in the program, will you expand it?" someone asked.

"No."

"Will you at least poll the parents and see how many want it?"

"If you like."

"And if there's an overwhelming demand . . .?"

"No. There will be only four classes."

"Why won't you consider the teachers who've written the proposal?" someone called.

"I'm going to staff those classes with good teachers. And I'll decide who the good teachers are. Just because some teachers run to parents all the time doesn't make them good teachers. Anyone can write a proposal, but it's the day-to-day work that counts. I don't want teachers who cut corners and don't give more of themselves than they have to. I don't want immature teachers. I'm the principal and it's my responsibility to choose the best teachers. I'd be shirking my responsibility if I let someone else dictate personnel decisions!"

There it was—a power struggle. And she had the power! We never polled the parents because it would have been dishonest. Since she would not honor parental requests, it was pointless to have parents make them. She had laid great stress on the need to strike the proper balance, in these four ungraded classes, between mature and immature children. That was her criterion. The child-centered program does not require any such balance. It only requires children. Yet when the time came to form the classes, she violated her own criteria by promoting the children, en masse, from the present kindergartens into the two first grades. (How the new kindergarten children were chosen I do not know.) She ignored her own standards and resorted, instead, to the most mechanical method available—whole class promotion. And this after she had laid such stress on the need to exercise her professional judgment.

The teachers she chose, in the exercise of that same professional judgment, were also a mixed bag. Neither Nancy nor Toni were, of course, selected. Nor was Marion Rich. The two first-grade teachers and one of the kindergarten teachers proved to be excellent. The other kindergarten teacher was none other than Mrs. Winter, Kathy's kindergarten teacher! The coordinator was a woman who had expressed hostility toward the child-centered philosophy and who ultimately fled back to a traditional classroom. I suppose one might argue that three out of four isn't a bad batting average, given the total teacher population. But when one considers that she had available to her three teachers who had already spent a great deal of time, energy, and thought on this program and who were by all standards, but hers, excellent teachers, then her batting average looks less impressive, and one is left with the inescapable conclusion that she acted not from the standard of professional judgment, but from pique (at best).

Thus ended, almost before it began, the close partnership between us and our principal. If we went in with illusions about the possibility for change under her aegis, we did not come out with them.

TWELVE

"Up With the Picket Signs—
Down With the Principal"

During this period there were two elections. The first was the PA election at our school on June 15 which was, as usual, marked by crashing apathy. Carmen Johnson, a Spanish-speaking parent who worked as an aide in the school, was running unopposed. At the election meeting we did make two historic decisions: 1) that we establish the radical idea that every parent in the school be a voting member of the PA—that dues-paying no longer be a prerequisite for voting; and 2) that we disaffiliate from the United Parents' Associations. The latter was necessary to effect the former. (The UPA constitution stipulates that member PA's limit voting members to those who have paid their dues.) In addition, we felt that UPA was more conservative, more establishment-oriented, than we liked.

The other election, which took place on June 15, was the election of the Joan of Arc governing board. There had been a meeting at our school to meet the candidates. It was well attended, but I had not found it terribly enlightening. I had gone to hear how the various candidates thought the school could be improved; but they had, by and large, never gotten beyond citing the need for improvement. They were all strong for community control, which was why they were running; but community control often meant different things to different speakers. Certainly it was a flag that was waved frequently, and anyone who wanted to be heard at a meeting had to preface his remarks with an invocation to community control. But there were factions in the neighborhood, apparently centering around degrees of control. There was a group for "responsible" community control (was there another for "irresponsible" community control?) who ultimately boycotted the election because "responsible" came to mean not now but in some nebulous future. There was the group for total community control (The West Side Committee for Decentralization), and there were all sorts of people in between.

There was also some confusion between community control and decentralization, the latter meaning simply the breaking up, administratively, of the central bureaucracy at 110 Livingston Street and placing the administration of the schools in the hands of the local districts, but still run by the professional staff from those districts. There were also those people who felt that total community control would mean that parents would run amok in the schools, charging into classrooms, telling teachers what and what not to teach, capriciously firing every teacher who displeased them (at the moment) on the spot, and altogether violating every tenet of civil service and academic freedom.

As far as I could understand it, the kind of community control that the West Side Committee sought was, first of all to decentralize the bureaucracy, but in addition, to make the schools accountable to the parent community. This did not mean that parents would run the day-to-day operations. Logically this is impossible. But the people who would be hired (notably the superintendent) would be responsible to the community, and obviously a person hired by the community would work for the kind of results that community desired. He would set the standards that the community wanted and would translate these into programs for teachers to follow. And teachers who knew that their ultimate employer was the parent community might gain some respect for the parents, and their children, instead of thinking of them merely as a necessary evil who produced the product that kept them in business. I don't think anybody had any illusions of setting up the kind of kangaroo court system that Shanker and the UFT sold to the public, subsequently, as the parents' definition of community control. That certainly was never my idea, nor that of any of the people I got to know during this period.

There was also the political struggle for recognition that the West Side Committee was engaged in. Since the Board of Education had decided against making the Joan of Arc complex into a fourth demonstration district, the election might have no validity. Consequently there was a great deal of lobbying, with city and state officials, to have the Joan of Arc complex specifically included in any legislation on the subject. At one meeting I attended at the FDR-Woodrow Wilson Democratic (reform) Club in the early spring of 1968, the proponents of "responsible" community control wanted the club to substutute their motion (to do nothing—hastily) for one endorsing the Joan of Arc complex and election. The responsible folk were resoundingly beaten back.

Since the demonstration districts were only an interim arrangement and legislation was then being considered for a comprehensive decentralization bill, the fate of our complex, as well as that of the other districts, had moved from the hands of the Board of Education to those of the state legislators. Senator Ohrenstein, an avowed advocate of community control, tried to effect a compromise and get us to accept the idea of a Joan of Arc planning, but not governing, board. He felt that he could get his fellow legislators to accept that idea where they would not accept another full demonstration district. But we felt that we had to go for the planning/governing board, and not for some half-baked compromise. As it ultimately turned out, we got killed in the legislature (both in the 1968 Marchi Bill and in the final 1969 version) by the simple expedient of being ignored. They never had the guts to spell us out of existence entirely. All the subsequent acts read "the demonstration districts"—never giving us birth by saying "the four districts," yet never quite killing us entirely by saying three. So we hung in, in a sort of limbo, for several years while the elected governing board had a modicum of power by virtue of its existence and of grants given it by foundations.

Against this background there had been a great deal of active campaigning, and now the election was upon us. Though I had not been too involved in it I had done volunteer work—typing of lists, getting out the vote in our co-op, and the like. I had also attended several of the meetings that were held to give us a chance to see and talk to the candidates. At one of these, held in the storefront that the West Side Committee had rented (a former bar that had been stripped of most of its furnishings but still retained the tiled floor and the polished wooden bar, as well as the aroma of beer and liquor) those of us who had become interested in setting up an infant school in the district had tried to get the various candidates to express their views on the program. It was disappointing. None of the candidates, including Jim Calvert, Nancy's husband, felt that the time had come to discuss educational programs. They all felt that first the board must be elected, and then they would have to look at the five schools and at various educational approaches before they could commit themselves to any philosophy. We argued that we would have a more intelligent basis for voting if we knew where the candidates stood on specific educationsl issues; but to a man—and woman—they did not see it our way, and we were left to vote for them on other bases.

The election itself took place on a Saturday. It was a bright, clear day, and the turnout was better than it is in some municipal elections. More than a third of the eligible parents voted, and this in spite of a boycott organized by the Committee for Responsible Decentralization, who said till the end that they could not vote in an election unsanctioned by the Board of Education. The West Side Committee had gotten a small grant from the Institute for Community Studies to run the election, and so the mechanics of it were administered by the Honest Ballot Association, thus assuring that the results would be aboveboard. The voting procedure was as follows: there would be one ballot permitted per family for each child they had in a public school in the complex. Each school would elect three people to sit on the board. Thus, each voter would vote for three candidates (or for one candidate three times) for each child in the public schools.

Walter left home early that morning, and with a small crew of cameramen filmed the process, interviewing candidates on their hopes for the board and their views of the schools, and interviewing parents who came to vote on their reasons for participating. And parent after parent—black, white, and Spanish—expressed the opinion that the schools were failing the kids, that the election seemed the only hope of reversing the trend of failure, that only with community control could the schools change to serve the children instead of the professionals. The only ominous rumblings of power, and struggle, and confrontation came from the boycotters who had come to watch. They were worrying about irresponsible elements seizing control and using the schools for their own sinister ends. And they spoke of Ocean-Hill Brownsville and the storm that was brewing there, which they feared would engulf us too if we elected a community board. They were very responsible—but obviously not for the children who were leaving the elementary schools for junior high school reading on a second grade level! When it was all over, and the ballots were counted, the winners from PS 84 were

Jim Calvert, Mike Goodman, and Isabella Hernandez.

The following Friday night I got a frantic call from Anne. She had been succeeded as president of the PA by Carmen Johnson, but she was still very much involved in the school. She had just spoken to Nancy Calvert who had told her that that day she and Toni Diamond had gotten an offer to teach in the IS 201 complex. They had gone to Mrs. Wachtel with their forms requesting a transfer, and Mrs. Wachtel had smilingly signed them. Both Toni and Nancy seemed dismayed that Mrs. Wachtel made no effort to dissuade them from transferring (which I think was an incredible indication of naiveté on their part); and so, undissuaded, they were going to process their papers and leave the school. They both felt they could not continue in a school that was so hostile to them and their ideas, where they were stifled at every turn from doing what they considered necessary to reach their children. I could certainly sympathize with them, but I hated to lose them.

"What can we do?" I asked Anne.

"I was thinking of picketing the school," she said. "It isn't only them. Mrs. Wachtel isn't rehiring about twelve of the best young teachers—most of the ones who've expressed interest in the infant school or who have made waves in any way. And she's letting a few good men teachers go, and lord knows we can't afford to lose men teachers."

She then named some of the teachers we were losing, and I groaned. It read like a list of all those who supported the parents, who cared about the children, and who managed, under adverse conditions, to make a difference. True we would not be losing every good teacher (some of them had tenure) but every good teacher who was vulnerable was on that list. On the other hand, not on the list were some of the teachers, also not tenured, whose names had come up again and again during the profile as being cruel and/or racist. It certainly seemed proof that Mrs. Wachtel protected the bigots and incompetents and punished the creative, effective teachers—yet another example of her willingness "to innovate and make changes."

"Has anyone tried to get her to rehire any of them?" I asked.

"Oh, yes. Some of us went to her. Some of the parents have written letters. No soap."

"What will picketing accomplish?"

"Well, maybe it will embarrass her into changing her mind. If we can get some press coverage, maybe Dr. Selig will even be embarrassed and do something. Anyway, I want to show her that I support Nancy and Toni, and that if I have to choose between her and them I know whom I'll choose."

"Okay. Count me in. What would you like me to do?"

"Call everyone you know and ask them to join us. Tell them to come to my house tomorrow and we'll make signs, and plan strategy."

So I got on the phone and called everyone I knew. The next day, in my travels, I buttonholed everyone I knew; and by the time we gathered at Anne's house that afternoon we had about fifty people committed to join us. Some of the people we had approached drew back; they did not like the idea of picketing the school. Others promised to come. Some agreed in principle, but couldn't bring themselves to join us. Others saw it as another move to oust Mrs. Wachtel—the charge that had been leveled at us when we began the profile—and would not participate for that reason. But there was quite a crowd at Anne's house, and we lettered signs with enthusiasm and Magic Marker. WE NEED GOOD TEACHERS MORE THAN BAD PRINCIPALS. MRS. WACHTEL KEEPS RACISTS AND FIRES GOOD TEACHERS.

And so on in that vein. We worked all weekend, lining up people for the picket line, making signs in both English and Spanish, getting in touch with the press, the school board, and the newly elected Joan of Arc planning/governing board.

On Sunday evening, the night before the picketing was planned, we met with the Joan of Arc board and members of the West Side Committee at the home of Jim and Nancy Calvert. Jim, Mike Goodman, and Isabella Hernandez (the three PS 84 board members), as well as six of the members from the other schools were there. The Calvert's sunken living room was fairly large, but we sat wedged on the sofa, on the floor, doubled up on chairs. Latecomers hung over the wrought-iron railing that separated the living room from the foyer or stood in the foyer itself, shifting from foot to foot. The light was dim, and as the evening wore on the room thickened with cigarette smoke so that it became increasingly harder to see across to the other side. And in spite of open windows, it was hot. I sat on the overstuffed couch, sinking, next to a gentleman whose name I never quite caught, and with whom, from time to time, I engaged in side conversation. He felt that picketing was hardly radical enough, and at the same time, too much to ask of the new board. I tried to convert him, unsuccessfully, to our point of view.

Anne presented our case in the crowded living room—a review of all the ills of the school that we had included in the profile, as well as a recital of the events since then, the meeting about the infant school, and the impending departure of Toni and Nancy. There followed intensive questioning on the part of the new board, dealing not only with our complaints, but also with our tactics—and, again, with our lack of representation of the school population as a whole. The questions flew fast and hard, and the room, not too cool to begin with, became heated with the crowd and the emotions.

"Why are the teachers leaving?"

"Did the PA discuss the situation with Mrs. Wachtel?"

"Are you talking as PA president or as an individual parent?"

"How come there are no black or Spanish parents participating?"

"Given the present rules, how will you get a better principal?"

"Why didn't you call a general PA meeting?"

And so on in that vein. Anne answered, and the rest of us as well, as best we could. We explained that there had been no time to call a general meeting, that if we waited the teachers would be gone. We did not claim to represent anyone but ourselves, and we were acting spontaneously, instinctively, because we were fed up with inaction. We had written the profile, and nothing had happened. We had tried to meet with Mrs. Wachtel, and nothing had happened. Now the teachers were going, and we were unwilling to wait longer—nice and polite—for nothing to happen. We hoped the governing board would support us; we hoped that other parents, when they saw the picket line tomorrow, would also support us. We were sorry we did not represent everyone, but we had called everyone we knew in the hopes that they would join us. Yes, we had called black and Spanish parents, too.

"You only called those parents who agreed with you," accused one member of our Executive Board [who had signed the statement of support of the school]. "No one called me. The Executive Board has voted several times against action versus Mrs. Wachtel. This goes against the expressed vote of the Executive Board. And why isn't Carmen picketing?"

ANNE: "She felt that since there was no time to call a PA meeting she couldn't participate since her presence would be construed as making this a PA action—which it isn't. She said that regardless of how she felt personally she represented the PA and therefore could not act without their approval."

There was more along these lines. The board members were very serious, very eager to do the right thing, the responsible thing. They wanted to support parents—but were we all the parents? They also felt that the eyes of the community and of the world were upon them, and that any action they took should be responsible and well thought out. After having asked their questions, they retired to another room to deliberate, leaving us facing the opposition. Stephanie Hale was there, and Irene Martins, and Norma Hill (whom I had heard of but had never met before) and several other members of our Executive Board, plus lots of people I did not know. Irene and Stephanie in particular felt our action was impolitic and ill-advised. Irene argued that the real enemy was not the principal but the Board of Education, a point I could not argue. However, since the principal was the agent of the Board of Ed, if I could not remove the employer at least maybe I could eliminate the agent. Stephanie again made her point that we would simply be trading one incompetent for another, that we must have control over who came in or it wouldn't be worth the effort of getting rid of Mrs. Wachtel. We said that might be true, but we would take it one step at a time; and if we could get Mrs. Wachtel out, then the next fight would be to get a replacement who really met the needs of the school.

Again they hit us with our lack of color.

"How come you're all white?" someone asked.

"We called everyone we knew," we said.

"You didn't call me, and I'm black," said Natalie Orr, our dissident board member.

"I don't know you," someone said.

"Anne does," she said.

"I used the PA chain," Anne countered. "If no one called you I'm sorry."

"How come you didn't call Norma Hill?" Irene asked me. "She's an active parent."

"I've never met Norma," I said. "Look, if I called Norma and said, 'Hey, we're picketing the school, and we'd like you to come because you're black' that would be pretty offensive. I know if someone called me and said, 'We need a Jew to round out our picket line—will you come?' I'd be insulted. I'm sorry, but I don't use people.

I called everybody I knew, and some were white, and some were black, and some were Spanish; but I called them because I knew them and they're my friends. Not because of their color or their national origin. Now if that makes me a racist then we have different definitions."

"Of course you don't do it like that," Irene said. "You call up Norma and invite her out for a cup of coffee, and you talk. And you listen to what she has to say—how she feels—and then, if she shares your point of view, you ask her to join you."

"Oh, come off it, Irene. Maybe you can call someone you don't know and do that. But I can't, and I won't. I'll call anyone I know; but I don't use people, not even politely over a cup of coffee."

Norma sat there during this exchange and said nothing, but the whole thing made me very uncomfortable. I knew Norma and Irene were good friends, but I thought it was pretty sticky. Irene was pretty mad by this time, and a few minutes later threw at me, "This picket line is nonsense. If you want to do something real, why don't you come in when there's a grievance. If you want to get to know black parents you should go along on some grievances. Then you'd know what the whole thing is about. Your profile is just more middle-class talk. Where are you when they're suspending black kids, or dumping them in junior guidance, or making racist remarks? Why aren't you ever there then?"

"No one has ever asked me," I said. "When a parent asks me to come along, I go—and I have gone. But just as I won't call Norma without knowing her, I don't go butting into meetings when no one has invited me."

"Okay," she said in a put-your-money-where-your-mouth-is tone. "Next time a parent goes in on a grievance I'll call you."

"Do that," I said, my voice trying to chill the room back down to a livable 90°. I was furious.

There was a bit more of this amiable conversation. Some of the people felt we were asking too much of the new board, that they hadn't even had a chance to get themselves together, and hadn't even elected a chairman or planned a course of action; and we were trying to plunge them headlong into an unwise struggle. Finally the board members filled back in somberly and told us what they had decided. They had agreed unanimously not to lend their support to the picket line. They said they wanted to see our profile; they wanted to call an open meeting, with the particular aim of reaching black and Spanish-speaking parents at PS 84 to see how they felt; and they urged Toni Diamond and Nancy Calvert to reconsider their decision to leave and to show their faith in the new board and the complex by remaining in the school.

And that was it. As we left Irene and Stephanie again urged us to call off the picket line. We said no. As we walked home, we reviewed what had happened and what it meant. Though we were disappointed that the governing board was not supporting us, we all felt that they had taken a responsible position, that they really could not go off half-cocked on the strength of our passions. True, the three members from PS 84 knew that what we were saying was true, as did Pete Worthem, a member from Joan of Arc Junior High who also had a daughter at 84; but the members from the other schools had to evaluate the evidence before taking a position; and though we would have liked their backing, we felt good that we had elected a board that thought and investigated before acting.

"After all," we told ourselves, "if another group, with which we disagreed, came to them for support, we'd certainly want them to get all the facts. This is a good precedent they're setting." And so we comforted ourselves. We were convinced that we were right, that we had to go ahead with our plans, Irene, Stephanie, and the others notwithstanding; but we understood the dilemma of the board and felt that once they had gotten all the facts they would support us. And there would be other fights, we knew. If they established their credibility now, if they did support us in the future, their support would carry more weight than if they had rushed in now.

Then it was Monday morning. I was awake early—and dressed before the kids, who were usually my alarm clock, awakened. I left them eating breakfast, and clutching my collection of bilingual picket signs, I met Anne downstairs for the walk to school. It was only eight o'clock, and not too many people were out. The morning was bright, clear, and, mercifully, not too hot. We were both rather nervous, worrying whether the parents who had promised to join us would show, whether the press—which one of our picketing parents whose husband worked for one of the networks had assured would be there—really would be there, whether other parents would join us, what Irene and her group would do, and so forth. We worried ourselves down the block and a half to the school; and since it was still too early for either children or teachers to arrive, we sat down on one of the benches in front of the playground and worried some more. Gradually, a few teachers began to trickle down the street, so Anne and I began walking in a large circle with our signs. Then other parents came to join us: Millie, Pete Worthem, Beth Barron, Meg Knight, Theresa Hunter, Mary George, and more. And more. And more. Other parents stood on the side and looked. A few asked for signs and joined us. After a while we even began to look slightly colorful. Mrs. Wachtel passed us, looking neither to left nor to right, teeth clenched, face set. Other teachers passed us. Some smiled. Others shook their heads in disapproval. One young teacher walked past us into the school and began sobbing. Nancy, who had been watching us from the entrance, threw her arms around her colleague comfortingly, assuring her that we did not mean her when we spoke of racist teachers.

We had all agreed that, though we would picket the school, we would not keep our children out nor attempt to keep other children out. This was not a strike, simply a means of stating publicly what we felt; and we wanted the kids in school. Walter arrived around eight-thirty with Kathy scrubbed and ready for school and Sam riding in the stroller (Maggie had been deposited at nursery school); and since it was still slightly early for Kathy to go into school, she took a few turns with me. And then, miracle, the press came. First the network, with its cameras and microphones, and then the newsmen. The TV man spoke to Anne, who outlined what we were doing and why. He then spoke to a few other parents. Irene and Stephanie were on the sidewalk looking on disapprovingly. We watched Irene make her way to the microphone, though we could not hear what she said as we did not want to break up the picket line. As we circled, we muttered under our breath about the fact that she was sabotaging what we were doing. It was dirty pool to use the press we had gotten to disagree with what we were doing. But there was nothing we could do about it, and we kept walking. A reporter from the *West Side News* came, with a photographer, and asked some of us to pose with our children for a picture, which subsequently appeared under the headline PARENTS PICKET WEST SIDE SCHOOL with the story. We had made it! We didn't know whether it would be effective, of course; but at least we had made the public statement we wanted, and now we would have to see what happened. After we had our picture taken, I took Kathy to her class, where Mrs. Winter, who had stalked past us into the building, greeted me with her usual warmth. This dual attitude, which I had often noted in the principal, never ceased to amaze me—and give me the creeps. I could never understand how, in the face of so much hostility, she could go on smiling and acting as though what happened on the outside had never happened. *Noblesse oblige,* perhaps!

Having deposited Kathy, I returned to the picket line, balancing the sign I carried on the handle of the stroller. I had tried giving Sam a sign, but he was more interested in chewing it or in dragging it under the wheel than in holding it proudly aloft; so I had retrieved it, slightly damp at the edges, and now negotiated the sign and the stroller in an orderly line of march. The 24th Precinct had sent several patrolmen who watched us with interest. They were most polite, as were the obvious plainclothesmen who stood on the sidelines. But we were conscious of their presence and took care to keep our line moving and orderly and took care also not to block pedestrian traffic. We may have been passionate but we did not want to get arrested, even though that might have made a better story. We kept marching until about nine-thirty, by which time the press had left, the teachers and the children were all in school, and our continued presence could serve no further purpose. We had decided to return at noon and again the next morning. At noon it was raining, so I left the kids home (it was, fortunately, a day on which I had household help), and Walter, Anne, and I walked a wet, lonely line. But at least the sun had shone on us that morning.

I watched the eleven o'clock news eagerly, wondering whether we would make it, or whether some cataclysmic local or national event would bump us. I sat on pins and needles through the world and national news—the talk of primaries and far-off wars. I sat half listening through the quota of robberies and other interesting crimes and endless commercials. During one station break I counted twelve commercials. And then:

"A group of mothers . . ." I perked up, sat forward in my chair, but no, it was somewhere in the Bronx where a child had been hit by a car and mothers had blocked traffic to demand the installation of a light. I sat back, disappointed. We had been edged out by a traffic light. But then I heard the welcome words,

"And in Manhattan, another group of parents . . ." and there we were. I could distinguish Anne, Inge, Millie, Betsy Worthem, and there I was, pushing Sammy. Then Anne was talking. She sounded great—reasonable, sincere, aggrieved. She presented our case with poise and feeling. I was impressed. It can't be easy to speak spontaneously into a TV microphone and come out sounding coherent, but she did. Then the reporter said, "But not all parents agreed with the picketing mothers," and there was Irene. I made a face at her on the set, but I listened to see how much damage she had done. As she spoke, though, I relaxed. She said that though she disagreed with our tactics—feeling we were picketing in the wrong place at the wrong time—she would back parents any time they had legitimate grievances, which we certainly had. She said that all we said was true; and though she differed with us on tactics, she could sympathize with our feelings of frustration. And the school board would ignore us at its peril. She said, further, that if the conditions we spoke of in the school were not remedied, then the school would see more and bigger picket lines. At that moment I revised my opinion of Irene Martins.

The following morning was in every way an anticlimax. Our numbers had decreased visibly, proving yet again that it is hard to wage a revolution with volunteers. Whereas yesterday we had been between thirty to fifty strong, this morning we were down to the hard core. All last night we had had calls from people who were backing out—children were sick; crises had developed; they had had second thoughts; they couldn't march on an unintegrated picket line. I began to dread the sound of the phone.

It was another glorious day, but we had more picket signs than people to carry them. We were almost outnumbered by the three policemen who had come to keep things orderly. Nevertheless we marched until all the children were in school and there seemed no further point in continuing. We decided to hold an impromptu council to plan strategy—should we continue picketing for the rest of the week, or had we reached the point of diminishing returns? Should we go to the district office as a small delegation and demand that Dr. Selig take action? As we straggled to the benches in front of the playground, we saw, hurrying toward us from across the street, Dr. Selig, Robert Goodfellow, and Elizabeth Dodge. Once again we had lucked out. Had they come five minutes earlier they would have seen our rump picket line and concluded that we were simply a small bunch of nuts and that they need not take us or our protest seriously. But when they came it appeared as though we had already dispersed, and they had no way of knowing that our numbers were not legion. Since the TV program had indicated considerable strength, they could no longer afford to ignore us. And so, instead of a desperation strategy session, we held, out there in front of the school playground, a serious meeting to determine what steps Dr. Selig and the school board could take to improve the parlous conditions at the school.

We talked at length, and it was as though the profile had never been written and they were hearing about the crisis at PS 84 for the first time. We repeated our stock of horror stories. We filled them in on recent events, including the non-meeting about the infant school and Mrs. Wachtel's inability to carry out a simple bureaucratic function such as a mailing without parental handholding. And we asked that Dr. Selig and the school board remove her before the entire school fell apart.

"But when you presented the profile, you didn't think her removal would solve anything," Robert pointed out.

"We've changed our minds," we answered "We still felt at that point that if someone looked at the school objectively maybe we could solve its problems together. But since that meeting on the infant school where she ignored the parents' and the teachers' ideas and made it quite clear that she would run the whole show single-handed, whether it works or not—we've come to realize that the split in the school can't be healed as long as she remains, and so we want her removed."

"You can't just remove a principal without grounds. Look what's happened in Brownsville. Unless you have charges, you can't just throw her out."

"You have charges," we said. "Read the profile."

"It's not enough."

"If you want more, spend a few days in the school."

It was agreed that Dr. Selig and the board would do just that. Elizabeth Dodge and Robert Goodfellow, our two representatives from the school board, were delegated to come into the school, talk to teachers, to parents, to Mrs. Wachtel, and to present a report to the entire school board. Dr. Selig would also poke around. The inference was that if their findings agreed with ours they would act, and so we parted. We had won more than we had hoped. The power of the press, apparently, cannot be underestimated. We were elated. We had hoped that our actions would embarrass Mrs. Wachtel into reconsidering her decision about the departing teachers. We had hoped that the school board and Dr. Selig might be mobilized into action. But we hadn't really believed it would happen. But it had, and we went home grinning that we had pulled it off.

That evening I got a phone call from Irene Martins. Two black mothers in the school were meeting with Mrs. Wachtel about their sons. Both boys had been in junior guidance since the end of the second grade. They had both served their three-year sentences and must now be placed back into regular classes. Both mothers had been informed that they had two choices. They could either have the boys go into a fourth grade at PS 84 (chronologically they should have been entering sixth grade in the fall) or they could transfer them to the district 600 school, a school for difficult children that is a continuation of the junior-guidance idea, with its attendant stigma. Both mothers refused to accept either option. They wanted the boys placed at PS 84, but not in the fourth grade. They would settle for fifth grade, but not in a 600 school; and so they had requested a meeting with Mrs. Wachtel which would take place at three o'clock the next day. Did I want to accompany them, and some other parents who were going along to support the mothers' demands?

Three o'clock was the worst possible time for me, and I'd been throwing the kids around to sitters a great deal over the past week. Still, it was put-up-or-shut-up time, and I told Irene I'd come.

"Good," she said, "we'll meet at my house at 2:30 to plan strategy. I'll see you then." She gave me her address and hung up, and I made arrangements for a sitter for the children.

It was raining when I walked over to Central Park West where Irene lived, and the water squished between my bare toes and my sandals. Central Park West in the rain looked as bleak, though there were now leaves on the trees, as it had on my first walk there when I had gone to visit the school. It seemed ages ago. Certainly on that other morning I had not thought that I would so soon be involved in picketing a school to remove its principal.

Irene's building was a narrow, gray-fronted seven-story place, tucked between two much taller, more impressive ones where doormen hovered under canopies out of the rain. There was a wrought-iron railing separating the sidewalk from steps leading to the basement. A shingle on the front door proclaimed that a doctor plied his trade in the building. I entered the glass door and found Martins on the registry. I rang and gave my name and was admitted. The lobby was a surprise after the unimposing exterior. The walls were wood-paneled, and several almost ceiling-high potted plants—real, by golly—thrived under the fluorescent lights. Next to the elevator was a cork bulletin board, proclaiming various house and community events, as well as a warning not to answer the buzzer without knowing who was there. (They, like our co-op, had also obviously not solved the security problem.)

I rode up and entered Irene's apartment, where I was greeted by two dogs, one an old brown anomalous creature with long shaggy hair and one cataract-thickened eye, the other, a sleek white long-limbed beauty who bounded up and put her paws on my shoulders and nearly knocked me backward.

"Get over here, Pandora," Irene called peremptorily. Pandora obeyed (it was hard not to obey Irene Martins), and I could proceed into the living room which, in addition to the two dogs, boasted a real brick fireplace, wood-paneled walls, and nondescript furniture. Irene introduced me to the two mothers, Elsa Henderson and Mrs. Beal. Also present were two other ladies, one of them a psychiatric social worker from a Harlem agency.

Over cups of coffee we reviewed the history of the two boys. Both had been in classes where the teachers were unsympathetic to boys and particularly to black boys, before, at age eight, they were recommended for junior guidance. Neither of the boys had ever received any medical or psychiatric workup from the school, either before or since their placement in junior guidance. On the few occasions when the mothers had come to school, they had been assured that the boys were doing well. Now they had been hit with the information that neither boy was capable of working on his grade level, and hence the choice. I was appalled. Mrs. Henderson said that she had placed her son in junior-guidance class reluctantly, but had done so when assured, by both the school and her friends, that he would do better in a small class. He had never been a behavior problem. In fact, he had been a silent, almost withdrawn child. She certainly did not want him in a 600 school where he would be associating with all sorts of behavior problems, drugs, and the like. Furthermore, she had, throughout the three years of his internment, had him tutored in math and reading, so that he was not behind academically in spite of what the school said. Mrs. Beal said that when the school called her and gave her the choice she had asked why, and had been told that her son was reading so poorly that he would be lost in the sixth grade. And yet, she said, his teacher, who had had him in the class for those three years, had never indicated to her that he was not reading. On the contrary, every time she had spoken to the teacher she had been told that everything was fine. And now this. Both mothers were insistent that they would not accept either alternative, and we backed them in their resolution. It was agreed that we would insist that the boys' teacher be present at the meeting and that we would not accept less than the boys' placement in a fifth grade class at PS 84. Then it was almost three, and we got our coats and left for the school.

When we got to Mrs. Wachtel's office, I thought that perhaps she would refuse me admission. After all it was only yesterday that I was picketing for her removal, but she made no sign that she even recognized me, although when she wrote down, as she always did for her records, who was present she acknowledged my presence and my identity. We sat around her conference table and I listened. Irene insisted that the teacher be present, and Mrs. Wachtel resisted. It was, after all, three o'clock, and the union contract stipulated that no teacher could be required to stay beyond her six hours and twenty minutes. At our insistence, however, she agreed to try to find her, though she could not force her to attend. Mrs. Wachtel left, and returned a few minutes later triumphantly bringing not only the teacher, but the guidance counselor, Mr. Olivieri, as well.

The teacher was a pretty, well-groomed woman in her early or middle twenties. Her hair was sleek and tied back in a bun. She wore a blue-and-white-striped seersucker suit, and she looked cool and crisp even though it was the end of the day. She also looked angry, and sat as far away from the parents as the circumstances permitted. I was sweating, Mrs. Henderson was sweating, Mrs. Beal was sweating. Even Mrs. Wachtel's upper lip was beaded with perspiration, but the teacher sat there, icy and detached.

Mrs. Wachtel said to her, "These parents want to know why we recommended that their boys go into fourth grade. Can you tell them?"

And she answered, "Oh, they couldn't possibly do fifth- or sixth-grade work. Jackson is reading only on a 2.2 level."

Mrs. Beal jumped. "That's what he was reading when he went into junior guidance. How come he's stood still for three years?"

The teacher replied, "I don't know. Whenever we have reading groups, Jackson just fools around. He doesn't seem interested in anything but playing."

"Why didn't you tell me that when I saw you?" Mrs. Beal asked.

"I sent for you lots of times. You never came," she answered.

"That's not true. I came whenever you sent for me, and I came during open-school week and you told me he was doing fine."

"Well, he was, except for his reading. Maybe he has some kind of reading block."

At that I nearly hit the ceiling. I had not intended to do anything but listen (a role I sometimes find difficult, if not impossible), but I couldn't sit there while she talked glibly of reading blocks without challenging it.

"The boy has been in your class for three years," I said. "Did you ever suggest he have a physical or a psychological workup?"

"No," she admitted.

"Then how can you talk about a reading block?" I asked.

Shortly thereafter Mrs. Wachtel dismissed the teacher, saying that she did not want to detain her further, and thanked her for giving us her time. She left, bestowing on us a scathing glance as she exited. Shortly thereafter we also ran out of conversation, and Mrs. Wachtel promised us that the boys could remain—in fifth-grade classes—at PS 84, even though it went against her better judgment.

"But I want to make you happy," she said.

We left. The next day was the last day of the term, and Kathy was promoted to the first grade. Her class was not chosen to participate in the infant-school (or ungraded) program, and what was worse, her first-grade teacher would be one of the women I'd hoped she would be spared—an old-line teacher who, according to Susan Barron who was presently in her class, "screamed a lot." I wanted to cry, but Kathy took it with equanimity, saying, "Susan says Mrs. Godfrey is a good teacher, even though she screams. And I want to learn a lot, so I don't care if she screams."

On that cheerful note ended my first full year at PS 84.

THIRTEEN

Thunder Over Ocean-Hill

During that summer of 1968 there were distant rumblings, news dispatches from a far-off war. On May 9, the unit administrator of the Ocean-Hill Brownsville complex, Rhody McCoy, had at the request of his governing board sent letters to thirteen teachers, five assistant principals, and one principal in the complex, telling them they had been transferred and asking them to report to the central board for reassignment. The history of community control in Ocean-Hill had not been placid. When the original plans for the complex had been drawn, there were teachers as well as parents and community people involved. However, because of a series of complex events—misunderstandings, politics, suspicion—many of the teachers in the district had withdrawn from participating in the plans. (The community claimed this was at the instigation of the UFT.) When the 1967 strike came, many of the Ocean-Hill UFT teachers stayed out, and the community saw this as a betrayal of their children. Furthermore, they felt that although the issues of the strike were, allegedly, more MES* schools and the right of teachers to oust disruptive children, the hidden agenda was to destroy the concept of community control; and so they saw the strike as a personal attack on their community by teachers whose loyalty they felt they should have had. This created a great deal of ill feeling between the community and the UFT teachers in the complex, and there were many incidents throughout the year that did nothing to dispel this. The teachers, for their part, felt threatened and insecure and believed that the only thing that stood between them and peremp-

*More Effective Schools (see footnote, p. 11).

124

tory dismissal at the hands of the community was the union and the tenure system.

The situation was further complicated by two factors. First, in creating the demonstration districts the Board of Education had never spelled out clear lines of responsibility—how much autonomy the districts really had before they got slapped down by central headquarters—and no matter how often the governing boards of the three existing complexes tried to have their actual powers delineated, they were never successful. Second, there has existed for years in the tenure laws of the New York City public school system an administrative expedient by which principals or superintendents get rid of teachers who cannot function or with whom they cannot cope. It's called "You take my problem and I'll take yours" and consists of transferring teachers from one school or district to another. This obviates the need to bring teachers up on charges, solves the administrator's headache, keeps the teachers within the system (and thereby causes them no loss in benefits), and hurts no one but the children whom they can continue to destroy someplace else. So when McCoy attempted to transfer the nineteen people, he had no reason to suppose it wouldn't work that way for him. But as black people have found before, the rules aren't always the same for blacks and whites; and what had been common practice in the system till now became suddenly, when attempted by the Ocean-Hill board, a violation of due process and a rape of the merit system.

The merits of the case have been muddied by the press and by defenders on both sides. Union friends of mine have told me that they have met the Brownsville teachers and that they are fine, dedicated, sincere people whose only offense was their unionism. Community-control friends have told me that if the charges against the teachers had ever come out they would have lost their licenses. I really cannot judge who is right, but I do know that most principals and superintendents have a great deal of leeway in transferring personnel they find unsatisfactory. When this leverage was denied to Rhody McCoy and the Ocean-Hill board, the stage was set for confrontation.

All through June there were almost daily reports in the papers about the brewing controversy. We, meanwhile, were busy with other things; and though the people most active in the community control movement in our district followed the Ocean-Hill developments carefully, I was at the time involved with the profile, the infant school, and the picketing and so was only tangentially aware of the struggle there.

At the beginning of July, the Joan of Arc governing board called a meeting of the PS 84 parents in order to assess their sentiments about Mrs. Wachtel. This was in keeping with the resolution that had grown out of our meeting with them the night before we picketed the school. The meeting was to be held in the auditorium at Goddard-Riverside Community Center, and heroic efforts were made to insure attendance by the black and Spanish-speaking parents who make up the majority of our parent body and who, by and large, did not attend PA meetings. Why this should be so—this lack of attendance of minority-group parents—has long been the subject of speculation and conversation, both at PA meetings and elsewhere. There are doubtless many reasons. In households where both parents work or where there is only one parent, and that a working one, the parent is often too tired at day's end to feel up to going to meetings, especially when, as had been the case for so long, those meetings rarely resulted in anything more than academic resolutions. But above and beyond fatigue at the end of a hard day, and a lack of confidence in one's ability to contribute anything constructive, many parents—especially, though not exclusively, black and Spanish-speaking parents—have been turned off by the PAs because they are run by groups of extremely verbal, articulate people. This is true particularly on the West Side, where we tend to talk and talk and talk and people who are less articulate begin to feel unwelcome. They have thoughts, they have ideas, but in the face of the verbal barrage they are hesitant to express them. Furthermore we have often been accused, and perhaps not unjustly, of being less than polite to people who express opposition sentiments, and again this acts as a deterrent to full PA participation. As a result our meetings were generally attended by the same inbred group, who spoke to each other and for each other, but not necessarily to or for the entire parent body.

Even recognizing all this, one is faced with the necessity of functioning, and we did. We tried to encourage other parents to come to meetings, but never with any great success. (The meeting at which we had asked for material for the profile was one of the notable exceptions to this.) At any rate, the governing board had also recognized this lack of a broad base, and it was that that had prompted them to call another meeting. The board members went around to the various projects talking to key parents in them. They sent out fliers. And in the end their meeting was no more representative than our PA meetings were, and we ended up with our same group saying the same things yet again.

Still, it was not lack of interest that kept the parents away, because once we were in crisis as a result of the strike they did come to meetings—and there were many meetings. Perhaps it was only at that point that they realized that their presence could make a difference—could effect changes—and so the fact that they felt less articulate than all of us talky people became secondary.

Be that all as it may, the governing-board meeting did not accomplish their desired goal; and so they went on, responsibly, to meet with Mrs. Wachtel and to hear from her her views of the situation at PS 84. Since I was not present at this meeting, and since none of the governing-board members has ever told us what she said, I can only conjecture. She was interviewed for the *West Side News* at the time of our picketing; and in that interview she said, "I guess we just have different philosophies of teaching."

She was quoted further as saying, "It seems too bad to me that such a relatively small group of people can divert public attention entirely from the overall excellent record of teachers and pupils in the school. . . . At the time [of the picketing] they already knew that I had approved the [infant school] plan for next year. What I did not agree to was the reorganization of the entire school in one sweep. I feel very strongly that such a scheme must provide for extensive teacher training if it is to have any success."

Of the charges that she was letting good teachers, especially male teachers, go, she said, "That is just silly. We are all required by the Board of Education to replace substitutes with regular teachers where possible. And as it happens, I only dropped seven substitutes. The excitement about Jim Brewer is something I simply don't understand. I am replacing both Mr. Brewer and the other male substitute with male teachers, so it makes no sense to say I am not interested in keeping men teachers at the school."

As for the complaints about reading achievement, she said, "If you look at the state survey made here in the last five years, you'll see a remarkable drop in the number of children reading below the norm, which is the key to success of a reading program. In 1965, 52 percent of our kids were reading below a fixed level of competence.

Two years later that figure had dropped to 39 percent. I think that's a measure of real progress."

If this interview at all resembles her interview with the governing board, it is understandable that they found her reasonable and plausible. For it is only when one has lived intimately with the school that one realizes all the holes in her arguments. And since most of the governing-board members had not lived intimately with the school and since they had only heard from that "relatively small group of people," it is understandable, I suppose, that they decided as they did: that they lacked sufficient evidence to warrant taking any action.

Had we been present at this interview, we might have asked a number of questions: How could she equate ungraded classes with a child-centered class? How did the drop in reading retardation from 52 to 39 percent have anything to do with her professional leadership, since both figures pertained to a time before she assumed the principal's position. Why did that 39 percent figure contradict the one she gave the parents and teachers at the conference on reading? Why was it necessary to replace a *good* male substitute with another substitute (even if he was also male) whose competence had not yet been proved? And we could have asked more, had we been present; but we were not present, and she satisfied the governing board of her competence as she had obviously satisfied the local school board of the same when they summoned her to answer the charges of the profile.

Does this mean we were wrong or, as some people charged, crazy? After all, we were contradicting the findings not only of the district superintendent, a man with impeccable educational credentials, and of the local school board, whose members included two lawyers, various other professionals, and others respected in the community; but we were contradicting as well, by our stubborn insistence that the principal was incompetent, a governing board we had ourselves elected, worked for, and in whom we had confidence. Was it conceit? Was it pride—refusal to admit error on our part—that made us persist in our views against the opinion of all those authorities? I think not. They all acted on the basis of what they saw, and we acted on the basis of what we saw, and as in *Rashomon*, where the same event, viewed by different people, comes out entirely differently, so here the principal, viewed in different contexts, was also entirely different. She had passed her exam to be a licensed principal, and all the interviews she had with the various boards were, in a sense, no different from the New York City licensing exams; so she knew what to say and how to say it. But passing an exam or being able to talk a good game is not necessarily related to performance; and whereas it may be possible to fool a board of examiners, it is harder to fake it on the job. Someone once said that if the facts don't fit the premise, don't throw out the facts—reexamine the premise. Here the premise was that since she had passed the principal's exam, she must be competent. The facts were that she was not. And while the local school board and the governing board were reluctant to accept these facts, we knew they were true. Consequently we had to challenge the premise that the exam that had licensed her as a principal was relevant.

So the summer wore on, and we expected that come September we would have to go on living in uneasy partnership with a principal in whom we had completely lost confidence. The rumblings from Ocean-Hill and from union headquarters continued. In the meantime I went about my business. It was a hot summer. Most of my friends, and my children's friends, were away, and we dragged endlessly back and forth from Central Park. Somewhere I picked up a virus which sent me to bed for two weeks with a temperature of 104°, and that took me for a time out of the playground routine. I was too sick to read or to talk on the phone, so I might have been in California for all my contact with the outside world. But as I recovered and people returned from their summers away, the storm in Ocean-Hill came closer and we began to talk of little else. The possibility of a strike became more real to me simply because we were talking about it constantly. The UFT had said that the Ocean-Hill complex must take back the teachers (there were by then only ten who refused the transfers). The complex refused. The union said that if the teachers were not in their classrooms on opening day the whole school system would be shut down by a strike. And we talked and examined our consciences and wondered what we would do in the event of a strike.

The Sunday before school began was one of those bright, clear days when the sun shines just warmly enough to be pleasant without being downright hot. You could stand on the corner of Columbus Avenue and see clear across to Jersey; and if there was pollution in the air, it was at least not the visible kind. We took the kids to the park; and after they had had their fill of the playground and Walter had bicycled around the park to his heart's content, we went to sit on the grass with Millie, Dotty, Anne, and their respective offspring. We were a prolific bunch with eleven kids among us but since they were all enjoying the park and each other's company after a summer's separation, they left us pretty much alone—with a minimum of refereeing necessary—and we could talk.

The grass smelled freshly mowed, and streams of bicyclists rode by. People strolled or sat on benches. It was a people's park again, and I thought, as I have done many times before and since, that if Mayor Lindsay had done nothing else in his term in office (and on bad days I sometimes think he hasn't) I would still vote for him again simply because he has given the parks back to the people. And there are so few things (institutions) in this world that serve people instead of vice versa, we should remember whence they come. As we lay in the grass enjoying the day and the park, we talked, naturally, of school and of what we would do if a strike came—which now appeared likely. Anne, who last year had honored the strike, had not changed her position. She felt that she could not cross a picket line under any circumstances. She was, moreover, concerned about the issue of due process: after all, teachers had certain rights as citizens; and if community groups could begin to fire teachers at will, who, worth his salt, would want to teach in that system? Dotty, on the other hand, felt that, though she did not cross picket lines lightly, in this case the union was absolutely wrong; and her children would be in school the next morning.

"The due-process issue is just a red herring. The union is out to kill community control. If they strike, it'll be a strike against the black community, and I won't honor it."

"But the hearing examiner found there was no substance to the charges," said Millie, whose husband is an officer of a civil-service union. "If you just start firing people because you don't like their politics, then no one is safe. Even if in this case McCoy is right and they were trying to sabotage the complex, in another area the same method could be used to get rid of liberals, or blacks, or Jews. You have to have safeguards."

"Sure you do," said Dotty, "but so does the community. If the Board of Ed hadn't tied their hands every step of the way, this wouldn't have happened. And Shanker is just using this for his own ends. Any teacher who goes out is striking against black people, trying to keep them in their place. As soon as they want to control their own schools, the establishment finds some excuse to knock them down."

"Aw, c'mon," I said. "I've spoken to a lot of my friends who are teachers, and they're not racists, and they're going out. They may not like it, and they voted against it; but if you believe in unionism, you have to go along with your union."

"Even if what the union is doing is racist?"

"Well . . . but is it?" I asked.

"Look, when teachers were transferred in other districts did the union go out on strike?"

"No," I admitted.

"Well then. When a black district—controlled by the community —does it, out they go! If that isn't racism, I don't know what is. And I can't support it."

That, in a nutshell, was the dilemma. On the one hand, I felt that teachers were entitled to due process, but on the other I could not contradict Dotty's argument. I had been saying and thinking the same thing ever since the teachers had been fired, or transferred, and if I argued with Dotty it was only because I knew too many teachers who were good and dedicated, who had been in the forefront of the fight for civil liberties as well as civil rights, who were in no way racists, and who would be on the picket line. I was really torn. I believed in community control. My experiences at PS 84 had made it quite clear that parents must have a voice in the education of their children. The helplessness I had felt for most of the past year had emanated from the fact that, knowing what was wrong (and knowing how it could be remedied), I was powerless to effect change. So I certainly sympathized with the community in Ocean-Hill. And yet . . . I was a teacher too, and I could not swallow the charge that only racists would be on the picket line. I am sure that had I not been a parent, and a parent in this particular school, had I not gone through the past year, I would have been on the line with my colleagues. Without my experience at PS 84, I, like most of my colleagues, would not have believed the community-control rhetoric. However, I had spent a year with PS 84; and I knew the rhetoric to be true, if not universally, at least for our school and for many others in the city. And there I was. I could not carry the banner that read "striking teachers are racists," and yet I could not carry the other that said "community control means chaos in the schools."

I spent a long time on the phone that evening, talking to many of my teacher friends. The more I talked to them, the more I realized how far apart we had grown over this past year, for they simply refused to believe the things I told them about our struggles. They could not believe that teachers would make openly racist remarks, or that the administration would back such teachers. They could not believe that children got put into junior guidance for any but the purest motives or that once they were so placed, the experience could be other than beneficial. They could not, in other words, see reality as I had come to see it over the past year. And so they were striking. They weren't happy about it. They didn't think strikes were good for the children, or for the system. But they were convinced that due process had been violated, that justice was on the side of the union, and that to do anything but strike would be unprincipled. A lot of them spoke about McCarthy days. They had or they had not (depending on the speaker) been silent then, but this time not one of them would be silent. They had learned their lesson from history. And as I talked to them, I felt sad that they had learned the lesson but were using it on the wrong side. Shanker had done his job well.

And so when morning came, I took Kathy to school, eating my words of the year before that I could not cross a picket line of my colleagues nor side in a fight with the Board of Education. Before the strike ended, I was to go even further.

FOURTEEN

Strike Breaking

September 9, 1968. The *Times* headline that morning heralded the school strike. The radio newscasts droned, in somber tones reserved for major catastrophes, the names and numbers of schools shut tight. The Board of Education proclaimed that schools were open. The UFT insisted they were shut. I left Margaret and Sam with Walter and walked with Kathy to the school where I ran head-on into a picket line. However, not one of the people on the line was a teacher at the school; they were all imported from elsewhere. I gritted my teeth, took Kathy's hand, and scabbed (the first picket line I had ever crossed in my life). I went with her into the cafeteria, where the children were to be met by their teachers on that first morning. They were met, instead, by utter confusion.

On the walls and pillars of the cafeteria were oak-tag cards with class numbers hand-lettered on them, and under these cards children huddled. Some of them were accompanied by parents, others were alone. I found Kathy's class number on a center pillar and walked toward it. There was no teacher there, but several children from Kathy's kindergarten class were, and she greeted them cheerfully. All over the cafeteria children scampered. Some talked to friends, some ran around. Here and there a teacher shepherded her children. Mrs. Wachtel, with a microphone clutched to her, intoned over and over, "Children, find your classes. Teachers, find your children." Many of the children, of course, had no teachers to find them, and they ran around or stood looking lost and bewildered. I went over to Mrs. Wachtel and asked her what she intended to do about the children whose teachers were out on strike.

133

"We'll put them in other classes, but I don't know where yet. I have to see how many teachers I have."

Little by little, children trickled in. So did teachers. By nine o'clock there were about twenty teachers there and about two hundred children. Mrs. Wachtel began sorting them out by grades, starting with the sixth, and gradually the noise and confusion diminished as teachers and children filed out and upstairs for the day. Kathy had grown increasingly nervous during this time. She kept wanting to know where she was going since her teacher was not there. For a while I kept telling her I didn't know, that Mrs. Wachtel would assign her to a class. As time went on, though, and as it became clear to me that Mrs. Wachtel was not assigning the children according to any plan, but according to chance, so many here, so many there, I decided that that was silly and that I could place Kathy with more sense and with more knowledge of her needs than Mrs. Wachtel's random selection could; and I took her over to Mrs. Austin, one of the teachers who had been chosen to teach the ungraded first-grade class. Dotty's and Millie's boys were in her class, as well as several of Kathy's other good friends, and I decided she might as well be happy as long as the strike lasted. I asked Mrs. Austin whether she had room for one more and whether she minded if I gave Kathy to her. She had room, and she didn't mind; and Kathy joyfully followed her friends and her interim teacher, as did several other teacherless children whom Mrs. Wachtel attached to the class as it filed out. I waited in the cafeteria until all the children had been assigned, then went home to get Margaret to nursery and to take care of Sam.

When I picked Kathy up at lunchtime she was happy and excited. She was full of talk of things they had done, of songs she was learning. Mrs. Austin, she told me, played the guitar. She needed a notebook and a pen—she would be keeping a log. She had painted a picture. And on and on. I had not heard her bubbling about school in this way all during last year. She couldn't wait for lunch to end so she could go back. I began to wish for a long strike.

That afternoon Dotty told me that Mrs. Wachtel had scheduled a meeting for the next morning with the four teachers who were teaching the ungraded classes, with parents interested in the infant school, with Mike Abraham, the director of the balanced-class project, who was interested in the infant-school idea because of its emphasis on individualized instruction, which, he had come to feel,

was the only method that would work in balanced classes, and with
Lillian Weber. Over the summer Mike had hired Mrs. Weber to
serve as consultant to the four classes at PS 84. She would come to
the school one day a week to work with the teachers, to help them
set up their classrooms along the lines of the child-centered class,
to help them select the necessary materials to make the program
viable, and to guide them in methods and procedures. In a sense,
then, Mrs. Weber was working not for PS 84 but for the balanced-
class project, which would pay her; but since the money was coming
out of the project funds allocated to PS 84, we were not taking
money away from other schools in the district. And if the program
worked, it would serve as a pilot project for other classes in the
school, and for other schools in the eight schools that were now part
of the balanced-class project.

I had never met Mrs. Weber. The one time she had spoken and
shown her film in our district, I was not even aware of her existence.
Now, after having seen her film, and having done some reading on
the subject of infant schools, I was eager to meet her and to hear
what she had to say. About ten of us arrived the following morning,
a few minutes early. We were met in the hall by Mrs. Wachtel and
by Mike Abraham, a tall, black-haired, stoop-shouldered man with
bushy brows and craggy face. With them was a woman in her late
forties or early fifties, with black hair and the shiny eager face of a
child. Even when she wasn't talking, her eyes glowed and her face
sparkled with intelligence and enthusiasm. Mrs. Wachtel, Mike, and
the woman, who I gathered was Mrs. Weber, were talking about
what the best place would be for the meeting. The ten or so parents
stood off to one side, waiting to be directed. As we waited and
eavesdropped, it became apparent that though this meeting was to
include the four teachers, they were nowhere to be seen, and the
reason for that became clear when Mrs. Wachtel turned to Miss
Federman, who had come along by then, and asked her to arrange
for coverage of the teachers' classes. I was incredulous. *She* had
called the meeting, which was to include parents, administration,
and the teachers, and had neglected to make it possible for the
teachers to be present by not arranging in advance for coverage.
Here was yet another example of her administrative ability (if I
needed any!). Surely, if one cannot ask that one's principal be an
innovator or a great thinker, one does have the right to expect a
certain minimal level of administrative competency. The result was

that the meeting was half over before the four teachers were assembled with us in the teachers' cafeteria, where we finally convened. Nevertheless it proved an instructive meeting, because Mrs. Weber outlined some of her ideas for making the four classes workable. The first thing she wanted—and which we backed her on—was to move the classes from their present location, which did not provide the kind of self-contained unit that Mrs. Weber envisioned, to the first-floor kindergarten corridor where they could share not only the corridor (away from other classes) but also a common courtyard. Mrs. Wachtel maintained that this was impossible; and though Mrs. Weber and the teachers, as well as the parents, argued that such an arrangement was essential to the infant-school concept, Mrs. Wachtel remained adamant. She said she would try to find four contiguous rooms, but the corridor Mrs. Weber wanted was out of the question. Mrs. Weber also spoke of the need to adapt the program to the particular character of the school. She said it would never work if we slavishly copied the British system—that what we had to do was see what felt right for this school, these children, and these teachers. For this reason she did not like to call the program the infant school, but preferred to call it an expanded-environment program. She also cautioned on the need to proceed slowly, to take things one step at a time so that the teachers would feel comfortable with what they were doing and why they were doing it. If we had come seeking instant change, we were disappointed. But she spoke with such vitality and such optimism that we left feeling that everything was possible. We even felt that she would be able to work with, and handle, Mrs. Wachtel so that, perhaps, the program might work in spite of her. In short, we looked upon Mrs. Weber as our deliverer.

When the meeting was over, I went to Mrs. Wachtel with a formal request: that she transfer Kathy out of her class into Mrs. Austin's. She refused, saying there was no room. I said that as far as I knew several of the children who had been programed into that class and who were on the register were, in fact, attending parochial school and that, therefore, there must be room. She said that that had been taken into consideration when the classes were made out, that every class had a number of such transfers, and that this would not affect the total first-grade register. Therefore she could not, on that account, transfer Kathy without upsetting the registers of all the classes. I asked that at least she put Kathy on the waiting list so that if a spot opened up in that class she could be transferred in, and she agreed, though she offered little hope that this would come to pass. Consequently, once the strike ended, Kathy would not be in the program. Just the same, I was most interested in its development, not only because I felt that the program could ultimately affect the whole tone of the school, but also because I had two other children who would eventually be going there; and even if Kathy could not be in it, if it could succeed, then perhaps they would be spared the experience Kathy had had. So my interest in the health of the program was not entirely selfless, even though it looked as though my child would derive no immediate benefits from it.

That evening the news told us that the strike was over. The Board of Education had insisted that the teachers who had been transferred out of the Ocean-Hill schools must be taken back and had given assurances to the union that the governing board would comply. The next morning, hoping for the best, I took Kathy up to her new class. She came home with the information that "Susan is right, Mrs. Godfrey sure does scream a lot." I asked whether the teacher had screamed at her.

"No, at the other children."

When I asked at whom and why, she told me that she screamed at the children who didn't behave—who didn't sit in their seats or who talked when they shouldn't. But withal she was cheerful about it, and I held my peace. Since I couldn't get her out of the class, I wasn't about to give her my opinion of it, not as long as she was happy. But I must admit that I wasn't too sad when, the following day, the strike was on again. Though the Ocean-Hill governing board had taken the teachers back into the district, they had not assigned them to classes. They said the classes all had teachers and there were no positions for them. So the union cried foul and pulled its teachers out again. Back to Mrs. Austin went Kathy, this time for the rest of the week, while the storm raged at Board headquarters, at Ocean-Hill, and in the press.

The situation at PS 84 was an interesting one. During the 1967 strike the teachers who had been out had been, for the most part, the young ones, the ones most concerned about the quality of education in the school, the ones with ideas that were not welcomed by the system. The others, who had gone in, had done so in the name of their professionalism and because of their professed concern for their students, who needed unbroken education and could not afford the chaos of a strike. Curiously, this year the situation was almost completely reversed. Those teachers who had been striking last year were now in the school. The others, who last year had been antistrike and anti-union, were now out on the grounds that the union must be preserved and that due process took precedence even over professionalism. It made one wonder. This is not to say, as some people did in the weeks that followed, that all virtue resided in those teachers who were in, and all vice in those who were out (or that all the "good" teachers were in and all the "bad" teachers were out). Certainly, among those whose consciences dictated that they honor the strike, there were some good, dedicated teachers, even at PS 84, and among those who came in there were some with motives less than pure; but certainly it was a strange reversal from last year, and by and large when the strike was on we were left with a core of excellent teachers. As a result, we had fewer problems in the school during the strike than one might have expected under such unsettled conditions.

The weekend ended and with it the strike, and again I took Kathy back to her original class. This time the truce lasted for two weeks, during which Kathy came home with daily reports of life with her screaming teacher. On one of those days I went to see for myself. I was greeted by Mrs. Godfrey, a short woman with fuzzy red hair and thick glasses, who told me, "Madam, you have a lovely child." I nodded agreement and took my place at the back of the classroom to observe. This was no informal visit. When I had decided to visit the class, I had gone dutifully to the office, where complicated negotiations proved necessary. Miss Federman first had to write a note to the teacher asking whether I might visit. The reply was that I could come the next day at 10:45, so that the teacher was certainly not taken by surprise by my appearance.

The lesson I witnessed was a reading lesson. Most of the class sat at their desks working in their workbooks and, upon completion thereof, sitting at their desks with their hands stiffly folded. A small group, which included Kathy, was gathered at the front of the room with the teacher for reading instruction. The group was diverse in ability, ranging from Kathy, who could read any *Dick and Jane* reader, to some children who did not know one letter of the alphabet from another. Mrs. Godfrey had put several words on the blackboard—"Dick," "Jane," "Come," "See," and "Run." She was calling on each child in the group to get up and point to one of the words as she called it. They were all attentive, all eager, but I was struck by several things: first, that I had been told there was no formal reading instruction until second grade, and if this wasn't formal instruction I don't know what is; second, that though Kathy was eager at this point, once the novelty wore off she was bound to be bored silly. I also noticed one boy in particular, who could not tell an *x* from an *o*, but who at this point raised his hand each time she asked "Who can point to the word *run?*" His enthusiasm was bound to be short-lived, for each time he answered incorrectly (as he did each time he volunteered) he was greeted by a brusque "Wrong. Who can show him?" And someone would pop up to point out the proper word. The teacher made no attempt at all to work with him. I am not a reading teacher; but my impulse, when he pointed to the wrong word, was to say "What letter does *Jane* start with. Sound it out. J-A-N-E. Now, what letter does *run* start with? Sound it out. R-U-N." But all he got for his pains was that barked "Wrong," and I cringed each time he raised his hand.

But while I was in the room, there was no screaming. Control, yes. Rigidity, yes. Boredom, yes. But there was no screaming, and no education, that I could see. I did not, however, have anything that I could take to Mrs. Wachtel to say "Get my daughter out of there." So I left with no more comfort than that I had a lovely child, a fact that I already suspected and that made me wish for her a better fate than the one I must consign her to. I found it ironic that, when hiring babysitters who generally attend the chidlren only when they are asleep, or about to be, I am always very careful in my selection. Yet, when it comes to someone who spends six hours and twenty minutes of daily waking time with her, I am forced to entrust her to someone I would never hire as a babysitter! With that cheery thought to sustain me, I went home to find from the paper that Albert Shanker had once again come to my rescue. The Ocean-Hill teachers were still without classes and had been harassed in the school auditorium by various members of the community and, until their safety and their assignments could be guaranteed by more than verbal agreement, there would be no union teachers in any schools in the city. This time the strike was to last for seven weeks, during which time Kathy was again in Mrs. Austin's class. And as the weeks wore on and Kathy adjusted to her class, I vowed that this time, come hell or high water, she would remain there.

Before that third strike Mrs. Weber called a meeting for all parents interested in the "expanded-environment program." She said at that meeting that the purpose of the program was to give the children all the tools they would get in a conventional classroom, but to give them, in addition, the curiosity that would enable them to learn on their own. In other words, at the very least, they would come out of the grade knowing as much as the children not in the program; but hopefully they would come out with a great deal more, both in factual knowledge and in intellectual growth. She then described, in a sadly funny manner, the conventional classroom as she saw it and then, by way of contrast, the expanded-environment program classroom. In her description of the traditional classroom, she cited all the things I had found so offensive in my observations of Kathy's kindergarten class, as well as of her first grade class: the closed questions that left room for only one right answer, the physical confinement that ultimately produces intellectual confinement as well, the busy work, the rote work. I thought of the day that Kathy had come home with an assignment to write her name in her notebook as many times as there were lines on the page (this during one of the few days her teacher was there—between strikes). Kathy had had a library card since her fourth birthday and could write her name quite well. Yet when she was forced to write it just so, as the teacher insisted, with each letter touching the precise spot on the line, she became paralyzed with frustration; and after five minutes of vain effort she burst into tears, saying, "I can't write my name." It took both Walter and me, together, almost half an hour to work her out of it, and then she managed to make each letter touch the appropriate spot. But it was this sort of thing that made this type of education lethal even for a bright child. As Mrs. Weber described the traditional class, I became determined that I had to get Kathy out of there. When the session with Mrs. Weber ended, I went to Mrs. Wachtel, again, and said to her, "You've got to let me transfer Kathy out of that class. I can't stand by and watch her kill my child."

She replied, "I can't do that. There's no room. Besides, I had to stand by and watch the school kill *my* child. You're luckier."

"How," I asked, "am I luckier if you won't take her out?"

"Because at least you can complain. My daughter attended a school where I was teaching, and I had to stand by and watch her being ruined, and I couldn't even say anything."

As the third strike continued, with negotiations stalled and both sides intransigent, attitudes hardened all around. Those of my teacher friends who were out and who were still speaking to me became more and more convinced that the union was right. The charges of anti-white and anti-Semitic sentiment were daily aired in the press; and though I saw neither in our own community (though anti-teacher feeling ran high), I could not convince my friends that every proponent of community control was not a virulent anti-Semite. I am sure that there were actual statements of anti-Semitism, but I felt, and still feel, that the UFT played up these individual statements for their own purposes, and made them seem to reflect the stated policy of the Ocean-Hill governing board. This is as fair as to take individual anti-black statements made by individual teachers, and use them as evidence of the stated policy of the UFT. Not that I condone such statements, wherever they come from, but I do feel they must be kept in context and in perspective. The union, though, got much mileage from the utterances of anti-Semitic extremists, and many teachers (and citizens not otherwise involved in the strike) lost whatever sympathies they may have had for the Ocean-Hill complex when they read the alleged statements emanating there.

Meanwhile, our school muddled along. Mrs. Wachtel was in, as was one of her assistant principals, a man who had come to fill in for Mrs. Young, the AP for the upper grades who, with her whistle, late-line, and ethnic survey, had become the subject of a petition to remove her and who had gone on a sabbatical in February—permanently, it was hoped by many in the school. We had, at this time, about thirty teachers, and they managed to cope with the two hundred to two hundred and fifty children who were then in attendance. Kathy, in Mrs. Austin's class, was happy and thriving. Unfortunately, there are about nine hundred children in the school so almost three-quarters of them were, during this time, left to their own devices. Since conditions were abnormal, there was an increased spirit of cooperation between Mrs. Wachtel and those parents who were not honoring the strike. She seemed more open, more willing to listen to parents during this time, perhaps because crises foster such cooperation or perhaps only because she needed us to fill in in some of the areas that normally were handled by her regular staff.

The local school board had passed a resolution on September 12, stating that all schools in the district should remain open, and since that time every one had; but in other schools in the district conditions were not quite as smooth as in ours. Most of them had far fewer of their regular staff and were forced, therefore, to rely on hastily recruited substitutes. Thus, all the schools in the district were limping along; but they were not providing education for most of the kids, and more and more parents grew increasingly bitter toward the teachers as the strike progressed. Though I had reason to be personally thankful for the strike and could selfishly have wished it to continue for the entire year, I was, of course, concerned about the kids who were getting no education at all (though for some in the classes of the worst teachers this may also have been something of an advantage). Thus, on October 16, I attended a meeting at Edna Garrett's home to discuss methods by which we could staff our school fully and get all our kids back into the school.

We sat around the living room, fourteen of us, while Sammy followed Edna's younger daughter, a pretty, bright-eyed little girl of five, into another room to play. Over coffee and cookies we discussed the present situation. Some of the teachers in other schools had attempted to set up classes in a community room of one of the co-ops and had been picketed by neighborhood residents who felt they should be teaching in the school or not at all. One of our own teachers, Mrs. Sumner, was meeting her class daily outside of PS 84, taking them to someone's home, and teaching them, without pay, until three P.M. when she returned them to their parents. This, too, met with the disapproval of the parents gathered in Edna's apartment, who felt she was salving her own conscience while refusing to take the "proper" stand on the strike. Truthfully, I could not quite see it. This teacher had been in at the outset of the strike, but then she had been convinced by Shanker's rhetoric (and by threats against teachers in the Two Bridges complex) that she could not abandon her colleagues, and so she had stopped coming. And yet she felt enough loyalty to her children not to want to abandon them and chose, on her own, to teach them. This was not earning her the thanks or gratitude of the community, which was harder on her than on some of the teachers who used the time of the strike to contemplate their navels (or go to the movies, or whatever), but she was doing what she felt she had to do, and I respected her for it. But I was a minority of one. Everyone else there felt that either you were with the community or against it, and there could be no fence-sitting, that if you were going to teach children you should do it in the schools. Personally, I could not see how, if freedom schools were all right during the boycotts led by Milton Galamison some years back, they could be so wrong now; but I was shouted down when I ventured this opinion.

Irene Martins said that it seemed we had two immediate problems: how to get the classrooms covered now, and what our long-range objectives should be in relation to the striking teachers. Theresa Hunter, the mother of five girls (four in the school and a fifth preschooler), a former teacher herself, and a woman who spoke at meetings with deep feeling—always on the side of the community —now suggested, to my dismay, that we send a letter to the striking teachers, appealing to them on the basis of the children that they come back. If their reply were negative (or if they did not reply), we should then hint to them that under community boards their jobs might be in question.

I said that though it was true that in our school the lines were fairly clearly drawn, that most of the good teachers were in and the bad out, this was not so throughout the city. I knew some fine teachers who were striking. A threat of this sort would merely confirm their fears that community control meant denial of due process. I certainly wanted the classes staffed, but I didn't think threats would staff them. I suggested that we try to find some compromise that would allow the teachers to teach without violating their conscience, perhaps asking them to come in without punching in so that they would be on record as supporting their union while at the same time not penalizing the children.

Meg Knight said, "That's a lot of hooey. If they don't want to come in, let them get the hell out!"

IRENE: "The teachers have to be made to decide on the real issues. This is not a trade unionism dispute. The character of the dispute is black versus white, and they must be made to see it."

It was suggested that before we sent the letter we have a meeting with the striking teachers, telling them how we felt, and listening to how they felt. There was to be a general membership meeting of the PA Thursday. If necessary, the parents would be asked to approve the sending of the letter to the teachers. Ronnie, Nina Gossens, and I agreed to set up the meeting with the teachers. I felt quite depressed. I knew that if such a letter were sent, it would not get the teachers to return, and yet I could not stop such a letter. Granted that some of the striking teachers were competent, others were not. How could I, in conscience, sign my name to a letter which said "We want you to return"? The truth of the matter was that I did not want Kathy's teacher to return. Nothing would delight me more than her continued absence. In fact, if I could have enforced the threat of no-return-no-job, I might even have been tempted to make it in her case. But though I did not want her in the school, this was not the way to get her out. She was entitled to a hearing on her merits or lack of them, not on her position on the strike. And if I was ever going to be in a position to challenge her merits at such a hearing, I could not very well sign my name to a letter asking her to return now. It was silly and it was dangerous—the very thing that had made my friends, reluctantly, man the union line.

I walked home with Natalie Orr. She was the PA treasurer and had been one of the people who had, last year, opposed the profile. Her husband had run for the Joan of Arc governing board and lost. Her daughter was in Mrs. Sumner's class, which infuriated Natalie because it set up a conflict in the little girl, who saw her classmates going off daily with her teacher while she went into the school to be taught by someone else. I expressed some of my feelings to her; and though I could not convince her not to draft the letter, at least I felt better about expressing my reservations again.

The following evening we had the general membership meeting, with fifty-eight—count them—parents present. Attendance at meetings had skyrocketed during the strike, proving that when there are real issues people will come out and be heard from. We had not been able to set up the meeting with the teachers for that afternoon, and I hoped that no action would be taken on the letter until we had had a chance to talk.

Carmen Johnson opened the meeting and introduced Meg Knight, one of the PA vice-presidents, as program chairman for the evening. Meg had invited Robert Goodfellow to report on conditions in the district; and Joe Gelber, the UFT district chairman, had requested permission to speak. Consequently there was some debate as to whether any outsiders would be permitted to speak, which was finally resolved affirmatively, and Robert, in his usual sweetness-and-light fashion, spoke of our neighborhood as the only one in the city where sanity prevailed. He felt that the strike had degenerated into a racial issue in other districts and hoped this would not be allowed here. He said that the local school board had agreed to hire substitutes for the duration of the strike. One of the parents questioned the wisdom of that, saying, "If we hire subs, we'll have conflict. The UFT demands that their teachers come back as if they had not struck."

Robert answered that any licensed substitute could be hired by any district to fill in for an absent teacher and that when the strike ended the school board would recommend that no extra teachers be removed from the school.

Then Joe Gelber spoke. That evening I viewed him with as much sympathy, I think, as I have ever felt for him, because I was closer that evening to seeing the UFT side than prior to that day or subsequently; but Joe was not a good spokesman for his cause. I would have wished the district's teachers had elected a more appealing chairman. He was pompous, smug, pedantic, always ready with the wrong phrase at the wrong time. He had a penchant for killing any latent sympathy for his cause merely by his espousal of it. I kept wanting him to shut up and sit down, not because I disagreed with him—for once—but because I half agreed.

First he gave us a lecture on the fact that only the finest career teachers were out and that those who were in were, at best, parvenus and, at worst, mercenaries. Then he told us that there was, at present, no education in the schools—only babysitting. He told us that he needed the support of the parents and that the fastest way we could end the strike was by siding with the union and shutting down the schools. He said that the union was only asking for fair play: hiring and firing by legal means and on grounds of competency, not on the basis of attitudes that could not be objectively determined. He said the teachers must fight or there would be no protection for any of them. He said the teachers in the district were willing to talk to parents and were not afraid of community control, but only of groups who threatened their rights. "We only want due process and the return to the job of all those exonerated after a fair hearing."

Pete Worthem, chairman of the Joan of Arc governing board, asked him what must be done to settle the strike to the satisfaction of the UFT. He answered that Mr. Shanker had said that we cannot have ten teachers removed without cause and then exonerated and then not allowed to return. "We must have them returned to their duties. If this means that the governing board and the district administrator must be removed, then that is the only way."

This statement prompted jeers, boos, shouts of "Shame on you, Joe Gelber," "Killer," and so on. Meg pleaded for order, and after several moments things settled down again. Joe stood, red faced and stiff, with a complaisant smile on his face that seemed to say "Well, what can you expect of *them?*"

A mother rose and said, "You have talked about due process and legality. Are not the teachers presently conducting an illegal strike?"

GELBER: "We recognize the illegality of the strike and are willing to take the penalties. It is the only way for us to protest injustices, and we believe this is an unjust law."

PARENT: "But due process is not at issue in District 5. The teachers could return to their jobs in this district." ("Little do you know," I thought.)

GELBER: "We are part of the city. We cannot negotiate separately."

PARENT: "You say the union is not opposed to decentralization, yet they have fought it every step of the way."

GELBER: "We sponsored the Marchi Bill [which did not grant any real control to the communities]. We are against the excesses that have occurred in Brownsville."

This last statement again elicited a great deal of booing; and Joe, having made his pitch for the union, left.

There followed a report of the meeting at Edna's house and then discussion from the floor on the suggestion to send a letter to the teachers asking them to return or else. Pete Worthem spoke first. He said that the governing board felt this was a strike against decentralization and pointed out that Gelber had said that it might be necessary for the Ocean-Hill board to be destroyed. "Then any other governing board that wants good teachers may also be destroyed."

He pointed out that if such a letter or telegram were sent, we should consider all the consequences. This would lead to a hardening of attitudes on the part of the teachers. On the other hand, after the Two Bridges governing board sent out a similar telegram, they had five hundred and ten more children in school and two hundred parents picketed Al Shanker. This action would mobilize the forces in the community.

MONA FRENCH: "We must support striking teachers. Six parents have agreed on this letter. One half of our student body is not in school, and their parents, at least, would not be in favor of this action. We must avoid confrontation. We must decide whether we are going to be motivated by negotiation or by physical intimidation." This again caused much booing.

MILLIE MILLER: "I am opposed to the proposal. We cannot dismiss teachers for an act of conscience. We must do it only on the basis of competency."

MORTY PLAUT: "I think it is wonderful that someone came up with a proposal. We will give the proposal due process."

FRED PEPPER: "I am only interested in having my child educated. Anything else is extraneous. I like a solution that will directly affect my child's education. I think this is a step in the right direction."

And so it went, with some parents arguing for the proposal, others against it. It was clear that the idea of action, any action, was satisfying. We had been caught in a situation over which we had no control, moved by distant forces. Here was a chance to do something that would directly affect our school, and it was understandable that so many parents were ready to grab at it. Nevertheless it disturbed me deeply, and I repeated what I had said at Edna's house: that I felt this was the wrong move tactically, that if we ever hoped to remove bad teachers legally, with due process, we could not provide them with ammunition by asking them to return now. Other parents voiced other objections: that we did not represent the entire parent body, that some good teachers were out, too, that we were directing all our hostility at the union against our own teachers, and so forth. Sarah Roberts said that she was unwilling to join in union-busting techniques.

"Teachers," she said, "are out in an illegal strike on the wrong side of history, but I don't approve of vigilante groups, either." Walter pointed out that, practically, we could not replace teachers we would fire, since we had no professional staff to evaluate new teachers as Ocean-Hill did. Thus we would merely compound the damage. Furthermore, he questioned whether our action was intended to get the teachers to come back and teach our children or whether we were asking them to come back as an action against Shanker.

In spite of all these demurrals, the question was called. Mona insisted the vote be done by roll call—which it was. The result was thirty-one in favor, eighteen opposed, nine abstentions.

During much of this debate I had noticed Mr. O'Malley, our custodial engineer, lounging in the doorway with Pete, the custodian, and two policemen with guns prominent in their holsters. As we left, both Mr. O'Malley and Pete were grinning broadly, almost smirking; and though this was an unusual departure from their generally unfriendly demeanor during the strike, I did not give the matter much thought. I was worrying about other things. I feared what the repercussions of the projected letter might be, and Walter, Millie, and I walked home glumly. I was almost ready to concede that Shanker might be right, and that community control, if given to parents, would indeed produce the kind of excesses that would make education impossible for anyone.

FIFTEEN

The Lockout

Friday morning, October 18. I was groggy from last night's meeting, and overslept so that there was a rush to get everyone ready and out of the house. I didn't turn on the radio, and missed the morning's news. As Kathy and I hurried down Columbus Avenue toward school, we met Nina Spiegel, who lived down the hall from us, and who was walking, not toward school, but toward home.

"Why are you going home?" I asked, knowing that her mother had already left for work.

"The school is locked," she answered.

"Why?" I asked.

"I don't know," she said, "but it's locked."

Puzzled, I continued toward school, a bit more quickly now. From half a block away I saw hundreds of children milling about in front of the school. Some darted between parked cars and chased each other up the street. Others stood outside the playground, looking in. I hurried down the block, and asked what had happened.

"The custodians locked the school last night, and we can't get into the building."

"Where are the custodians?" I asked.

"Gone."

"Where's Mrs. Wachtel?"

"She's out here somewhere."

"Doesn't she have the keys?"

"Yes, but they don't work. They changed the locks."

That explained the presence of Mr. O'Malley in the school last night. No wonder he had been smiling. He had been listening to us planning how to restaff the school, all the while knowing that he was about to pull the school out from under us. I had long felt that the schools were run, not for the children, not even for teachers, but for the custodians. Now I was confirmed in this opinion, and I was furious. How dare he lock *our* school! How dare he lock out our children! I heard later that Edna, from her window, had seen the custodians leave the school at two in the morning. She had no way of knowing why, of course, but she too had wondered at this unusual display of devotion to duty on their part.

Cursing the perfidy of the custodians, I walked closer to the school entrance where a small group was gathered around Mrs. Wachtel. She looked absolutely distraught. She stood with the useless keys dangling in her hand, talking to various parents and teachers. Occasionally she stopped talking and turned to children who had gathered around and waved her hands at them ineffectually saying,

"Go home. School is closed today."

"You can't do that," we said. "Where will they go?"

"Home," she said. "The school is locked."

"Let's gather them in the yard," someone suggested. "Then we can decide what to do. But we can't send them home, and we can't let them run in the street."

"Call the 24th precinct," someone else suggested. "Tell them to get a man over here to close off this street."

Someone went off to make the call. One of the fathers, meanwhile, went off to divert traffic off the street so that the children darting in and out would not be killed before the arrival of a patrolman. Some of us began gathering the children from the street and sidewalk and shepherding them toward the yard, which was also padlocked. However, since the fence had various good-sized holes, we were able to let the children into the yard where their teachers could watch them; and then all we had to do was watch the holes to see that the kids didn't slip out. With Kathy still in tow, I returned to the group around Mrs. Wachtel. She was frantic.

"Now what shall we do with them?" she asked.

"We've got to get the school open," one of the fathers said.

"But I don't have the keys," she said.

"Then we'll have to break in," we said.

"But that's illegal. You can't destroy school property."

"Listen. That school belongs to the children and the community.

The custodians have no right to lock us out. The children belong in there. Let's go."

A few of the fathers then separated from the crowd and went off to see how the school could be opened. Mrs. Wachtel stood, still clutching her impotent keys, and wringing her hands.

"What will happen if you get the school open?" she moaned.

"We'll go in, and school will continue."

"I can't go in," she said.

"Why not?" we asked.

"It isn't safe without the custodial staff."

"It isn't safe for the children if they're sent home. They're better off in school."

"I can't go in. I can't be responsible for those little children in a building without a custodian. What if there's a fire?"

"There won't be," we said grimly. "We'll patrol the school. But you should be there. We need a principal."

"I can't go in without the custodian," she said.

"You've got to," yelled John Rollins. "Listen, don't you care about those children?"

"Of course I do. But it's not safe for them in there."

"It's safer if you're in there than if you're not."

"I can't take that responsibility," she moaned.

"You're paid to take responsibility," yelled Edna. "This is the school you're supposed to be in charge of. If you give a damn about these children, you'll go in when we get it open. If you don't, then I've had enough. You'll be turning your back on those children, and you'll be through as far as I'm concerned. If you abandon them, you quit, and we'll know how to interpret that."

Mrs. Wachtel's lips trembled. She looked, as she always did in times of stress, as though she was about to drop her teeth. Her voice rose, but she spoke slowly.

"I won't be talked to like that," she said. "I care more about your children than you do. That's why I can't take responsibility for them."

John, whose black skin had grown almost purple with rage at this, said, "You care more about our children than we do? But you didn't even have the sense to call the precinct to get the street closed. And you were sending these little children out into the streets. You don't give a damn about our children, and you never have. Since I've been in this school, you've never treated me with respect—nor any of the other black parents, either. Don't you stand there and tell me you care about our children."

"I don't have to stand here and listen to you, Mr. Rollins."

"You'd better listen. We're going to open that school. And we're going in. And if you won't come in and take responsibility for those children, we'll find someone who will."

"Do that," she said. "I can't. The school isn't safe without a custodian."

Meanwhile the fathers had been busy with the locks. Someone had had the wisdom to call the district office and the school board, from whom it was learned that the lockout of custodians was city-wide. They were thus showing their allegiance to Al Shanker and the teachers, rather than to the children in whose service they purportedly labored. The rule was that a set of keys to each school resided in the district office, which accounted for the changed locks. In some schools, the custodians had gone even further and had smashed locks and light switches and removed key parts from boilers to render them inoperable. If they were not running their domains, they were making pretty sure no one else would. (After all, once it was learned that schools could be operated without them and their firemen's licenses, their job security might be slightly diminished. They might show their solidarity to their union brethren, but they weren't taking any chances with their property!) The school board and the district superintendent, who were also infuriated by the lockout and the ensuing chaos, authorized parents in each school to proceed to enter them. They suggested we hire locksmiths to break and then change the locks and to leave the new keys with the principal or with whoever was in charge of the school. Before a locksmith could be reached, however, our inventive fathers, under the watchful eyes of several policeman (who made no effort to interfere), were inside the school. From there it was only a matter of minutes before they found the master light switch, turned it on, and thus, lighted and opened, the school was ready to receive the children. A cheer went up from the children. Mrs. Wachtel blanched.

We then led the children into the cafeteria where they waited with their teachers while several of the men, with the policemen in their wake, went upstairs to examine the premises. They returned and reported that the gates leading to the second- and third-floor halls were also locked and that these locks, too, were new. We held a hurried conference and decided to open only the second-floor gates. Since not all the classrooms had been utilized since the strike in any case, we decided that rather than scatter the children and teachers we would concentrate them on the first and second floors, thereby obviating the need to break more locks and also making the problem of security somewhat easier. With the classes concentrated they would be easier to keep safe. The fathers went off again to jimmy the locks to the second-floor gates and returned a few minutes later rather proud of their new-found skills. We had been saying for a long time that the parent body had untapped skills that the school could utilize. Our fathers were proving it.

We again asked Mrs. Wachtel, who had followed us into the cafeteria, along with Mr. Sussman, the acting assistant principal, whether she would assume her responsibility for the school. Again she refused, as did Mr. Sussman. In that case, we said, they might as well leave, since we had work to do. Mrs. Wachtel then turned her keys—useless though most of them were, it was a symbolic gesture of investiture—over to Mrs. Warner, one of our teachers who had a bona fide assistant principal's license and who had, during an earlier sabbatical of Mrs. Young's, served as acting assistant principal in the school.

"Sylvia," said Mrs. Wachtel, "I can't do it. The school shouldn't be open without a licensed custodian."

"But the children are here," answered Mrs. Warner, "someone has to be responsible."

"I can't do it," answered Mrs. Wachtel, and she and Mr. Sussman left. They returned only once during the remainder of the strike to look around and to engage in a half hour of useless confrontation with those of us who were manning the desk at the front entrance.

After they left, we gathered around Mrs. Warner, a pretty, light-skinned black woman with a marvelous, impish smile, flashing black eyes, and a combination of warmth, competence, and humor that were to stand her in good stead in the days that followed.

"The first problem is lunch," Mrs. Warner now said. "Apparently the kitchen staff has also found strength in unionism."

"Is the kitchen open?" someone asked. It wasn't.

"There's not much point in forcing the lock," someone said. "There's probably nothing there anyway. Most of the food gets delivered daily. And as far as I know, the refrigerators are kept locked too."

"But the children have to eat," someone said.

"Let's go buy some stuff. We'll make sandwiches. And we'll buy some fruit and some milk. It won't be gourmet food, but at least they won't go hungry."

Irene turned to Mrs. Warner. "Sylvia," she said, "can we send someone around to the classes to count heads? Find out how many kids are there who eat the school lunch. The ones who normally go home can go home today, but we have to know how many sandwiches to make."

"That's a good idea," answered Mrs. Warner, and several people were commissioned to poll the children. Meanwhile we passed the hat around and within a few minutes had collected enough money to take care of lunch for a few days. We then began to plan a menu, deciding on peanut butter sandwiches for simplicity, plus apples and milk. We also realized that paper cups and napkins were missing, and added these to our shopping list. In the meantime our scouts had returned with the information that we needed about one hundred lunches; and armed with that we sent out shoppers to get the stuff. Because of the general confusion, we had agreed that children whose parents were there would be better off out of school for the day, which would allow the teachers to concentrate on those whose parents were not around, so Kathy and some of the other children with us set the tables with napkins, cups, and apples, while the rest of us slathered peanut butter onto bread. When the sandwiches were made, the kids put one at each place, and in about a half hour lunch was ready.

We then huddled around to make plans. We decided that the school could not be left untended over the weekend, lest the custodians return and do further mischief.

"We'll have to get a list of fathers who are willing to sleep in the school. During the day mothers can be here—in shifts—but at night we should have men."

"Can we get lists from the office, Sylvia?" Irene asked.

"I don't see why not," she answered. Then she went off to see about running the school.

"We'll need people who can stay after school today, too," said Irene. "Let's get started on those lists. First we'll call people we know and that we know we can count on. After that we can work out some schedule."

Thus the community school of PS 84 was born, out of necessity and the abdication of Mrs. Wachtel. Had she stayed, things would probably have proceeded as before, with minimum parental participation. When she left, however, a new sense of community developed among those teachers who remained, Mrs. Warner, and the parents. We had a common crisis, and we worked it through together. As we manned the school, we became more and more aware of how disastrous the reign of Mrs. Wachtel had been; and this led, finally, to the conclusion on the part of the parents who had not backed us in the profile and the picketing last year that we had been right and that Mrs. Wachtel was, indeed, not the principal we needed. Only in that sense, then, were our subsequent attempts to remove Mrs. Wachtel a result of the strike. We were accused, of course, of ousting her as a reprisal for her strike action. This was not really the case. Those of us who had wanted her out before the strike could point to our actions of last year as proof that our feelings predated the strike. For Irene, Carole, Stephanie and others—who had opposed us in the spring—their subsequent actions were motivated, not by vengeance, but by the tangible evidence that our occupation of the school provided of her gross incompetence as an administrator.

That morning marked another turning point for me, too. After the events of last night, my feelings about the strike had become more clouded. I was even half toying with the idea of keeping Kathy out of school and casting my lot once again with my colleagues over the issue of due process, which I feared we in District 5 were about to deny to our teachers. And then, when I had come to school this morning and seen the place padlocked and the children running around unsupervised, everything crystallized for me. Kathy was safe with me. If the school was locked, she would return home with me, out a day's instructions but otherwise no worse for it. On the other hand, there were all the children whose parents worked and who, locked out of school, were left completely stranded. Who cared about that? The lockout, then, did not affect my child or the children of the parents who were home or who had maids to take care of them. It was only the children of the poor who were really locked out. And for the first time I saw the strike for what it really was— a strike against all those black and Spanish-speaking and white children who depended on the school to be there for them. The strike and the lockout might not have been racist in intent. I doubt that Shanker sat down, or that most teachers did, and said, "Let's sock it to them." But though it was not racist in intent, it was certainly racist in effect, so it came to the same thing. This was what I had not truly understood till that morning. This was what my high school colleagues still did not understand. (Conditions in high school are different, and students locked out there are not as vulnerable as grade school children.) But seeing the children abandoned on the street I saw the lockout for what it was, and though I still did not want to send threatening letters to anyone, I no longer had ambivalent feelings about which side I was on. When they locked the schools, the custodians blasted me for good over to the side of the community.

SIXTEEN

A Community-Control School

We had a hurried supper that night; and after packing the kids into bed with less than the usual full ceremony, I picked up Millie and we went over to the school. All the gates were still locked, so we entered via the gaping holes in the playground fence, and then made our way to the front entrance, where we rang the bell. A head appeared in one of the lighted windows, and a voice told us to go back to the side entrance, which someone would open for us. There we were greeted by Stu Robbins. With Stu was Brutus, his mastiff, who, along with the Martins' two dogs, was to form, during the weeks of our sleep-in, the backbone of the PS 84 security force. What we feared, in those first days especially, was some sort of sabotage from the custodians. Perhaps we were slightly paranoid, but the papers were full of stories of custodian-initiated violence; and if the other side was willing to believe the worst of the community, we were equally willing to believe the worst of them. And not entirely without reason. After all, if they were capable of locking out children, and, in some instances (though not at our school) of walking off with essential parts of boilers so as to render the premises uninhabitable, then they might also be capable of worse. So the dogs, as well as the fathers, took turns sleeping in the school to keep out unwelcome visitors.

The hall was dim and the school strangely silent as we made our way to the office. The office itself was ablaze, with all typewriters manned, some people on phones, others composing fliers to alert the community to what was happening. On one of the secretary's desks the remains of a Chicken Delight dinner proclaimed that it was not business as usual. The entire office had the aura of a com-

157

mand headquarters, with General Martins very much in charge. We went to her and reported for duty and were promptly set to work in the office anteroom, which normally housed the rexograph machine but which had been converted into the typists' pool. There the two of us typed up parents' lists from the office cards. We had never, until then, been able to get those lists because of the resistance of Mrs. Wachtel. My first involvement with the school had come about in my attempt to get just such a list for the Joan of Arc governing board election (of such tiny acorns mighty revolutions grow); and had Mrs. Wachtel but known where her refusal might lead, she would certainly have given them to us, and good riddance. We were not now going to pass up this glorious opportunity. Indeed, without those lists we would not have been able to reach more than a nucleus of parents, and without the support of a large group of parents the subsequent history of the school might well have been different. As it was, throughout this period we had more than two hundred and fifty parents actively involved; and when you consider that there are about nine hundred children in the school, and that many of these are siblings, the parent involvement was substantial.

One of the immediate effects of getting the lists was that we were able to increase student enrollment from about two hundred and fifty to about five hundred children; and since about half the staff was in, the teacher-pupil ratio remained more or less the same as it normally was. But because only half the teachers and half the children were in, we closed off the entire third floor, and the composition of the classes was visibly altered. Though our classes were allegedly balanced, some of them, especially in the upper grades, were anything but. Nancy Calvert, for example, had told us in June, when she got her class list for the following year, that her class was entirely black and Spanish and that, moreover, all the children in it were at least three years retarded in reading and math. Consequently, another teacher on the same grade had what amounted to an IGC class (though these were supposedly being phased out when the last group—then in the fifth grade—graduated), and this one was predominantly white. What many of the parents in that tacit IGC class did when the strike came was to put their children into Nancy's class, thereby integrating it both ethnically and academically. Similarly, Evelyn Moses was teaching a fifth grade "citizenship" class (a euphemism for junior-guidance postgraduate study), and many parents of children in the sixth grade IGC put their children into her class at this time, so that she ended up teaching a fifth-sixth combination. This class worked so well that when the strike finally ended all the parents (those of the IGC, as well as those of the "citizenship" pupils) petitioned the principal and then after she refused, the district superintendent, to allow the class to remain together—a proposition he gloomily accepted with a "the sins be on your head if it doesn't work" letter.

At any rate, the lists were essential; and Millie and I typed for several hours, and promised to return the following day to do some more work and, at the same time, to keep the school secure with our presence. By the time we left, Irene and a few others had also set up a roster sheet for fathers willing to sleep in, and I volunteered Walter for the 11 P.M. to 7 A.M. shift for the following evening. Thus the pattern of our occupation was set, and it continued in this fashion until the custodians returned and grudgingly gave Sylvia Warner a set of keys and the school board the assurance that they would not again evaporate.

I returned Saturday afternoon with the kids to take a couple of hours of guard duty. The halls were dim, and the school eerily silent, but the kids had a good time running up and down the halls from the office to one of the classrooms. Beth Barron came with her three children and someone else with a couple, and we put the oldest ones in charge of the younger ones and let them play school in the classroom. They took it very seriously, assigning classwork and homework, and came into the office every five minutes to announce another infraction of the rules. We sat in the office drinking coffee—someone had brought an electric percolator—and discussing plans for the coming week. There were lots of details that needed to be worked out, and an executive board meeting had been planned for the following day. Guarding an empty school was one thing; running one with real children in it was another; and though at that point we were not sure whether Mrs. Wachtel would return on Monday—whether her cold feet would have warmed sufficiently after a weekend's reflection to allow her to assume responsibility— we had to make plans in the event that she did not.

At this time I was not yet a member of the Executive Board. I had been asked to run for one of the vice-presidency spots in the spring, but had turned it down because I didn't feel I knew enough to do the job responsibly and because I didn't want to make that kind of commitment to an organization whose effectiveness I still questioned. And, finally, my kids were still quite young, and I just didn't have that much time to give. I did agree that I would serve on the Executive Board as chairman of one of the standing committees, providing I could find one that wasn't too time-consuming and at the same time wasn't too insipid. I expressed some interest, after attending the meeting with the mothers of the junior guidance children, in serving as chairman of the grievance committee. This was vetoed by two members of the Board (both of whom had voted against the profile) on the grounds that I was too critical, and so I looked around for something else I could do constructively. When Anne asked me whether I would co-chair the newspaper committee, I agreed. This was to be voted on the following day, as would all the other committee heads. If accepted, we would all serve on the Executive Board along with the elected officers.

The changing of the guard around five left me free to go home and make supper, and we had a few hours of a household before Walter departed, armed with a flashlight, a thermos of coffee and a slab of cake, an old army blanket, and a pile of books. He returned the next morning and fell into bed, and when I left shortly before noon, he was still sleeping. I left the kids plunked in front of the television, the phone off the hook, and warned them not to disturb Walter except for a national emergency. Then, fingers crossed that they would cope, I made my way back to the school by the now familiar route through the hole in the fence. The side door was open and I went into the office where people were on the phones rounding up those board members who had not yet been reached. Carmen was there, looking anxious. After a while the officers retired to the teachers' cafeteria, where they were to vote on whether to accept the committee heads as voting members of the board. That done, they called us in, and the meeting began.

The first order of business was a discussion of whether Mrs. Wachtel would be in the following day. If she would, there would not be much planning necessary since she would then, presumably, continue to adminster her school. But if she continued to take the position that she could not come in without the custodian, then we would have to formulate a plan of operation. So Carmen went to call her and returned saying thay she was noncommittal, that she would return if the custodians did. Celia Cohen, a new member of the local school board, had come by with her dog (we were practically a kennel club by this time) and had told us that the school board had ordered the custodians to return. The custodians had said that they would come back if ordered to do so by their principals. This seemed to be a game of ring around the rosy, but I suggested that Mrs. Wachtel be called back and told to call the custodian and order him to return. He would then have his orders, she would have her custodian, and she could come back and do her job. Apparently, though, there's many a slip 'twixt cup and lip, because she was either unable or unwilling to order his return, or he was unwilling to obey her orders. Or else someone wasn't telling us somethng. In any case, since her presence was a matter of question we decided to proceed with plan B—who would be where, who would do what, and when. We set up committees to take charge of various operations. The teachers and Mrs. Warner would decide on the deployment of children. We would be in charge of patrolling halls and doors, of providing lunches, of serving as custodians, of manning the office and performing the various clerical functions that would continue to be necessary. As it turned out, our duties were expanded: we became, in addition to hall patrolmen, guidance counselors, and deans, shoulders for upset children to lean on, and disciplinarians to back up the teachers. We also learned a lot about office management, and the myriad forms that consume the time of the office staff. But the fact is that we managed—though we were amateurs—which proves, perhaps, that it is not quite so necessary for people to go through the infinite and ridiculous testing process that the Board of Education would lead us to believe is necessary to the successful running of a school.

So we made our plans, and finally left without knowing whether we would use them. Carmen was to keep on calling Mrs. Wachtel throughout the day to try to get from her a commitment as to her intentions (she never got it); and we would all be at school a half hour before the children were due to take up our spots and to see that the children were received in an orderly fashion. We were all determined that there would be no repetition of Friday's chaos, and to that end we enlisted as many fathers as possible to be on patrol in the halls and on the stairwells during the time the children were arriving. We also scouted around for a licensed fireman (Board of Ed requirements) who could work the boiler. Though the weather was still mercifully mild, we had no assurance that it would last; and once it turned cold, we had to heat the building. Unfortunately, licensed firemen belong to the same union as the custodians, and though we did find one who was sympathetic to what we were doing, he could not risk his union's displeasure by taking the job. He did, however, show one of the fathers, a licensed engineer, how the boiler worked. And when the weather changed we had heat, provided by some kind gremlin whose loyalty lay with the children. Technically, of course, this was a violation of the law, since only someone with the proper license may handle Board of Education boilers (and gremlins are rarely licensed), but since we did not want frozen children we were willing to overlook this technicality. Unlike the shoemaker and his wife, we never peeked to see who the elf was, and consequently our heat remained constant until the custodians returned.

SEVENTEEN

Some Inconclusive Confrontations

Monday morning we rose early. Walter left shortly before eight to take a tour of duty on one of the stairwells. When we talk of the sacrifices we made during this period, we cannot omit the fact that Walter, who prizes that hour of sleep from 7:30 to 8:30, gave it up willingly all those days to ensure the safety of the children. Some of us are morning people, and wake up bright-eyed. Walter is not one of these, and yet he staggered over for guard duty, along with many of the other fathers. I deposited Maggie at nursery, and then Kathy, Sammy, and I went over to school. I was curious to see whether Mrs. Wachtel had recovered her courage (or her sense of survival) sufficiently to have put in an appearance. She had not. The custodians were also still conspicuously absent, and so we learned to be janitors, too. Perhaps we shouldn't be too angry at Shanker and the custodians. After all, they gave us an opportunity to acquire a wealth of on-the-job training in such a variety of capacities that I am sure we are all much more employable than heretofore. I have learned how to wash four-letter words off bulletin boards, how to clean bathrooms (including the wads of wet toilet paper that adhere so beautifully to the ceilings), how to man a desk at the front entrance of the school and keep unwanted people politely but firmly out of the building, how to answer a telephone, run a mimeo machine, write a flier, and a host of skills necessary to the smooth operation of a public school. Actually, since I had spent six years in the actual paid employ of the New York City Board of Education, I had already acquired most of these skills (save the latrine detail), and for me it was only a chance to brush up on them. But for parents less fortunate than I, it was a veritable Job Corps. We even considered applying for OEO funds.

163

I, and many other mothers with small children, were able to work in the school because from that Monday morning until the teachers returned we established a community room. Here some of the mothers with infants stayed all day and provided day care service for those of us with toddlers. Sammy was thrilled at the idea of going to "school" and for a long time afterward he referred to Phyllis Miles, Ruth King, and Violet Morton as his "teachers." I would drop him off in the room and then go and put in my time and energies wherever they were needed that day. After Maggie came from nursery, we would all go for lunch to the community room, and then Maggie and Sam would stay for the afternoon while I returned to my duties. In addition to providing day care, the community room did something far more important. It said to the parents who for years had felt excluded (and this meant mainly the poor and the black and the Spanish-speaking parents), "Welcome. This is your school, too." And, though this should not really be surprising, they came. For the first time since I had been involved at PS 84, we began to have real communication among disparate groups of parents. You cannot share a room and children and not become friends. Suggestions were made and put into effect. Behold! Not only middle-class parents have ideas! As a result of this increased participation on the part of parents, the Executive Board was greatly expanded. We got committees for housing, welfare, health—all the areas that are so important to the whole child that education courses always talk about and the schools always overlook. These things are important to all children, but in neighborhoods with a large population of poor people the schools must certainly provide help in these areas if education is to be possible for the children. This we now proposed to provide, using as our experts (and here we were certainly following the guidelines of the federal government) not those people who had acquired their expertise from textbooks, case studies, and field work, but those people who knew the problems from living with them. And so people with housing problems could come to parents who were in the same boat, but who knew where to go to get out of it. And so forth.

There was another benefit to the increased participation of parents and their presence in the school. During this period many of the children were angry and acting out. They read the papers. They watched the news on TV. And they were not immune to the volatile emotions in the community and in the city. The presence of the parents served the children well. We were there—a steady, large, stable group of adults who cared. We were there, and we didn't disappear. And so, when a child struck out and could not be controlled, the presence of a parent he knew and trusted often made the difference that allowed him to vent his anger verbally and then be able to return to class calmed down and ready to learn.

During this period Sylvia Warner was superb. She ran the school efficiently. The necessary forms got filled in and sent out. People got paid. She used the parents with skill and tact and leaned on their strengths without giving up her own. And she was great with the kids. I would see her in the hall with a child in the throes of a tantrum. She was firm, yet she was never brutal. The kid knew who was boss—there was no question of that. She never backed down, but at the same time she never lost her sense of humor, and so the kids never lost their pride. And it wasn't easy. It's one thing, when you're a licensed principal, to give orders to a paid staff. It's quite another to work with a body of independent volunteers. And parents on the West Side, as anyone will tell you, are the most independent bunch of people imaginable. Yet Sylvia managed to make things move, and I think everyone admired and respected her more at the end than at the beginning of her tenure (no small accomplishment).

The meeting with the striking teachers that had been planned the night before the custodian lockout was to take place on Monday afternoon in our co-op community room. Since the strike was still on, and the teachers obviously would not come into the school, this room offered a location close enough to the school to make it possible for parents to attend. What we hoped to accomplish, naively it seems to me in retrospect, was to convince the teachers that their children needed them and to ask them to return. If they felt they had to support their union, perhaps we could work out some kind of device whereby they could do this without abandoning the children any longer. It was now October 21, which meant that five weeks of school had elasped. Though we had about five hundred children back in school with enough teachers to teach them, we were increasingly concerned about the other four hundred who were not in and who desperately needed to have their education resume.

We set up the chairs in a semicircle for "gemütlichkeit" and waited for the teachers to arrive. Promptly at one o'clock they filed in, en masse. I'll say one thing for the power of the union. It got a lot of teachers who had never voluntarily met with parents before to come into hostile territory and to talk and to listen! The UFT chapter chairman was Jenny Silverman. She was new to the school and had just been appointed there in September. This was the first time I had ever seen her. She was tall, about my height, and young, not more than in her early twenties. She wore her brown hair loose, and she was dressed in a miniskirted corduroy dress decorated with several strings of beads. She looked very eager, very earnest. Her large brown eyes focused with great candor on the collected parents.

It had obviously been decided that she was to be the sole spokesman for the teachers, and she addressed us at some length, telling us how important it was for the teachers to be unionized, how the union had gained for the school system untold benefits that were as important to the children as to the teachers. She cited specifically: decreased class size, prep periods, increased guidance personnel. I could not argue with any of this. Certainly, where teachers are dedicated and conscientious, all of these things will benefit the children. But where they are not . . . And besides, all of this was beside the point. We had not come to discuss the pros and cons of unionism, or even of the UFT. We had come to present our feelings to the teachers, and to listen to theirs. I don't know how all the other parents felt, but I was rather annoyed. I really wanted to hear from the teachers individually, to see how they viewed what was happening. Maybe I was being naive. Maybe in the climate which then existed, the teachers were really frightened to expose themselves individually. Perhaps they had so swallowed the propaganda that Shanker was disseminating that they felt that only in collective anonymity could they be safe from reprisal. I suppose it was heroic of them even to come.

After Jenny finished, Nina Gossens, who was chairing the meeting, asked whether any of the other teachers wanted to add anything. There was an uncomfortable silence. Then Natalie Orr spoke, with great anger.She said that she certainly wanted the teachers to know how she felt about the strike, and what she felt was that the strike was racist and that teachers who were out were striking against her black child and that she could view it in no other way. She continued, "How do you think my child feels every morning when her teacher isn't at the school? She feels rejected."

At that point Mrs. Sumner (who was the only one teaching her class—but outside of the school building) interjected, "But she needn't feel that way, Mrs. Orr. She's welcome to join the class."

"You belong inside the building," Natalie shot back. "That's where my daughter is, and she's waiting for you to come back."

"Look, Mrs. Orr," Mrs. Sumner said. "I'd love to come back. I didn't want this strike, and no one will be happier than I when it's over. I was in at the beginning, but then when I heard what was happening to teachers in other districts I had to rethink my position. And so I made my decision to stay out. If you make your decision to send your daughter into the school, then I respect that decision. But I think you should respect mine, too. And certainly I'm not rejecting your child or anyone else's. They're all welcome."

One of the other parents spoke up "But if your quarrel isn't with our school or our district, then why are you striking? Why should all our kids be penalized for something that should be settled locally elsewhere?"

"Don't you see that I can't do that?" she replied. "That's saying that as long as I'm all right I don't give a damn about my brother. That's what happened in Germany. Everyone thought, 'Well, it's not happening to me, so it doesn't concern me.' But unless we care what happens to our colleagues, then what will happen to us?"

Her words disturbed me. Though I certainly didn't equate what was happening in Brownsville with what happened in Germany (and I thought it an unfortunate comparison), still she was obviously sincere in her position. Not only was she dedicated enough to the children to teach them, daily, without pay, but she had, obviously, thought long and hard about her stand. She was pained. She wished it were otherwise. But she was doing what she had to do. And though she was given a harder time than some of her colleagues, whose convictions were, to me at least, more suspect, I could only respect her for her honesty and her pain. In fact, I felt that the teachers would have been better off if they had made her their spokesman. While Jenny delivered the union position, it was my feeling that she had not arrived at that position through any dark night of the soul, and it came across as glib, a party line.

Another teacher, stung apparently by the racism charge, strode to the front of the room. Her voice shrill, her hands shaking, she began to talk about her more than twenty years of teaching—all children. She had, she said, never noticed the children's race. She couldn't care less if they were pink, blue, green, black, white, or purple. All she cared about was children and teaching them, and yes, it was harder now than it had been. But what could you expect? It had nothing to do with race or color, but if children didn't come from homes where learning and culture were valued, then how could we expect the schools and the teachers to teach them. But racist—no sir! Another teacher at the back of the room rose. As she spoke she began to pull on her long white gloves; and as she spat out each word she gave one of the fingers a tug, as if for emphasis.

"You ask us to come back. How dare you! We belong to the union, and we won't be a party to union busting."

'Where were you last year,' I thought. 'You've found your union rather late in life.'

"And if you care about your children, you won't want us to turn our backs on the union. Because Al Shanker, the UFT, and the teachers care more about your children than some of these political agitators."

She gave her glove a final yank, turned, and began to march to the door. She was followed by her friend, who pulled on her own white gloves as she marched. Most of the other teachers also rose to leave. It had been an exercise in futility. No one had changed anyone else's mind. We parents had had a chance to say very little. Most of the teachers had been equally voiceless. Obviously this was not the time for meaningful dialogue. I stayed for a while to talk to Mrs. Sumner, and to tell her that I for one did respect and understand her position and that I certainly didn't subscribe to the theory that her absence from the school made her a racist. So we talked, earnestly and long, without either of us convincing the other of our viewpoint. But at least I think that we parted friends. As for the rest of the assemblage, I was thoroughly depressed. We had said come back and they had said no. So nothing had changed, everyone was as angry and bitter as before; and if we had thought that we could convince the teachers by our calm and reason and by virtue of our mere charming presence, that we were not the rabid fanatics they feared, and that, even if they entrusted their fate to our hands, they would be safe because we were sane, responsible, and reasonable, then we had failed. And from their point of view, who could blame them? After all, if you felt your job was on the line and you could choose, on the one hand, due process to protect it and, on the other, the whims of the community (a variable, at best), you too might choose due process. And in so choosing you might even feel that you were both right and righteous. By choosing you would not be defending something so narrow as your job, but a principle. And for principle men have gone gladly to their deaths.

It was a hard argument to counter, somewhat akin to being against motherhood and peace and apple pie. Who can be against due process, after all? What no one on the other side even bothered to remember was that we weren't against due process at all, but that we wanted a little due process of our own. So the meeting changed nothing (though one teacher did return to school the next day). Why had the teachers come? Were they as naive as we, and did they hope to change our minds so that we would support the strike and close the school? Or did they come only because Jenny convinced them that to stay away would be a tactical blunder—that they need say nothing, but that they must be there to show the parents that they were reasonable and ready to listen? I do not know. But whatever their reason, it was not the time for dialogue, meaningful or otherwise.

The parents left the meeting angrier than they had entered. The overwhelming feeling was, "Well, we gave them their chance, and they muffed it. Whatever happens now is their own responsibility. We tried." They were angry at what they considered the arrogance of the teachers in refusing, for the most part, to talk, and angry that they had refused their final offer to return without reprisals. And now they felt the die was cast, and whatever happened was out of their hands. Fortunately, in this case, our inefficiency saved us, for I truly feel it would have been a grave mistake to send out letters or telegrams giving the teachers an ultimatum. As I had said at the meeting last Thursday (Was it less than a week ago that the custodians left us?), I didn't want to hang out a welcome sign for Kathy's teacher or for others of her ilk, but we had no right to fire them.

Actually, since the parents had voted at the general membership meeting to send such a telegram to the teachers (even before the meeting with them), I'm not quite sure why it was never sent. I think the lockout simply diverted our energies, and we became too busy with the actual daily operation of the school to have time to compound our problems. And there is no doubt in my mind that such a telegram would have compounded them. Besides, from a pragmatic point of view, we didn't even have the power to enforce the threat.

One morning I was sitting at my by now familiar post at the desk in the corridor outside the cafeteria. From this vantage we could watch the entrance from the playground and the stairs (providing we left the stairwell doors open). On the left were the swinging doors that led to the office corridor, and by leaving these open as well we could also see down that entire corridor. In this way we were able to maintain fairly tight security. This was one of our big headaches. Not only were we worried about saboteurs, but when we had opened the school we had made a commitment to the parents and the children that we could keep them safe. One incident and boom. So we wanted to make sure that no one wandered in off the street; and though we were now community school 84, any member of the community had better have a good reason for walking in. And at that, unless he was known, or a bona fide certified parent, chances were that he'd have an escort while he conducted whatever business had brought him there. We usually had two or three parents at each of the posts. In this way we could provide escorts where necessary and still not leave the spot unguarded. Also in this way we always had company, and the rapport we established in those days helped us in the ensuing battles. It was yet another way in which we got to know and trust each other. On this particular morning as we sat, a young lady entered, notebook in hand. She identified herself as a reporter for a city newspaper, and we offered to take her on a tour of the school to show her how well things were going.

"Don't you have any riots?" she asked.

"No," we said, "but we'll be glad to take you around and show you how well the classes are functioning."

"Well, actually . . . hasn't there been any violence?" she asked hopefully.

"No. Everything's going remarkably well. We'd be happy to show you around. Any class you'd like to see."

"I think not," she said. "I was really looking for a story." And she left, leaving us speechless. Since I certainly don't want to cast aspersions on her paper, I must say here that we never demanded her credentials, nor did she offer them to us. So it is possible that she was not only not from that newspaper, but conceivably not from any paper at all. The world is full of nuts. However, on the theory that only violence makes news, it is also quite possible that she was a genuine representative of the fourth estate; and so, since we could not provide the story that confirmed the prevailing prejudice, that nothing good could be going on in a community run school, our lady friend left. Perhaps she wrote for the UFT journal.

On several other occasions parents who had been keeping their children home, but who knew we were running the school, came to look around. We showed them around, assured them their children would be safe and that there were teachers who were teaching—that we were not simply running a glorified babysitting service. Most of these parents, after a tour of the school, then brought their children in. During this time there were frequent meetings between parents and staff. Mrs. Warner and those teachers who were in were doing a superhuman job. They were short of help in various ways; and though the parents helped wherever they could, the main burden still fell on the staff. Lunchtime was especially critical, for this was the time when there were fewest parents available and when they were most needed. Lunchtime is a madhouse under normal conditions. Now with all the aides out in support of the teachers and the kitchen staff also depleted, it could have been disastrous. But it wasn't. The teachers gave up their lunch period. Parents pitched in. Nan Sergeant organized some of the older children into monitor squads. And so we muddled through. As Irene Martins put it at one of our meetings at which we were all engaging in some self-congratulation, "This is community control. The professional decisions are being made by the professionals, but they are listening to the community to find out what *they* want."

And it really was that way. The teachers were happy, the parents were happy, and the kids were happy, except for the ones who weren't in school at all. As one of the teachers put it, "Our school has never run so well."

And I really don't think she was exaggerating. For a while there we really had a sense of community. We had problems too; but we tried to solve them together and there was no contempt for parents' suggestions as there had been in the past. There was no attempt to deny facts as there had been in the past. And if one thing didn't work, we tried something else, as we grappled with the problems of wandering children, no hot water, children who were going "teacher shopping," and so on.

On October 31 the custodians returned as suddenly as they had gone. This proved to be a mixed blessing, for while they had been out the school had been ours. Now, suddenly, it was their school again. They went around grumbling about damage, vandalism (we had broken their brand-new locks), and filth. Considering how hard we had worked to keep the school clean, that was the unkindest cut of all. They were interminably slow in making repairs, refused to speak to us at all, and insisted that we not speak to them but make our requests through Mrs. Warner, who could relay them to the custodial engineer. This might not have been too bad, except that he hardly deigned to speak to Sylvia either. As for our not issuing orders to the maintenance staff, that was fine. You can't very well have one hundred and fifty bosses, all issuing contradictory orders. It assumed ridiculous proportions, though, when we were so thoroughly intimidated that we would not have reported a major catastrophe to the nearest custodian.

It was certainly nice to have the custodians assume responsibility for the boiler, nor were we sorry to give up our latrine detail. But suddenly we were made to feel like intruders again. When three o'clock came and the children went home, the grumbling grew louder. Not only was the parents' presence unwelcome past three, but pity any poor teacher who wanted to stay and do some preparation for the next day. There was no question that once the custodians returned, they wanted their building back and they wanted it back as it had been, unencumbered by the bodies of fathers by night or mothers by day. Probably they would have preferred it without children at all times; but alas the millennium is not yet, so they had to put up with the children, though they did not suffer them—or us —gladly. Their comments on subjects educational and social were illuminating. They knew just what to do with that little S.O.B. who . . . And when one of the kindergarten teachers complained that her floors never got mopped, she was told that if she would keep her children in their seats like Mrs. Rudley did, then her floors wouldn't need to be cleaned so often.

We didn't know what had made them return—worry about their building, probably. Neither did we know how long they would stay. We had no guarantee that they would not again disappear, this time leaving the fort impenetrable; so we decided at a large meeting that, for the duration, the sleep-in would continue. Sure the custodians promised they were back to stay; but we had grown wary over the past few weeks, and we wanted more than words before we ceded the fort. So far all we had gotten were words. Furthermore, the contempt with which the custodians treated us and, worse, the fact that this same contempt was heaped on Sylvia Warner too (just this side of insubordination) made us reluctant to trust their assurances that they had come back to serve the community.

The fact that the custodians returned presented another interesting situation. When Mrs. Wachtel had left the morning of the lockout and when she had refused, the following Monday, to return, she had given as her grounds for refusal the fact that she could not enter the premises without the presence of a licensed fireman. Now they were back. Up until this point her absence had not, technically, been a strike action. She could stand upon the legality. With the return of the custodians, her situation changed. If she remained out any longer, she would by anyone's definition be on strike. And indeed, the day before the custodians returned, as I sat with several of the other parents at my usual ground-floor post, who should walk by but Mrs. Wachtel, together with Mr. Sussman. She had come, she said, to see how things were going. We told her they were going fine, thank you, and when was she planning to return? She turned to Carmen Johnson, who was walking down the hall toward the office with her and said, "Why don't you put that question in black and white?"

They then went into Mrs. Wachtel's office (at the moment it was Sylvia Warner's) and Mrs. Wachtel puttered around for a few minutes looking for some papers. According to Carmen, while she was conducting this search, she said that as long as parents like Irene Martins remained in the school she would not return.

Meanwhile, back at our table, we were having a conversation with Mr. Sussman. I had had high hopes for him when he had come, for he seemed to like the kids and they him. He seemed both firm and kind, and he also seemed interested in better parent-school relations. In fact, we had, before the strikes hit us, intended to do a joint school-parent paper, with the promise that the parents' material would not be censored by the school. This had seemed like a good way of working for educational change. Because of the strike the Executive Board had voted not to get involved in such a joint venture, but as a result of this beginning there was a slight rapport between us, and I had been truly sorry when he had joined Mrs. Wachtel in refusing to come in without the custodians. We could have used his presence, and besides I was disappointed in him.

A rather large group of parents had gathered around the table as word of our rare guests had spread quickly through the school. The questions put to him were hostile, and he flushed at times, blanched at others, as he tried to justify himself. As he spoke, he turned to me periodically, appealing for help. He wanted to be a good guy, he wanted to be liked by everyone, and now he was facing the hostility of a whole group of parents. He spoke of his anguished reflection, how he had to stick by his principles. He did not consider himself on strike. He was merely expressing his solidarity with the concept of due process. The argument got angrier. Someone wanted to know what principle had changed when the custodians had gone out. If due process was the issue, it was the issue from the outset, and the custodial lockout didn't make it more or less of an issue. He stammered over that one. Someone else asked when he was coming back. "When the strike is over," he answered.

"But you said you weren't on strike," someone reminded him.

"I'm not," he answered.

"Oh, brother," someone groaned.

The subject turned, as it inevitably had to, to the fact that this was a racist strike. At this he turned to me and said, "Tell them I'm not a racist, Mrs. Hess."

Poor guy. For a moment a scene from a B-movie flashed through my mind. This guy is up against the wall, and only the chief of police can exonerate him. He turns, pleadingly, to the chief, who shrugs his shoulders and walks away. Fade-out as shots are heard. . . . The only trouble with that scene was that I couldn't exonerate him. I have no idea whether or not he is a racist, so I answered, "You tell them."

I must say that though this won me the applause of the gathered group, I didn't feel particularly good about it. He was in an unenviable position, and I was the only friendly face around. On the other hand he had made two choices, and he was now paying the price for both of them. The first choice, of course, had been to stay out when his boss left (that was obviously the safe, the politic, thing to do). His second choice had been in coming in with her this morning. I still don't know why they came. Was it curiosity? masochism?

Shortly thereafter Mrs. Wachtel came out of the office; and gathering up her faithful retainer, she left. Someone muttered under her breath, "Goodbye, and don't hurry back." We stood around for a while, reviewing the conversation and wondering what it all meant. It also reminded us that the strike would not last forever and that we had better start making some decisions about our course of action once it ended.

EIGHTEEN

"We Cannot Go Back"

On Thursday evening, October 31, we had another Executive Board meeting. We wanted to take stock of where we were and to begin thinking collectively of how we would deal with the return of the teachers and the principal. Earlier that day a film crew had arrived, and Sylvia Warner had asked me to act as tour guide. One of the crew told me he was doing a film for NET on how community control was working. Since this was a welcome change from all the press and media people who were trying to show the opposite, I was happy to take them around the school. The crew was interested and sympathetic, and I thought it would be lovely if their show ever saw the light of day. Perhaps then the public would see that parents are interested in education rather than in power for its own sake.

When I arrived at the Executive Board meeting that evening, the TV cameras and the sound equipment were set up. I assumed they had cleared it with Carmen, and I guess everyone else did, too, because no one said anything about their presence. And so our meeting began, and the cameras and tape equipment recorded. Stephanie Hale wanted to send a copy of a Jimmy Breslin column to the striking teachers (which column pointed out the racist nature of the union and the strike) with a note asking them to return. Several parents recited incidents of teachers' lack of concern for their classes. One teacher had left strict instructions with her children that they were to do no work in reading or phonics until her (eventual) return. The children were so to instruct any substitute; and to give teeth to these instructions, she had locked up her readers. What the children were to do in the meantime was obviously of no interest to her, presumably because she felt they should not be

175

there without her in any case. Incidents like that made it hard for me to defend the striking teachers. But since I saw no realistic way of preventing the return of those we could have lived without, I was still opposed to sending such a letter. And this time my arguments prevailed. Though we did not vote officially, it was the sense of the meeting that no letter be sent.

We then turned to a more pressing problem. How would we deal with the returning teachers? Would they be given their original classes? Would they get new classes composed of those children who were out during the strike? Some of us suggested that they deserved each other; but obviously that was impractical since the majority of the children who were out were Spanish-speaking,* and we did not want to unbalance our classes. On the other hand, I and many of the other parents felt that we could not go back to the September class organization since that would mean taking children out of stable situations where they were functioning and learning and forcing them to make another adjustment.

I said that I for one would not allow my daughter to be moved back to her original class, that she had made a good adjustment, that she was happy, and that since it was not her fault that her teacher had left, she should not be penalized by having to return to her original class. Furthermore, since her original teacher was one I would not have chosen in any case, I was not going, any longer, to consent to her presence with the body of my child.

"But what do we do about the classes?"

"I make a motion," I said, "that no child be forced to return to his original class."

"What about classes that have been having a great number of subs —classes that aren't really stable?"

"And what about racial balance?"

Carole Arnowitz pointed out that the classes hadn't been balanced to start with in many instances and that they had become more heterogeneous, not less, as a result of the strike. The motion was amended to include the provision that parents did not have to keep their children in their present classes, but basically the motion, which was passed with only one abstention and no opposition votes, said that the parents would determine the placement of their chil-

*Their absence did not indicate sympathy for the strike, but rather a fear on the part of the parents that the opened schools were unsafe.

dren when the strike ended. This was revolution, for it took from the principal the right to determine the organization of her school, and we knew she would not accept it without a fight. But we were determined, too.

The discussion then turned to the principal. Irene Martins pointed out that three more principals in the district had returned that day.

"We have had a meaningful relationship with the professionals who have been in. The problem is that Mrs. Wachtel will want this to stop."

MIKE GOODMAN: "Let's consider the alternatives: 1) the parents can all go away; 2) we can refuse to allow her into the building; 3) we can institute a legal procedure against her; 4) then we have to consider a replacement."

As to the last, somebody suggested that Sylvia Warner, who had been doing such an outstanding job, could be asked whether she would be willing to continue after the strike ended.

Carmen said that when she had asked Mrs. Wachtel whether she was planning to return, she had replied that Carmen should put the question in black and white.

"I have the feeling," said Carmen, "that she is not coming back. I think we should send her a letter and ask her."

"Send her a letter requesting a reply before the general membership meeting tomorrow night," said Mike Goodman.

IRENE: "The CSA* under the new legislation now has the right to arbitration. But we could request that Dr. Selig institute a disciplinary action against her—insubordination and neglect of duty are possible charges."

"There are two areas of concern," said Carole Arnowitz. "One is what to do about Mrs. Wachtel's permanent position in the school. The other is what to do if she comes back in now."

EDNA GARRETT: "Are we really afraid of what Mrs. Wachtel will do?"

And so we decided that we could not turn back, that we had accomplished too much to give it up. We then turned our attention to our immediate problem: how to deal with the newly returned custodians. Carole Arnowitz reported on a meeting she and a small group of parents had attended with Mr. O'Malley, our custodial engineer, and with Mrs. Warner. Mr. O'Malley had said that his

*Council of Supervisors and Administrators.

union had directed that parents could not stay in the school after 3:00 P.M. He also complained that parents were smoking in areas of the building where it was prohibited, and he asked that this be stopped. In short, he was dictating the terms of our surrender, and we were all pretty mad, especially since he still had not given Mrs. Warner a set of keys to the school, although the school board had ordered that she receive one set and that another be left with the district office. While we were fuming about this arrogance, Pete, one of the custodians, came into the cafeteria and peremptorily turned off the lights. It was no longer our building!

We all went into the office where the lights were still on, and the discussion turned to the presence of the TV crew. Carmen was furious.

"Who invited them?" she wanted to know.

"Didn't you?" someone asked.

"I did not. I'm sick and tired of people making my decisions for me. I'm the president, and no one ever bothers to consult me on anything. It's pretty insulting, if you ask me."

We all stood around looking embarrassed. It turned out that it had been no one's decision, that we had all assumed someone else had made the decision. In fact, the crew had called the district office and asked Dr. Selig for permission to film the meeting. No one knew what his answer had been. In any case, it was after the fact, and the question now was whether we should sign the releases permitting the use of our part of the footage. Since this seemed to be on the way to becoming a full meeting in its own right, and since Pete now stood in the doorway of the office glaring at us, it was clear that we would have to move elsewhere. Only two parents would be permitted to remain through the night. So the rest of us relocated to Selma Wood's apartment where the discussion continued unabated.

"We don't want all that on TV."

"How do we know how they'll use it?"

"At least we should have the right to screen the stuff."

"Reprisals."

"They say they're in favor of community control, and then they come in and shoot without ever consulting the community. Humph!"

The producer looked rather pained by the entire discussion. My own feelings were that signing a release at this point was a pure formality—that anyone who had come in and seen the cameras had

had, at that point, several options: he could have protested their presence (which might have obviated the need for all of the subsequent negotiations); he could have refused to say anything as long as the crew was there; or he could have participated, knowing full well that the cameras and tape were running. We had all opted for the last, but now some of our feet were fast cooling. I was rather annoyed that we were taking so much time for this when it seemed clear to me that we had all made a choice, and I said so. The result, after several hours of this, was that only Edna and I agreed to sign the releases; and the producer, after saying that he really could use the footage even without the signatures, said it wasn't worth the hassle, packed up his gear, and left, saying in parting that he could have done our cause a service. And perhaps he could have and would have. But on this issue I think there were few converts in either direction, and had the show seen the light of day it would, at best, have been solace to the already convinced.

The following night, at the general membership meeting, the concept of the resolution I had made at the Executive Board—that children be allowed to remain in their current classes—was accepted. Furthermore, it was agreed that before *any* interclass transfers were made, both the child's parents and the child's present teacher must be consulted. What we voted that night was, in effect, a declaration of war, for by this vote we said that the power to organize the school no longer rested solely with its administrator.

Having thus voted, we turned to the matter of Mrs. Wachtel. Carmen reported on her visit two days earlier and stated that she had asked Mrs. Wachtel her intentions. Mrs. Wachtel had asked Carmen to put that in writing, which had now been done. Carmen also reported Mrs. Wachtel's comment that she would not return as long as parents like Irene Martins were in the school, which infuriated everyone, since it was both an insult to Irene and an assumption that she could decide which parents would be permitted in the school.

IRENE: "Good. I'll be the secret weapon. I'll come in, and she'll stay away. But seriously, since we've been here, we've increased student attendance from three hundred to five hundred. We took responsibility for the school when Mrs. Wachtel wouldn't. Now we're ready to work with teachers on plans for the future. The custodians say they won't leave again. Mrs. Warner has tremendous potential as a principal—she's flexible, intelligent, and human. I say Mrs. Wachtel should be brought up for disciplinary action—insubordination to the district superintendent and neglect of duty."

Bob Goodfellow (of the local school board) who had come, apparently, to give us the broad view we lacked, said, "These problems are also true for the other schools in the district. There have been teachers and supervisors there, too, who have not only been out but who have taken actions that warrant drastic measures by parents. But any drastic action would be playing into the hands of Shanker and the legislature. The legislature will vote in March on a new decentralization bill, and they're waiting for us to do something drastic so they can discredit the community. All the settlements have a clause against reprisals at the end of the strike. There are legal steps we can take through the present law: withholding tenure, bringing people up on charges. We can do the legal and the right thing and still maintain control, but if we act illegally we would be defeating ourselves and our cause,"

ELLEN LODGE: "We don't want to panic our teachers by doing something illegal. There are plenty of legal grounds to remove Mrs. Wachtel."

MIKE GOODMAN: "I'm not very happy with Bob's legal opinion. He misses the tone of what's going on in the school and the tenor of parent opinion. Nothing will happen here unless we organize, and unless we get a consensus of parents. We should make a statement of what it is we wish to do, and we should seek additional legal advice."

PETE WORTHEM (chairman of the Joan of Arc governing board): "The teachers and supervisors are out illegally. The local school board has not been providing leadership at a time when parents have been working to keep school open. A way has to be found in which the organized will of the parents can be exercised. The parents are the only group who cares—and they know who is doing the best for the children. The local school board must help the parents organize."

SELMA WOOD: "What are the legal grounds for the removal of Mrs. Wachtel?"

BOB: "That's no problem. She doesn't have tenure."

EDNA GARRETT: "You don't want to get your hands dirty. We won't get anywhere being legal. They have the laws stacked against us."

IRENE: "Charge insubordination. Mrs. Wachtel told the children to go home when she was ordered to keep the school open. We must stand behind the charges. Let's think about it—get a committee with an educational lawyer, and let's bring charges that are really charges."

JOE DREIER: "I'd like to make the following motion: It is the recommendation of the Parents' Association that Mrs. Wachtel be removed as principal of PS 84 because of incompetence." The motion was passed overwhelmingly. Yes: 41. No: 0. Abstentions: 5.

MARY DEGREGORIO: "Will there be support from the entire parent body?"

MIKE: "We need it. We need organization to get parental support. The parents must have an opportunity to express themselves."

BOB GOODFELLOW: "It really doesn't matter how many parents do or do not want her. It's simply a question of whether or not she's doing her job."

IRENE: "I move that the Executive Board set up a committee to implement the previous resolution, and report its findings to the parent body. I further move that the resolution be brought to the attention of the local school board and the Joan of Arc governing board."

This was passed unanimously.

TONI DIAMOND: "The teachers voted today to give full support and cooperation to the efforts of the parents to remove Mrs. Wachtel."

GLADYS WEAVER: "The Joan of Arc governing board gives its full support to the parents in this effort."

There was one further motion, that a letter be sent to the local school board with a copy to Dr. Selig, asking them to instruct Mr. O'Malley to take his orders from Mrs. Warner and to treat her with proper respect. This was also passed unanimously. And so we adjourned, having voted out the old order. It remained to be seen whether we could make it stick.

We called another general meeting for Wednesday evening, November 12, and the cafeteria was filled with parents. The strike was winding down, and our mood was one of urgency. We had to take some action before Mrs. Wachtel and the teachers returned, and things went back to their impossible (for us) prestrike state. A petition had been prepared calling for the removal of Mrs. Wachtel. After some discussion as to the wording, we amended that to read:

"The parents of PS 84 feel that Mrs. Hilda Wachtel should not continue as principal of the school." Millie and I went into the office to type up sufficient copies, and we returned and circulated them, gathering over two hundred signatures on the spot. The wording on the petition was important, since to speak of "firing" Mrs. Wachtel or to suggest bringing her up on charges would entail a drawn-out legal procedure. Because she was untenured, however, to ask that she not continue as principal was within our rights; and that no one present wanted her to remain as principal was clear from the testimony of parent after parent. Everyone had a story to tell, and each story reinforced the panic we were feeling at the thought of Mrs. Wachtel's return. A lot of the incidents we had read in the profile. Others were new. But the cumulative effect was to convince us that we could not return to normal. Theresa told how, when she had tried to discuss methods of teaching reading, Mrs. Wachtel had replied, "We must face the fact, Mrs. Hunter, that some children simply cannot learn."

Parents are not supposed to discuss methodology with professionals, and the fact that Theresa had been a licensed teacher before she was a mother was irrelevant to her present role—ignorant parent. Meg Knight recounted how, when they were working on the budget and parents wanted to hire a remedial reading teacher for the upper grades, Mrs. Wachtel had refused, preferring to put the person into the lower grades in spite of the fact that the worst rate of failure was in the upper grades where there was, also, the highest concentration of black and Spanish-speaking children. Other parents told of the contempt with which they had been treated by Mrs. Wachtel. One father, with an appointment, had cooled his heels in the outer office despite repeated reminders to the secretary that Mr. Smith was waiting. When he grew tired of waiting, he decided to pull rank, and he told the secretary to announce that *Dr.* Smith was waiting, whereupon the door immediately opened and he was unctiously summoned into the presence of Mrs. Wachtel.

At this point there was a whispered conference between Tom Cabot, who was chairing the meeting, and one of the parents. Tom interrupted the speaker to say, "I understand we have some uninvited guests this evening. Will all those who aren't parents, friends, or invited teachers please leave."

"What does that mean?" someone asked angrily.

"It means," said Tom, "that an announcement of our meeting

was on the CSA hotline* and that all supervisory and UFT person-nel in District 5 were told to come to our meeting tonight."

"Ask them to leave," "Throw them out," "We don't crash their meetings," came from various people throughout the cafeteria. Mr. Cannon, one of our dissenters who thought Mrs. Wachtel was just fine and that we were all bomb-throwing revolutionaries who were ruining what used to be a fine school till we got the upper hand and abolished IGC classes and forced his children to hobnob with just anyone no matter how dumb or how antisocial, now rose and said, icily, "I thought this was a public meeting. This *is* a public build-ing."

"This is a parents' meeting," Tom replied. "It's for parents and their *invited* guests."

"Then I think the teachers should all leave," said Mr. Cannon.

"There are teachers here whom we've invited," said Tom. "But I must ask that anyone who isn't a parent, or an invited guest, leave before we continue the meeting."

Two or three little gray men rose hesitantly. "Stay," commanded Mr. Cannon. They froze like obedient setters.

"I'm afraid I must ask you to leave," repeated Tom.

At this second command they began to come back to life and to thread their ways to the exit.

"I thought this was still a democracy," shouted Mr. Cannon. "You don't represent anyone. You can't throw people out of public meet-ings."

"This isn't a public meeting," Tom answered coolly. "It's a par-ents' meeting. But if you're worried that I'm ramming something through, let's vote on it. But remember, only parents of children in the school can vote. All right, all those who want these gentlemen to remain, raise your hands."

"Mr. Cannon's hand shot up. Two other parents diffidently raised theirs.

"All those who want this meeting restricted to parents and their invited guests . . ."

Every other hand in the room went up.

"Sorry, gentlemen," said Tom with a smile. "The majority has spoken."

*An information service for supervisory personnel, informing them of items of interest throughout the city.

So we lost our uninvited guests, and Mr. Cannon, too, who put on his coat and stormed out, shouting about kangaroo justice.

"Now, where were we?" asked Tom, and the horror stories continued.

Teachers rose to tell how their efforts to improve education were stifled, how they were caught up in bureaucratic regulations and protocol, how they could only make changes if they so couched them as to make it appear that they had originally been Mrs. Wachtel's ideas. They complained that supplies were withheld from them if they were on the s-list. The meeting began to assume the flavor of a revival meeting, with one saved soul after another rising to tell how he had found salvation and with the rest of us swaying to the rhythm. All the anger we had been storing, all the frustrations, all the hopes that we had for making our school into a viable place instead of an institution and that were constantly being rebuffed, all the personal insults we had encountered came pouring forth. They reinforced each other, reminded us of others, drew a picture of a school in crisis and of a principal who neither would, nor could—nor even cared to—change it. Norma Hill rose. The mother of seven bright, lively, well-behaved children, she had long been active on the Executive Board, but I had never heard her speak in public. Now, her voice trembling slightly, she began:

"Last year they suddenly dropped my daughter from the IGC class without any explanation. I tried to go to see Mrs. Wachtel about it, and I could never get an appointment. It wasn't till I took Stephanie Hale with me that I even got into the office. Mrs. Wachtel won't see black parents if they don't take a white parent along. When I finally got in to see her and asked why she had dropped my daughter from the IGC class, she said it was because of her reading score. I asked how they could do that on the basis of one test, and she answered, 'You know, Mrs. Hill, you people expect more from your children than they're capable of.' Then the assistant principal turned to me and said, 'Mrs. Hill, the trouble is, you don't stimulate your children enough.' Now how does she know that? She doesn't know I take my children to the ballet, to the theater—but she looked at me and told me I don't stimulate my children enough."

Lila Emerich, a new parent in the school, who had until then listened to what sounded perhaps like the rantings of lunatics, asked, "What did she mean by 'you people'?"

Norma said she hadn't asked her to spell it out—maybe she meant you parents, maybe she meant you black parents—but all she knew was she resented being called "you people" in any case.

"Look," Tom said, "we can go on like this for hours, and it's all important. But the school board is meeting at PS 75 tonight, and we should all go over there and give them the petitions. How many of you can go?"

It was by then close to ten, but about fifty of us raised our hands.

"Good," Tom said. "Now the thing is we should have one spokesman, and he should tell them why we've come and present the petitions. Then, if it's necessary, those of you who are there can fill in with what you've been telling us tonight. And we'll also write it down so it's there as evidence."

It was decided that Jim Calvert should be our spokesman to the school board, and we prepared to leave. We trudged through the cold to PS 75 to present the school board with our just demands.

We had informed the school board that we were coming, but I think they were taken aback by the size of the group that piled into their office. After a hasty conference with her board, Jessica Malamud told us that they would move into the auditorium and that they would then hear what we had to say. We found seats in the auditorium—while the board composed itself at the front, the cool, responsible experts come to hear what the bothersome clients had to say.

Jim opened by saying that he had a petition from the PS 84 parents asking that Mrs. Wachtel no longer continue as principal. He handed the petitions to Jessica, who put them on the table where they lay like a vial of cholera germs. Then the questions began—and the note dominant in all of them was fear. We were asking them to act; and if our complaints had validity, they would have to. Ergo—question the validity. Was this a strike action? The settlement would contain a no-reprisal clause. Were we representative of the parents as a whole? We threw Bob Goodfellow's argument back in his teeth. At our last meeting he had said that if we were right it didn't matter how many of us there were, and there were "only" fifty or so of us present at close to eleven P.M. What evidence did we have to warrant such a petition? When we had written the profile, we had not asked for Mrs. Wachtel's removal. Why had we changed our minds? What about all the parents who had disagreed with the profile? What about their feelings?

So we tried to answer their doubts, to break through their fear.

We began to rise again, one by one, to recite our litany. Theresa spoke. Meg spoke. Norma spoke. I spoke. Millie and Dotty did a duet, recounting how they had tried to get together a meeting requested by Mrs. Wachtel, and how they had had to nurse the procedure every inch of the way, down to stuffing, stamping, and mailing the envelopes, and how, after all that, they had been accused by the assistant principal of breaking into the office and rifling her letter box. Many of the parents said nothing—but they were there, testifying with their presence and their applause to the justice of what we were recounting. Irene pointed out that the reason she had not originally backed the profile had been a tactical one—that it was the wrong effort at the wrong time. Stephanie Hale said she had opposed the profile because she was unwilling to exchange one Board of Ed incompetent for another, but that now, with the new decentralization bill impending, she felt there was a better chance of getting the kind of principal our school needed, and so she was now willing to consider a replacement. Ronnie Rubin pointed out that when Mrs. Wachtel had first been presented to the parents as a possibility, they had had serious doubts about her, based on reports from the school where she had been an assistant principal. But the parents had been told to give her a chance. At that time they had told Dr. Selig the criteria they were seeking in a principal: someone with vision, competence, and the ability to buck the system. Now we had given Mrs. Wachtel her chance, and she had proved that she had none of these qualities. We were still searching for someone who had them, and we were no longer willing to continue with someone who didn't. Silence from the board.

Carmen rose, and with tears in her eyes said that she had been willing to give Mrs. Wachtel a chance because she felt it was important not to prejudge people; that if that could happen to Mrs. Wachtel, it could also happen to black and Spanish principals, but "I've worked for her for a year and a half, and her reputation was right. I work in that school. There are some teachers there that I love. I've seen Mrs. Wachtel give them the business, just because they don't agree with her."

Silence from the board. Here we were, on a cold November night, spilling our guts to them, and they sat impassive—detached. It wasn't their kids in there.

"What are you going to do?" we finally asked.

"We need documentation," they answered. "You can't remove

someone just like that. Do you want to bring her up on charges?"

"But she doesn't have tenure. You don't need charges. You can simply deny her tenure."

"You still have to have documentation," they said.

"We gave you the profile," we countered. "That should do for openers."

"It's not enough," they said.

"What about everything you've heard tonight? For God's sake, what do you want, a novel?"

"It's not enough," they said.

"We'll give you more," we said, "but we don't want her to go on being principal. With her there the school can't function."

At this Victor Gonzalez-Patron came to life. With a smirk he asked, "You mean that all the problems in the school are her fault?"

"No," I said, "but she doesn't even recognize that there are problems. When we gave her the profile, she said 'I don't know whether to sue for libel or ignore it.' And then she ignored it. She never even tried to see what the problems were or how to solve them. And she never will. As long as she's there, the problems won't get solved, don't you understand that? As soon as anyone tries to suggest anything, she just gets defensive."

Ho hum, yawned the school board. Give us the evidence and we'll consider it. Class dismissed. Dr. Selig had said not a word, but had been sitting there smiling smugly throughout. Some of the parents were beginning to wonder whether he could speak at all, or whether he was, truly, a ventriloquist's dummy who sat there simply to make people think they had a superintendent. Those of us who had heard him speak knew, of course, that he was real, but for all the decisions he made he might as well have been a dummy. His *modus operandi* seemed to be that if you delayed doing anything long enough, most things would resolve themselves, and those that didn't could be dealt with at some later time. And who could blame him? In the bureaucratic mess that is the Board of Education, if you attempt to deal with everything that comes across your desk, nothing will get done either, so you might as well wait and let the important things rise above the trivia. The trouble with it, of course, was that while the important things were rising so were tempers.

So the meeting ended, and we walked home warmed by our anger. We realized once again that if anything was going to get done, we would have to do it ourselves. Some of the board members might be sympathetic (others obviously were not), but none of them was living in the school, and at best they lacked our sense of urgency. Nor did they want to face the inevitable confrontation with the CSA and the Board of Education. They would act if they had to, but we would have to see to it that they had to. Our next move was to get ourselves a good lawyer.

The following day a group of parents met with one of the lawyers from MFY* who gave them advice on the legal ramifications of our position. She said that according to the law charges are not necessary for the removal of nontenured personnel. They can be transferred, their services can be discontinued, or they can simply be denied tenure at the expiration of their probationary period. The superintendent writes a report to the central board recommending that tenure be denied. She suggested, therefore, that our school board ask the superintendent to do this. She also said that our profile and our picket line were helpful, as was the fact that Mrs. Wachtel had allowed the ethnic-attitudes test† to be given to our children, since all of these proved that our actions were not motivated by the strike. She also suggested that we be careful in our wording to avoid "charges" and talk of firing, since that would immediately bring the CSA in with all their legal machinery.

The parents asked whether there was any possibility of preventing her return, and the lawyer thought there was no legal way. But he advised that we continue to document both how well the school was running in the absence of Mrs. Wachtel and any further idiocies committed by her upon her return. And he promised to look at our

---

*Mobilization for Youth, an antipoverty agency that provides legal service to the poor.

†This test, devised to probe the degrees of racial prejudice of children in grades two through six, was in the form of a series of hypothetical situations. For example: The teacher leaves the room for a minute. The entire class behaves well, with the exception of Joe, who hits Fred in the stomach. The children were then asked to tell, from this situation, what color Joe was. What color Fred was. This they did by filling in one of a series of circles with black for black, striped for Spanish-speaking, and blank for white. Other typical situations dealt with stealing, dishonesty, aggression, and "proper" behavior. In each case the children were to ascertain the race of the participants.

When the parents protested Mrs. Wachtel's administration of this test, she replied that she had been ordered by the district to do so.

documentation to make sure it was not libelous. Our work for the next few months, then, in addition to trying to keep the school from going to pieces under the administration of Mrs. Wachtel, would consist of documenting each new instance of inadequacy or incompetency on her part. On a human level, over the next few months, I felt rather sorry for Mrs. Wachtel. She was in a situation she did not understand. She had been trained for another era when professionals knew everything and parents kept their respectful distance, and she was suddenly faced by daily meetings with angry parents, all of them taking copious notes when they weren't yelling at her. I wondered why she stayed as long as she did. Her public protestations that it was "her" school and that she would not be moved made no sense to me. But then, I've also never understood the psychology of the wife who, knowing her husband wants a divorce, still hangs in. I guess it takes a special kind of doggedness, self-righteousness, or something.

NINETEEN

The Old Order Changes

On Friday, November 15, the UFT and the Board of Education brought Ocean-Hill to its knees. We were all terribly depressed. The terms of the settlement were that the teachers fired from the Ocean-Hill complex were to be reinstated and given back their classes. There was to be no further harassment of union teachers. A state administrator, and union and Board of Education observers, were to be in the schools to insure compliance. There were to be no reprisals against any of the striking teachers, and any school, or individuals therein, who in any manner or fashion threatened any teacher, would be brought up on charges by the union. Furthermore, to restore the lost education suffered by the children, the school day would be extended for forty-five minutes daily, and ten holidays would be eliminated, until the lost time was recovered. The teachers were to be paid for this additional time. This last provision particularly stuck in our craw. It seemed like a thinly disguised method of paying the teachers for the time *they* had lost, rather than like a real concern for the children's education.

Learning is a qualitative, not a quantitative process. Besides, after the 1967 strike the teachers in District 5, when the same suggestion had been made, had unequivocally opposed it on the grounds that it would in no way make up for the educational time lost. Now, one year later, they had changed their minds. We hadn't though. We felt, moreover, that since our children had been in school during the period of the strike, and had been learning, they should not be burdened with additional school hours simply to recoup the pay losses of the strikers. The entire settlement had been arrived at without the presence of the Ocean-Hill Board, or any other parent

190

groups. The Board of Education and the union had hammered it out and were now preparing to ram it down the throats of the communities. And we did not like it. Not only was the settlement a large defeat for community control, but it also spelled the end of our school as we had come to know it. We dreaded the return of Mrs. Wachtel.

That afternoon some of the teachers came into the school to get things ready for Monday. Our community room had been set up in one of the first-floor kindergarten rooms. Violet Morton, Phyllis Miles, Emily Anderson, Millie Miller, and a few other mothers and their children were there when the "owner" of the room walked in with one of her colleagues. Mrs. Rudley was a lady who gave the impression that she loved order above children and who had always run her kindergarten with the thought that cleanliness is not only next to, but far above, godliness. On afternoons preceding holidays she always asked her children not to bother coming because she would be cleaning the room, and woe betide any child who failed to heed the suggestion. Furthermore, even on normal days she kept the children nailed to their seats lest they dirty themselves or the floor, and she would have suffered a coronary had anyone ever suggested allowing the children to use paints. It was of her that Mr. O'Malley had spoken when he had told another kindergarten teacher that if she kept the kids in their seats the way Mrs. Rudley did, she wouldn't need her floors mopped so often. On that Friday, then, Mrs. Rudley walked into her room and saw—horrors—parents and children. What was worse, some of the children were toddlers, black ones, and some of them had bottles. And worse yet, there were signs of food in the room! It was only with the most heroic effort that Mrs. Rudley kept herself from passing out on the spot. She could hardly be blamed, though, from gasping to her colleague, "We'll have to fumigate the room."

This incident, word of which spread quickly around the school, did nothing to soften the feelings toward the returning teachers, and there was much talk of having a screening committee to interview all those who returned to ensure that they would pledge that they would remain for the rest of the year and not walk out again if Shanker had another fit of moral indignation. It was another move I opposed, smacking both of vigilantism and naiveté. No teacher who had been out would submit to such a screening. We would simply be brought up on charges by the union. Furthermore, an assurance of that sort was meaningless, since we obviously could not bind anyone to it even were he so foolish as to give it. Therefore, the whole procedure would at best be a waste of time. Nothing came of the idea, fortunately, but it showed the feelings of even decent, rational people toward the striking teachers, and the "fumigation" incident simply confirmed for many the racist nature of the strikers.

At an emergency meeting held the night before the teachers' return, a resolution was passed, fifty-nine to nothing: "As a sign of our nonacceptance of the settlement terms of the strike, we shall enter the school as we have since October 18 and shall attempt to run the school as we have been doing."

We voted overwhelmingly, also, our opposition to the makeup time. Various parents said that they had instructed their children to leave at 3 P.M. as usual, and that they would not send them on the canceled holidays. I suggested that we withdraw our children at 3 P.M. on religious grounds, and that we state our religion as Disgruntalists. It was the only note of levity at the funeral.

Our final decision was that the community room had become too important for us to give up, since it had become a center for parents to come together, not only to plan for the school, but also as people. We decided, however, that the room we had been occupying was not the best choice for a community room, and since it had a bathroom it really was necessary for the kindergarten class. There was another room on the first floor, though, that was a natural.

As a classroom it had always presented problems for the teacher. It was isolated from the other rooms on that corridor by a set of fire doors, and because it was right next door to the main entrance to the school, it invited the curious to stand and gawk, thereby distracting the children. For us, though, it was perfect. It was right off the only school entrance that had a ramp instead of steps, so parents with strollers and carriages could come right in without disrupting the rest of the school. It offered a good location for parents to serve as a security guard, and because it was set off from the other classrooms, our activities would not create a disturbance to them. All in all it was ideal for us, and so we moved our various possessions— our signs, our reading material, and children's toys—from the kindergarten room into room 134. We taped a sign, "PS 84 Community Room," on the door, and we prepared to defend it vigorously against the attempted ouster that we knew would soon be forthcoming.

Monday came, and I walked Kathy to school feeling as though I was on the way to my own funeral. We had been living, for these past two months, in an idyllic world where we were in control of our own lives, and now reality was about to descend once more. I was concerned—equally—about two things: what would happen to Kathy (our grand pronouncements on the subject of class changes notwithstanding); and what would happen to the school with the return of Mrs. Wachtel. I took care of worry number one first by telling Mrs. Austin that I wanted Kathy to remain in her class, and that under no circumstances did I give my permission to have her moved. With her assurance that she would keep Kathy, I left to attend to worry number two.

Someone had torn our sign off the door of our community room. All that was left of it was one triangle still taped to the glass. I walked in, and there was Mrs. Wachtel sitting stiffly at one of the tables, surrounded by shouting parents. 'What's *she* doing in *our* room?' was my first thought, and then I remembered—the fairytale was over. There was no happy ending; and ding-dong, the wicked witch was very much alive. She wasn't even a wicked witch, only a Board of Education principal. And she had returned to assert her claim to our domain. Here we had been, for over two months, equals and partners in the school, making decisions concerning curriculum, guidance—policy—our opinions respected, our counsel considered, and in one fell swoop Mrs. Wachtel was plunked back in our midst, expecting us all to go back to our hat-in-hand roles. I expected her to say, any minute, "Good morning, boys and girls."

I wasn't the only one who felt this way. In the parent pecking order I was probably considered, by Mrs. Wachtel and her ilk, to be closer to the top by virtue of my middle-class status, my skin color, and my education. Though I was generally treated like a kindergartner (Millie theorized that parents in the school were treated according to the age of their children), still I could pull my rank: high school English teacher, and don't you forget it, Mrs. Wachtel, and be, if not listened to, at least not treated with unconcealed contempt. Other parents, though, especially the poor, the black, and the Spanish-speaking, could not even expect that much. Norma's story ("You people expect too much from your children") typified this attitude. No one in the school administration expected her to have any intelligent views on education. During the period of the strike, though, she and other parents who in the past had been, or had felt, frozen out were listened to with respect. They, too, had been directly involved in the decision-making. For them a return to normal would be equally devastating.

So when someone asked Mrs. Wachtel why she hadn't returned when the custodians had, what they were really asking—angrily— was why she had returned at all. She, of course, answered the spoken rather than the implicit question and said she had come in but that she had felt threatened.

"Were you threatened?" someone asked.

"No, but I felt threatened."

The unspoken answer to the implied question—why had she returned?—was evident in her manner, which was one of patient irony toward her inferiors. It was her school. Her presence made it so. It was to this attitude as well as to her presence that the anger of the parents was addressed, and it took the form of badgering her with specifics. What were her plans? She had to see what the situation was. Was she planning to allow children to remain where they now were? Her inclination was to go back to the September organization. What about the makeup time for children? If the parents didn't want their children to attend, she would take it into consideration. We wanted a parent in every classroom to insure that there would be no reprisals against children who had been in school during the strike. How did she feel about that? She would have to consult her teachers. We had a liaison committee to act as a bridge between the parents and the school. We wanted them included in the consultations with the teachers. How many parents were on the committee, she wanted to know. Six or seven? All of us, we said. Why hadn't she returned with the custodians? She had felt threatened.

"You didn't really care about the children."

"You must respect that I am a person with feelings, too. I am an individual person with emotions, feelings. You must respect that."

This brought snorts of contempt and guffaws from several of the parents. The fact of the matter was that had she responded to our emotions, to our anger, with genuine emotion instead of with words, had she even gotten angry in turn—in short, had she responded as a human being instead of as an institution—she might have been able to salvage something. But she sat smug and straight, teeth clenched in a let's-get-this-over-with-so-I-can-get-down-to-real-business manner that betrayed her utter contempt for us. She had no interest in what we had learned during the period of her absence. She didn't want to know what plans, if any, we had for the transition period. She only wanted to consult "her" teachers and make "her" plans and evoke our sympathy by talk about her feelings and emotions. She only succeeded in making us angrier. We already felt betrayed by the strike settlement. Her presence was the seal of that betrayal.

During the strike I had been busy in the school. Kathy was happy and I was needed elsewhere. Now, to protect her placement, I made arrangements to stay in her class till the question was settled. This was the first time I had spent any time in an open classroom. My first impression of it was "Where are all the children?" A fast head count indicated that there were more than thirty kids in the class; and they were a diverse bunch, both ethnically and intellectually, as I soon saw. But there was no sense of a mass of children, as is the impression I always get from a traditional class. Also, at first, everything seemed random. Some kids were lying on the floor in the corner reading. Others were watching the turtles. Others were playing with cuisenaire rods. Some were counting buttons and beans. A few were taking a survey of everyone's favorite color and marking the results on a sheet of paper. One boy was playing aimlessly with a sheet of paper that he had folded into a shape that, when shaken, made a most noisy and—to him—satisfying pop. A few girls sat talking quietly. And one little boy with a broad, friendly face flitted around on the periphery of everything, trying everything, touching everything, and only occasionally becoming bothersome enough to draw a quiet but firm reprimand from Mrs. Austin.

The other thing that struck me again and again was the indifference of the children to my presence. I had told Mrs. Austin that as long as I was riding shotgun I might as well do something useful; and during the several days that I remained, I helped here and there, but my presence was accepted in a most matter-of-fact way by all the kids. In every other class I had ever been in—both as a student and as a teacher—visitors had been very much noted; and either everything had stopped dead during their presence, or there had been an on-your-best-behavior eagerness displayed. But here everyone went about his work, and I was as much a part of the scenery as the turtles. I was there.

What also became apparent very soon was that though things seemed random there was a good deal of planning. Mrs. Austin was very well aware, not only of who was working and who wasn't, but also of what each child was doing and where he was supposed to be going. To the paper-popping young man, she soon said, "Jeremy, do you have any plans for the day?" When he shrugged negatively, she said, "Well, here's what I have planned for you," and she led him over to a table and sat him down with a reader. To two girls who were wandering around, she said, "When it's time to write in your log about what you did today, what will you write?" They looked abashed and hurried off to find some more worthwhile pursuit. She read with one child, and the rest of the class remained occupied. There was a constant hum of talking, but there was no disorder. The problem of keeping the whole class interested while a teacher tried to clarify something for one child—thereby losing the rest of them —seemed to have disappeared here. And then there was Jorge, the little fellow who wandered around like a friendly puppy. I learned that he had come into the school with less intellectual experience than the average two-year old, and that though he had already come a long way, Mrs. Austin felt that he needed time to explore as a toddler. She left him pretty much alone, unless he got too obstreperous. On this occasion I was pretty impressed with her handling of Jorge, and of the rest of the class; but when I went back during open-school week a few months later, my respect for her really grew. On that occasion she had a group gathered for show and tell, and lo and behold, Jorge was no longer on the fringe, but a part of the group. He described something he had brought. And when he was finished, he answered questions. Then he remained a part of the group and listened. He raised his hand to ask a question. At that point my impulse would have been to call on him, but Mrs. Austin didn't, and I realized she was right. Part of his learning had to be to be able to wait. He did, and it was only then that I realized how far he had come, and how skillfully she had brought him there. He was, at last, a first-grader. That boy would have died in a formal class. Here he was functioning. Throughout the year Kathy came home with stories about Jorge, and sometimes they were that he had been a pain (which I hear frequently from both my girls about all members of the male species); but sometimes they were also about his brilliant work in math, for it seems that in spite of his original educational handicap he was a mathematical genius.

Those few days that I spent in Mrs. Austin's class did two things: they reassured me that Kathy would not be removed, and they gave me concrete confirmation of my feelings about the open classroom approach to teaching. I had been convinced by the rhetoric. Now I was convinced by the reality.

Because I was busy guarding Kathy's position in her class, I did not attend several of the meetings that took place over the next few days between Mrs. Wachtel and the parents, but I was filled in by various of the parent participants. The substance of these meetings was similar to the one I had attended. The parents were angry, hostile. Mrs. Wachtel was contemptuous. The parents pressed her for details of her plans for the transition back to a state of normalcy. She was unable to come up with details.

"Let me say first what we observed," she said. "A number of classes are overcrowded. Some adjustments should be made in the registers for the good of the children. If we consider the present state of classes a beginning, then we must reorganize. If we prefer to continue as classes stand, then there's no problem. We *might* be able to adjust the classes when the children come in from the new buildings. I think it would be better to have smaller classes than overcrowded ones."

Pushed for further details she said, "My feeling is that children should return to their originally assigned classes except in certain radical cases, special situations where children can't adjust. Children are flexible."

IRENE: "In other words, you'd like to keep classes as low and as balanced as possible. How would you go about effecting these changes?"

MRS. WACHTEL: "I'd have to look at the registers, and take each case into consideration. I am interested in your children and perhaps am more objective about them than you are."

IRENE: "Have you worked out procedures for shifts?"

MRS. WACHTEL: "No. Not yet."

IRENE: "What techniques will you use for balancing classes?"

MRS. WACHTEL: "My own techniques."

But she seemed unwilling or unable to take the necessary steps even to return to a prestrike condition. She spoke of the need to keep balanced classes, condescendingly pointing out that it had been the parents who had—rightly, she allowed—agitated for them in the first place. She ignored the fact that the classes had become more, rather than less, balanced as a result of the strike.

She wanted parent participation in the school, she said. She welcomed it, in fact. And then she spelled out her vision of parent participation: a bulletin board committee and parent patrols in the halls and the lunchroom. She brought in reinforcements in the form of Jenny Silverman, the UFT chapter chairman, who painted *her* picture of parent involvement: parents could be most helpful in the lunchroom and yard—to patrol, to organize games. Parents could also help teachers gather instructional material, run off material, make illustrative materials. Some teachers might want parents in the classroom. The parents were talking of involvement in the decision-making, and Mrs. Wachtel came back with KP.

Carmen, speaking for the entire parent body, told her, "We no longer want you to continue as principal of this school," a gutsy statement in view of her role as a paid employee of the school.

Mrs. Wachtel smiled tightly at this before answering, "I have been assigned as principal of this school, and I intend to remain here until I am legally told not to remain."

When someone asked her why she would choose to stay in a school where parents felt so opposed to her philosophies, she replied again, "I am principal of this school, and I will remain here until under due process I am subsequently removed."

She was asked why she had appointed Mrs. Warner to take over after the custodial lockout if she thought the school was unsafe. She replied, "I didn't appoint her. She said she was staying so I transferred the functions to her." A bureaucrat's nice distinction!

STEPHANIE HALE: "Many of us who supported you last year don't trust you any more. The first day of the third strike you said the building was unsafe, and you said you would return when a licensed fireman returned. Yet when the custodians returned *you did not return,* nor did you inform us by word or phone that you had changed your mind."

JACK MARTINS: "Our first priority is to remove this principal."

ANOTHER PARENT: "You have no plans. I don't think you can administer a school."

"Last year when the parents wrote the profile, I was willing to give you a chance. But now I know they were right," said another parent. "We need a new principal here."

She answered with a shrug of indifference. Christine Reilly accused her of refusing to work with parents.

"I am always willing to work with parents," she replied.

When this was greeted by derision, she simply sat up straighter and clenched her teeth. She was called a racist. She said nothing.

The parents had called in members of the school board and Dr. Selig to be present at these meetings because we wanted all of these encounters to become part of the public record. We were determined that if Mrs. Wachtel continued to prove incompetent, she should do so in full view of those who had the power to remove her. We had also decided that we would not cooperate with her by giving her our ideas as to how the school should move back to a normal condition, since she could then use our plans to prove her own efficiency. This was not easy for any of us. We on the West Side are a talky group, and in the face of her lack of planning it would have been easy to jump into the breach and tell her what to do. On one occasion, in fact, one of the parents said, "We don't want children moved from one class to another without their parents' permission"; and the parent was jumped on by the rest of the group. We were maintaining strict radio silence. Mrs. Wachtel must make her plans, and then we would react. The result was that though we held almost daily meetings with her on the subject of her plans nothing happened. Things muddled along. Some teachers, thinking they had orders from Mrs. Wachtel to retrieve the children who had originally been on their registers, actually did pluck them out of their strike classes. We yelled like hell. Mrs. Wachtel complained to Dr. Selig that we were "ensconced" in the community room, "conniving and plotting with teachers," and she wanted us out to make room for an additional first-grade class. Dr. Selig and Bob Goodfellow said we could not be removed unless it could be proved that the room was really needed. Thwarted, she ordered her teachers to stay away from us and from the room. Some of them disobeyed.

She spoke a great deal of "her" school and "her" teachers, but very little about her plans. When we appealed to Mrs. Dodge on this, she said, "Be fair, she just got back"; to which we retorted that she had known the strike was ending, had had three weeks to think of a transition, and had come up empty. "That's what we mean by incompetency." Mrs. Dodge offered herself as mediator between Mrs. Wachtel and the parents. We accepted her in that capacity because it meant that she would be present at meetings and would see Mrs. Wachtel in all her glory. Why was she willing to accept Mrs. Dodge in that role? I can only assume that she realized that she could not refuse and that, further, she was confident that she could weather the storm in any case. And she had good reason to believe this. She enjoyed the continued confidence of Dr. Selig. Further, she had been trained in an era when there was a tacit agreement between the Board of Education and the staff that anyone who passed the necessary tests and lasted out his probationary period could, provided he did nothing outrageous, keep possession of his fiefdom till death or retirement did them part. Divorce had not yet been legalized. True, there had, of late, been some ominous rumblings in the papers of duly certified principals being thrown out of schools by disaffected parents; but these had been in ghetto areas where the communities were black and the principals white and where the principals had, according to the supervisory association, been callously sacrificed to buy off the militance of the parents. We at PS 84 were in a different situation. True we had expanded our Executive Board to give greater voice to the active black parents. Nevertheless the Board was still predominantly white and middle class. In the last analysis we were her kind of people and would not turn against our own. After all, she was looking out for our children. Could we be so sure that a militant principal would do the same? I don't know whether this was her line of reasoning or whether it just never occurred to her that we could prevail. If the former, she misjudged us. She was not one of our own. She believed that not all children could learn. We felt not all children had been taught. We wanted remedies for children's failure. She was satisfied with excuses for it. But above all, what we were seeking was not simply her removal but the right to decide on the kind of successor who shared our vision of what our school could be, and who would travel with us to translate that vision into reality.

One morning, after a series of these meetings with Mrs. Wachtel had taken place, we were presented by a petition signed by the black and Spanish parents who had been active during the strike. They said that no one had as yet really addressed herself to the question of racism that was a central issue of the strike. They said, further, that if we did not support them in confronting Mrs. Wachtel with this issue and with the issue of her lack of a stand against open instances of racism on the part of some members of her staff, then they would take our continued silence as an indication that we condoned the offensive practices of these teachers. They concluded, "If the black and white parents are going to continue to march together, it is imperative that you support our position on this issue as strongly as we have supported you during the conflict of recent weeks."

My first reaction to the petition was one of surprise that so many of the parents with whom we had been working so closely should have felt this way and said nothing. There was also something of the feeling, "gee whiz, we've tried." We had expanded the Executive Board to include all the black parents who were actively involved so as to give them a voice on the Board. We had shared recipes and frustrations. We had diapered our kids together. We had fought together. Now they were threatening to separate at a time when unity was vital. Then I realized the essentially racist nature of these thoughts. What I was saying to myself was no different from those people who say, "What do they want now, after all we've done for them?" The fact of the matter was that we had done nothing for "them." We had done whatever we had done for our kids and for the school as a whole. And I realized, too, that what the black parents were saying, in effect, was, "We've followed you. Now will you follow us?" The answer could only be yes. And I realized, too, that it was, in a sense, like the old joke about the Frenchman, the Englishman, and the Jew who were each asked to write an essay about the elephant. The Englishman wrote about the elephant and the Empire; the Frenchman wrote about sex and the elephant; and the Jew wrote about the elephant and the Jewish question. We all see issues from our own perspective. Though we had worked closely with the black parents, we were not black. We did see the racism in the system and in the strike, but we were not black. And if we were seeing Mrs. Wachtel's incompetence as the overriding concern, the petition made it clear that the black parents saw the racism as paramount. And I realized that they were right, and so I said that though I could not sign their petition since it began "We, the black and Puerto Rican parents of PS 84," I certainly supported their position and felt that racist teachers had no place in any school—and certainly not in ours. I would, I said, therefore write a parallel petition for the white parents, which I did, and we all signed it.

Thus, on November 22, with all sides gathered*, Gwen Palmer read the following memo, which had been unanimously approved by the Executive Board—all thirty-three of us:

*Celia Cohen was there for the school board. Jenny Silverman (the UFT chapter chairman), Miss Federman, and Mrs. Wachtel represented the school, and most of the Executive Board members were present for the parent body.

To: Mrs. Hilda Wachtel, Principal
FROM: Parents' Association PS 84 Executive Board

I. As racism was the primary factor in the strike you chose to support for four weeks, we, the concerned black, white, and Spanish-speaking parents feel that you must state your position regarding this issue.

II. As we are all aware that these perverse and discriminatory practices exist in our school, we insist you come to an agreement on the disciplinary measures to be taken against those teachers who have clearly demonstrated their inability to control their racist attitudes. Your continued silence on this issue can only be taken as an indication that you condone the offensive practices of these teachers.

III. Every parent with a complaint in this area will be accompanied by Executive Board members at a meeting with Mrs. Wachtel.

IV. New personnel that is hired is to reflect the ethnic balance of the school. We support the October 17th policy statement of the Local School Board in this matter.*

V. It is the responsibility of the principal to be sensitive to the racism that exists in the school and to take appropriate action to eliminate it.

VI. We support the concept of balanced classes. We do not accept the present criteria for balancing classes. At present, we demand that classes not be organized for balance alone, but for the stability and best interests of the children. We demand a state investigation by the State Department of Education of the balanced class program to insure proper guidelines for the future balancing of classes.

VII. No child is to be removed from a class without the prior consent of his parent. The teacher must be in agreement with the change.

VIII. Your June commitment to eliminate the junior guidance program as presently constituted must be adhered to, and appropriate programs, with provisions to repair the educational damage already done, must be adopted.

IX. The regular school day (8:30–3:00) is to be kept. Schools are to be kept open on the proposed ten days for those parents who wish to send their children to school and for those teachers who wish to work.

X. Parents have the right to be in school, and to go into classes to observe their children. All classrooms shall be open to all parent volunteers.

XI. Parent volunteers, who will sign up and be given badges in the community room (134), will also be in the school as their schedules permit. This community room shall be equipped with telephone, file cabinet, desk, and tables.

---

*The resolution said that in the hiring of personnel for the district special efforts should be made to hire black and Spanish-speaking teachers and administrators.

When Gwen finished reading the terms of the surrender, there was dead silence. Mrs. Wachtel, who had listened grimly, with lips compressed and teeth clenched, made no reply. Instead, she began to talk of a school community council that the school board had said should be set up for each school. There were several new parents present at this meeting (from buildings which had just been opened to occupancy) and their reaction to the memo was one of puzzlement. They had not been involved in the history of the last year, nor were they used to hearing principals called racists by parents. But they were also puzzled by the lack of reaction on the part of Mrs. Wachtel. They felt, as I did, that though there were many points in the memo to which she could not easily agree, a decently developed survival instinct should have prompted her, in some way, to respond to the charges of racism. She could have denied it. She could have asked for specifics. She could, herself, have made a ringing denunciation of racism and have said that she would deal forthrightly and peremptorily with any such acts when they were brought to her attention. In short, she could have come away, if not smelling like a rose, at least not tainted by the charges. But on this occasion, as on so many others, she chose silence, and it was no defense.

Irene asked her whether she would give us her reactions to the memo Gwen had just read. She replied that she would not react until she could read it.

IRENE: "Why can't you tell us what you think about it?"

MRS. WACHTEL: "I would like to read it and think about it."

And like Miniver Cheevy, she went on thinking. Though we did give her a copy of the memo, it was never mentioned by her again. Apparently she decided that, like the profile, it was best ignored.

However, though she had at present no thoughts on the subject of racism, she did want to give us her plan on the transition of the school from the strike situation to a normal situation. To wit: "The first grade has a problem—some of the classes are overcrowded and some are under register. We're sending out letters to parents explaining the situation. We tried for many years to make first-grade classes small. We're sending out letters with a tearsheet for parents, so that if they wish to send a child to another class they may, and then we'll have six first-grade classes as originally planned. Some parents will want their children in smaller classes. They'll have that choice.

"The second grade is all right. It's functioning except for the inexperience of some teachers, and we're working with them.

"The third grade is more stable.

"The fourth grade. We will check into ethnic imbalance there. It seems a little contradictory that only the fourth grade is unbalanced. All classes should reflect the school's ethnic breakdown.

"Fifth grade. With one exception this is functioning well. That exception is that the citizenship class is keeping six children from an IGC class.

"Sixth grade—intact except for the six children from an IGC class."

It should be remembered here that what Mrs. Wachtel referred to as the problem of the IGC-citizenship class was, in fact, a problem only to her. The parents and the children in there were pleased with the arrangement.

Mrs. Wachtel, having presented her plan, sat back, satisfied. We were still bound by our vow of silence, so nobody pointed out to her that what she had just presented was not a plan at all, but merely a description of how things stood at present. With the exception of the proposed letter to first-grade parents there was not a word of how she planned to solve what she saw as the problems in the other grades. But as we said nothing, she must have assumed that we did not notice that the emperor was not wearing clothes at all, and it must have increased her contempt for us that she could so easily put us off. Notice we did, though we merely asked whether she had a written plan.

MRS. WACHTEL: "Oh no, you have the notes. I have a school to run."

MEG KNIGHT: "The Executive Board requests a written plan."

MRS. WACHTEL: "No! I'm sorry. You have your secretary."

MEG: "The full Executive Board wishes to consider your plan in writing. Is that your answer to the Board?"

MRS. WACHTEL: "Yes. That's my answer."

And she rose and walked out haughtily to run her school.

On December 3, more than two weeks after the strike had ended, the promised meeting of first-grade parents and teachers was finally held. It was evident from the good turnout—there were more than sixty parents present—that this was a subject of serious concern. From the outset the meeting was heated, and parent after parent spoke angrily about the delay, about unauthorized shifts of children, and about the general incompetence of Mrs. Wachtel. She was loudly and repeatedly denounced, shouted down, and insulted. I was embarrassed by this, though I could understand the emotion that prompted it. Her lack of candor, and her inability, even at that meeting, to come up with a solution for the grade made the yelling and the insults inevitable. Shortly after the meeting, Jim Calvert wrote a letter which summed up both the content and the feeling of the meeting, and which ended

"They [the parents] could not understand why you did not have this information [on class sizes] while the parents who have been coming into the school have had this data for weeks. They find it difficult to accept the fact that such gross incompetence is possible. This is where I differ from them. Although my initial reaction was similar to theirs, after due consideration and process, I feel that you were honest with the parents. I accept your explanation that for two weeks after the strike, you had no idea what was going on in your school."

He sent carbons to the entire central school board, to the local school board, to the governing board, Dr. Selig, and the PS 84 Parents' Association. No one ever replied.

TWENTY

Another Attempt at Reconciliation

When we had presented the profile to the school board and to Dr. Selig, the answer had been that we should learn to live together (if not love one another). Clearly, nothing that had happened in the past six months had brought that possibility closer to realization. And now the school board and the superintendent were being barraged, once again, with communications from individual parents at PS 84, and from the Executive Board. In addition, members of the school board had been spending an inordinate amount of time there, and since school board membership is an unpaid position, they were neglecting other duties to be there. Elizabeth Dodge, in particular, was at the school almost daily, and she had already made it plain that she was seeing what we saw. However, she had not yet been able to persuade enough of her fellow members that we were not simply ranting pests. From the volume of mail, though, it became plain that some action was called for, and so, on December 6, Dr. Selig requested a meeting with Carmen Johnson to present a proposal. Carmen asked that the meeting be held with the entire executive board.

Dr. Selig, a tall, slim man with wavy black hair that was just beginning to be touched with gray, greeted us with a little smile. In his gray suit, white shirt, and old school tie, standing before us relaxed but erect, he exuded professionalism and confidence. We had come a long way, though, and were no longer awed by his professionalism. We waited. He thanked us for coming on such short notice.

"I wanted to address a group that is in a position to give serious consideration to a proposal. I hope you will consider this and bring it to the body of parents quickly in order to move it forward.

"The situation at 84," he continued, "gives me reason for concern as the educational head of this district. It is serious. I have been personally involved for some hours. I am looking for a reasonable way to find a solution to the problem.

"We need someone objective to act as fact-finder to assess the situation. He should find out what are the key differences, consult experts, come up with recommendations. In this interest I have approached the West Side Mental Health Center.* They would be willing to nominate such a person and provide the resources necessary. After the fact-finding period, this person would make recommendations to be implemented in order to move forward to a resolution of the problem. This person, presently unknown to all of us, would want an advisory committee to provide leads and pinpoint areas of concern. The composition of this committee should be a representative group. The advisory committee would have no power to make decisions."

He then outlined the composition of the committee: three parents of children who attended during the strike (preferably white, black, and Spanish); three parents of children who did not attend during the strike (also preferably one from each group); two teachers who taught during the strike; two teachers who did not teach during the strike; Mrs. Wachtel; Mrs. Warner; Dr. Selig; one member of the local school board; one member of the Joan of Arc board (maybe) —for a total of fifteen persons in all.

Carmen asked whether the problems he spoke of were educational or whether they were the problems with Mrs. Wachtel. He answered that this would be an all-inclusive evaluation, and repeated that he would like it to get underway as soon as possible. He had already spoken about this proposal to Mrs. Wachtel and to Mrs. Warner, both of whose reactions, he said, had been positive. He was meeting with the teachers the following Monday to present the proposal to them. He estimated that the study would take four weeks to complete.

SARAH TYDINGS: "This is once again band-aids when emergency surgery is called for."

*The Jewish Board of Guardians, who were already involved in the school (see p. 45).

DR. SELIG: "I can't respond to Mrs. Tyding's comment because it's all negative."

We objected that Mrs. Wachtel's role on the committee would make things difficult, that teachers would not speak out for fear of reprisals. He answered that there would be no reprisals while he was in office. We said that dividing staff and parents into strike and nonstrike groups would further polarize the school when what we needed was to unite. He replied that each group could provide input. We asked why he should start now. We said his observations and those of the school board should enable him to make a decision. He said he could not make one on the basis of his present observations. We asked whether he would be willing to delegate his authority. He sidestepped that one, saying only, "This would be a third force, a neutral observer to give me a recommendation."

JULIA STEIN: "He can't be objective. He has his own interests. He'll see what he wants to see."

JEAN PEPPER: "An outsider can't pinpoint as well as those who are inside. You don't seem to believe us. Everyone will behave themselves and we will look like nuts."

SELMA WOOD: "Parents are always put on the defensive."

DR. SELIG: "Everything parents have said is noted. There are other things, too. Your testimony is not the only testimony. Other testimony is being given and it too is being heard. It is difficult to determine the situation. An objective person is needed."

RONNIE: "This would have been a proper, rational way to proceed after the profile was presented last spring. Now we have no time for leisure because the day to day situation is so serious."

MEG: "The proposal is fine to present to a new administration with material to settle this situation. It is futile to do it with Mrs. Wachtel."

RONNIE: "Can you put in another administrator while this is done?"

DR. SELIG: "This was one of the things considered."

RONNIE: "Why can't you put someone else in here?"

DR. SELIG: "Because of what I have in my files." He never divulged what mysteries reposed there.

RONNIE: "How do we operate in the meantime?"

DR. SELIG: "You give the leadership of the school a chance to operate for a month. You do your activities as you have been doing. There would be no drastic change."

RONNIE: "We need a drastic change. The fourth grade is being departmentalized. The kids are rebelling. What shall we do?"

DR. SELIG: "You cast your dependence on the administration of the school to carry out what is best."

RONNIE: "But what is being done is directly opposite to what we think is right and proper."

ELIZABETH O'SHEA: "You are asking us to do what we have said we will not accept. I hope you know we are restraining ourselves minute by minute.

SELMA: "You're asking a great deal of the parents."

DR. SELIG: "I know."

MEG: "This is a good plan, and we need it. But now is no time. We feel an urgency. We feel you don't believe us. What have we got to lose? Only another month of our kids' lives. You seem to hope for a reconciliation of views with the parents and administration. We can't do that."

DR. SELIG: "A month would be well spent to get expert thinking on the problem."

RONNIE: "I don't think you know what is happening if you are going to let it go on."

DR. SELIG: "This would be to gather facts and file a recommendation. There would be no preconceived notions except to gather facts into a cohesive report. No, not to conciliate, but to be as objective as possible. You see only your side. The administration sees its side."

JULIA: "Again the children are lost."

RONNIE: "You saw all sides last year."

MEG: "If we reject this, it is because we think it is reasonable to remove Mrs. Wachtel now."

DR. SELIG: "I hope to hear from Mrs. Johnson as soon as possible. Time is of the essence."

RONNIE: "Meanwhile the situation at 84 remains the same?"

DR. SELIG: "The situation at 84 remains the same during the study, yes."

And the situation at the school was fast deteriorating. The potential for violence rose daily. Kids were being beaten. There had been a few episodes which, though fortunately not serious, were unpleasant. One little girl had been pulled into the boys' bathroom by several bigger boys and had been thoroughly scared. Mr. Sussman, the acting AP, had sent the terrified child home—alone—to get her parents. We were all incensed at this, and Mrs. Wachtel had not reacted at all. The whole tone of the school was growing more chaotic daily; and, in addition, as Ronnie had said to Dr. Selig, departmentalization* had begun in the upper grades. Thus the study, even if it was truly objective, even if it came out with the inescapable conclusion that we had already reached, was a luxury we felt we could not afford at this time. But beyond that, we saw the study as an attempt to cool us off and to divide the parents. By putting parents on the committee, though they would only be there in an advisory capacity, this plan had the further bureaucratic advantage of neutralizing us, for if the observer found that Mrs. Wachtel should remain we would be in the position of being a party to that finding. If, on the other hand, the observer advised that she must go, then Dr. Selig still had the out of saying he would now consider the observer's findings, and then act as he chose. In either case we could only lose, and we therefore wanted no part of his plan. Besides, we were beyond reconciliation. It is interesting to speculate how we would have viewed Dr. Selig's proposal a year earlier. Then it would have contained the same trap for us, but I think then we would have fallen into it. But we had learned a lot over the past year, both about what we needed and about how a bureaucracy works to perpetuate itself, and so we were no longer flattered by talk of being responsible people and decision makers. We saw the hook and we didn't bite. But it was a cool maneuver on the part of Dr. Selig, and it failed only because we no longer were what we had been and what he was used to dealing with. Had he not underestimated our growth he might, perhaps, have come up with another ploy that would have worked.

In spite of our immediate negative reactions to Dr. Selig's proposal, we were responsible enough to call a full Executive Board meeting to consider it, and out of that meeting came our counter proposal: 1) that before any study is made of the school, Mrs. Wachtel be removed; 2) that after her removal the study be done by the elected planning/governing board and the Parents' Association, and such consultants as *they* deem necessary; and 3) that following such an investigation the governing board should make specific proposals for the reorganization of the school.

*Grouping of children according to math and reading ability within their heterogeneous classes—a violation of the spirit if not of the letter of balanced classes.

I then moved that we propose to the planning/governing board that they place an ad for a principal for PS 84, "a community-oriented, integrated school in Manhattan that will have a vacancy in February of 1969." The motion was passed with only Mona French abstaining because she felt this was a political rather than an educational move. The rest of us, though recognizing the political nature of the act, felt that it was also educational. We did need a principal. One of the weapons that is constantly being used against parents when they try to change things in the schools is that they are political—political being used, in that context, as a dirty word. And the charge usually works, because parents then spend all their energies trying to deny the charge. In fact, everything that happens in a school is political (dealing with power relationships). Every decision a principal makes is a political one. If the principal is any good, the decision *may* also be educational. But the point is that in order to effect educational changes where parents have no power, the means employed are, by definition, political. And parents have to stop being scared off by the thought of their own power if they are going to make the changes that will provide their children with an education. This is not to say that the ends justify the means, but rather, that anything that changes power relationships is political, and the answer, when parents are charged with politics, is "so are you." It's as simple as that, and once everyone has accepted that each side is political, then perhaps we can get on to the real issue: political to what end? And here is where the difference lay. We wanted to use whatever power we had to effect educational change, to make learning possible for the many children whom the system had failed. Mrs. Wachtel and Dr. Selig were using their power to maintain themselves.

We had already rejected the proposal, but Dr. Selig had also already called his teachers' meeting, and so he presented the proposal to them with the information that the parents had turned it down. From the minutes of the teachers' meeting came the same reservations we had expressed: the divisive nature of the committee (into striking and nonstriking groups), the fact that it was really Dr. Selig's responsibility to investigate the school, and that the "facts" were already there for anyone who wanted to see them. The upshot of the teachers' meeting with Dr. Selig was that they wanted time to study the proposal, and Dr. Selig said he would put it up on the teachers' bulletin board. But that was not so simple either, for it turned out that there was a UFT bulletin board and not all the teachers belonged to the union. Therefore, which bulletin board should receive the proposal? In true Solomon fashion, Dr. Selig offered two copies, one for each bulletin board. It was to such silliness that the divisions in the school had reduced us all. Thus died the final attempt to bring us all together in peace and harmony.

During these past few months we had been having almost daily meetings on some crisis or other, and the community room was a godsend. Without it we could never have gotten ourselves together. At this time, Sam was not in school at all, and Maggie was still in nursery; and had we not had a room where we could come with our kids and where they could play together without getting into mischief and without interrupting the proceedings, I could not have been in the school as much as I was, and neither could many of the other parents. There were always several babies sleeping in strollers or carriages while we went about our business. Since getting to meetings in the evening is difficult for many parents—and impossible for others—it was daytime meetings or nothing, so the community room allowed for broad participation during this period and kept the PA decisions from being made by a small clique of parents who had the leisure to allow them to participate. There developed among us all a real sense of camaraderie, that cut across class and race lines. We began to see that we all faced the same problems, and that our reactions, on most things, were pretty similar. In short, we became friends, which is no doubt why most principals resist the idea of a parents' room in their schools. When power is the name of the game, a divided parent body puts a principal at a distinct advantage.

Since most of our meetings were held during the day, and since Carmen was working in the school, she was not present at many of them. Furthermore, the fact that she was both president of the PA and an employee of Mrs. Wachtel put her in an uncomfortable position. To complicate her life still further, she was also a member of the Joan of Arc governing board. The combination of all this began to tell on her, and because she was absent at so many of the meetings she was beginning to feel excluded. This was not intentional, but decisions *did* have to be made, often on the spot, and there was not always time to consult with her. The sentiment she had expressed when the film crew had come in—that nobody cared what she thought—combined with the pressures she was under vis-à-vis Mrs. Wachtel, surfaced again, and she resigned as president. Meg Knight became acting president, and because another vice-president had also resigned, it was decided that we would have an election at the end of January to fill the vacancies. In the meantime, Meg was in charge.

TWENTY–ONE

The Curious Case of Mrs. Carroll

One of the factors that had led us to picket Mrs. Wachtel last June had been that she had, in addition to agreeing to the transfer of Nancy Calvert and Toni Diamond, failed to rehire some excellent teachers who had been outspoken in their criticism of her. Now she seemed eager to rectify that error, for after the strike there appeared two, one a gym teacher who was hired as a regular substitute (to take a class), and the other a per diem substitute (to cover classes when teachers were absent). That they were both strong teachers could not be doubted. Mr. Trumbull, the gym teacher, appeared on his first day of service wielding a baseball bat, because "none of those little bastards is going to get tough with me." They didn't. He was given a class that had been vacated by one of the teachers who had retired after the strike, and his methods must have been effective because no one in his class moved. They didn't learn to read, either, but you can't have everything. Kathy's assigned teacher had also retired after the strike, so I was no longer faced with the prospect of having to defend her presence in Mrs. Austin's class with my body.

At any rate, with the departure of these teachers we got some new faces, and one was the above-mentioned bat-wielding Mr. Trumbull. Another was Mrs. Carroll. Mrs. Carroll first came to our attention through the complaints of various children who commented on her behavior. She talked—muttered—to herself a lot. She was arbitrary in her punishments of kids: kids having to stand with their hands extended and similar things. After a few of these complaints, we went up to look for ourselves. Mrs. Carroll was not in her classroom when we went up, but had left the class covered by Mary, one

214

of the custodial staff (a clear violation of law), while she had gone to visit with another teacher across the school. When we reported this dereliction to Mrs. Wachtel, she got very excited and angry—at us. What had we been doing on the third floor without a pass? Where were our badges? Why were we spying on teachers anyway? When we pointed out that no matter how improper our conduct may have been in her eyes it still did not change the fact that Mrs. Carroll was AWOL and that she ought to react to that, she turned her back on us and went back into her office.

As a per diem sub, traveling from class to class as teacher absences necessitated, Mrs. Carroll got maximum exposure to the school. Thus one day Violet Morton got a summons from her about her son. Evan, though only in the fifth grade, already towered over his mother. As a result he had a problem with desks—his long legs refused to stay neatly tucked under them without knocking his knees against the top. He solved this problem by putting his legs into the aisles, but Mrs. Carroll deplored this posture (perhaps, having read Greek mythology, she would have preferred a Procrustean solution), and thus the summons to Violet. Violet is a concerned, caring mother who disciplines her children when they need it, and, summoned, she promptly climbed the three flights to hear about her son's misbehavior. However, once upstairs, she was completely ignored by Mrs. Carroll. Instead of telling her of Evan's sins, she began to lecture the class as a whole on proper behavior—at great length—and so Violet left, shaking her head in disbelief. It was only when she asked Evan what he had done to incur Mrs. Carroll's displeasure that she found out why she had been called, but during the ten minutes or so that she stood in the room, listening to the speech about what a bunch of uncouth, ill-mannered children they were, Mrs. Carroll made no attempt to talk about her son to her. Another item for the log.

And then there was the incident with Mary Cooper, who was also called into the presence by Mrs. Carroll. Mary's son, Colin, was at that time in the second grade, under four feet tall, and couldn't have weighed more than forty pounds soaking wet. But, apparently, Mrs. Carroll found him more than she could handle, so she called for Mary. When Mary arrived, she was accosted by Mrs. Carroll, who began to yell at her about what a "terrible" child Colin was and that what he needed was to be put into a German school, with real German military discipline. She then went on to tell Mary that she was nothing but "a poor, ignorant, black woman, and unfit to be a mother." And then she pushed her out of the room.

I was in the community room when Mary came back down from this encounter. She was shaking. We asked what had happened, and she burst into tears. It took some time before she could even talk, and then she related the experience.

It was shortly after this that Mrs. Carroll paid a visit to the community room. Violet Morton, Ruth King, Phyllis Miles, Mary Cooper, and a few other black parents were there with their kids. Mrs. Carroll came shrieking into the room and accused the startled ladies of being racists. She went on for several minutes in that vein, and then ended with, "Why don't you do something useful like patrolling the bathrooms, instead of sitting there on your asses and plotting."

Then she wheeled and stalked out of the room. When the mothers recovered from their initial shock—they were not used to being thus addressed, and certainly not by "professionals"—they took pen in hand and began to write up the incident. This had become standard operating procedure for everything untoward that happened to us or to our children during this period. If the school board required documentation, then we would provide it. We didn't make anything up, but when it happened, by god we noted it—in duplicate. So the incident was duly noted, and Mrs. Wachtel was informed of it. No answer.

The following day, Jack Martins was standing outisde the community room. A group of us were inside when we suddenly heard raised voices. Joe Dreier and I stepped out to see what the commotion was about and there was Mrs. Carroll yelling at a speechless Jack.

"I'm not afraid of you. My husband was in the paratroops, and he can take you. I saw you outside, looking at my car. Well, let me tell you, if there's so much as a scratch on my car I'll know who did it. And my husband will come after you. I'm not afraid of you. My husband was a paratrooper."

Jack is a tall man, well over six feet, and I'm sure he could handle even an ex-paratrooper. But he simply looked puzzled by the unprovoked outburst. I don't think he even knew who Mrs. Carroll was, much less what her car looked like. Jack's silence did nothing to abate Mrs. Carroll's fury, and she went on repeating the fact that she had seen Jack eyeing her car, and that she wasn't afraid of him. Finally Joe simply led Jack into the community room, and Mrs. Carroll went muttering down the hall. I don't know who was covering her class that time, because Mary was mopping the hall.

We wrote up that episode, too. Irene was really shaken by it, not because it involved Jack but because it seemed that anyone whose behavior was as peculiar as that had no business being in a school. Mrs. Wachtel refused to meet with us about it, however, and so she continued to appear almost daily as a per diem.

The morning following the encounter between Jack Martins and Mrs. Carroll, we were greeted, as we entered the school, by a sizable contingent of police. There were two squad cars parked outside. In the office, in addition to some uniformed patrolmen, there were several plainclothesmen. I wondered what had happened, but since during that period there was no one in the office who would give any of us any information, I went into the community room, there to wonder with several other parents what had caused this sudden mobilization on our doorstep. While we were still wondering, two detectives appeared in the room, asking if any of us was "Irene Morton." We said there was no Irene Morton, but that there was a Violet Morton and an Irene Martins, and who wanted the one or the other. At that point they introduced themselves as Detectives Somebody and Other, and they said they wanted to talk to Irene Morton, but maybe it was Irene Martins.

"Is she white or black?" we asked.

"White," they said.

"Then I guess you want to talk to me," Irene said. "Why?"

"Well, we just want to ask you some questions. A teacher claims you threatened her."

"Oh, no," Irene said. "I'm not going to talk to you. I'm going to call a lawyer. You're not going to violate my rights. Who says I threatened her?"

"We don't have the name. We just got a call that a teacher here says she was threatened."

"Did she say I threatened her?"

"No. Someone just gave us your name."

"Oh, no. I'm not going to take this. I'm going to call a lawyer. I'm going to call Jessica Malamud. She's a lawyer and she's the chairman of the school board. She'd better get down here. They can't go around intimidating parents."

And she left to make her call. We tried to get some further information from the detectives, but they simply repeated that someone had called and said a teacher had been threatened, that there were many incidents of this sort throughout the schools since the strike, that it was not their job to make judgments, but simply to follow up all calls of this nature, and that they were sorry Mrs. Morton had gotten so upset. Meanwhile, "Mrs. Morton" had returned. Jessica had said she would try to come. Irene refused to talk to the detectives, except to say that she would file a countersuit of harassment if they didn't go away and leave her alone, and they left the room, still saying they were only doing their duty by following up all such threats.

Ronnie and Meg also left—to call for reinforcements. They began by calling everyone on the Executive Board, and then everyone on the school board, to come down and show their solidarity. Quickly the room began to fill with parents, but no one from the school board or from the district office came. So much for the rights of parents! But Father Cody dropped his razor in the middle of his shave and hurried to Irene's support.

He walked in, half-shaved, the lather decorating his face like a partial Santa Claus, and began ribbing the detectives still standing outside. With his arm around Irene's shoulder he said, "You fellows had better arrest her. She's dangerous. She talks to me, and you know what a troublemaker I am."

The detectives smiled uneasily.

"In fact," he continued, "maybe you'd better arrest them all. Get 'em for loitering on school property—something like that. You fellows are inventive. Look at them. You can see that they're subversive."

The detectives shifted uncomfortably, the fixed smiles still on their faces. At that point another detective appeared. A member of the youth squad, he knew Irene and Father from their Stryckers Bay Neighborhood Council involvement. He greeted Irene and Father with hearty enthusiasm—ho ho ho, what have we here? a little misunderstanding, obviously—and then, *sotto voce,* he told the other detectives to split.

We never did find out who, if anyone, was threatened, or how they had come to Irene. But we all suspected it was Mrs. Carroll again. We also began to wonder whether Mrs. Carroll was a union or a government spy (we were getting a little paranoid by this time). Tales of her strange behavior kept coming in, though nothing on a scale as grand as the scene with Jack or with Mary. We kept writing them down and putting them in our file, along with the file of other parent complaints that we were amassing. Then one day the entire file disappeared from the community room, and then we really got scared. We even began to worry that the community room was bugged, and we became careful about what we said there.

And still Mrs. Carroll was in almost daily attendance. Finally, Meg wrote a letter to Mrs. Wachtel saying that we had tried, repeatedly and unsuccessfully, to meet with her regarding our growing concern about the continued presence of Mrs. Carroll, and asking that, until we could meet with Mrs. Wachtel to discuss our fears, she not employ her. Since she was only a per diem sub, she was not entitled to any job, and no contract would be violated by her not being called for service. In spite of the letter, she continued to be called.

At the same time, several other young teachers who had been in during the strike were not enjoying the same protection from the administration. In these instances, or so it seemed to us, Mrs. Wachtel's aim was not so much in getting effective teaching as it was in removing people who had been on the "wrong" side of a hot issue. And Mrs. Carroll still remained.

After failing to get the meeting with Mrs. Wachtel to discuss the continued presence of Mrs. Carroll, Fred Pepper, Tom Cabot, and I made an appointment with Dr. Selig to discuss the situation. We sat in his office and presented all of the episodes regarding Mrs. Carroll's strange behavior. Dr Selig listened with a bemused smile until we had finished. He then told us that he could not supersede his principals and that hiring of substitutes was in the principal's domain. He suggested we take up the matter with Mrs. Wachtel (channels again). We replied that we had already tried that and that we would not have come to him had she been willing to meet with us.

"Then I suppose she thinks, in her professional judgment, that she is a good teacher."

"We don't," we said.

"Well, then there's a difference of opinion," he said with that same bemused smile.

"Indeed," I said. "I think her behavior is unusual, to say the least, and it scares me that she's in contact with kids. If you won't do anything and something happens, you'll be responsible."

"I'll take that chance," he said, still smiling. "Thank you for coming."

The epilogue to the tale of Mrs. Carroll came a few months later.

After Mrs. Wachtel left us, she was no longer in our school, and we had almost forgotten her when we learned that a substitute in another school in our district was being sued by the mother of a boy whose arm the teacher had twisted—and dislocated. The teacher was our Mrs. Carroll. It was fascinating that in spite of all of our experiences no one in the district had ever investigated her behavior, and that she kept her license—merely going from school to school—until she did *visible* physical harm to a child. And she wasn't even tenured! If subs like that can float around unchecked for years, how many tenured teachers are removed on the basis of that kind of behavior?

TWENTY–TWO

Action—Finally

The Christmas holidays were approaching, but there was little joy to our world and even less goodwill toward men—at least toward some of them. Nothing had changed in the school, and though we were still busily documenting we were beginning to feel a sense of futility. We would go on writing forever, and when our children graduated other parents would take up the pen in an unending compilation of a modern doomsday book.

In addition to our continuing problem with the presence of Mrs. Wachtel, we were also having our differences with the Joan of Arc governing board. Up until this point they had not been terribly active. In fact, when we had gone to them for help at the time of our picket line, they had been about as responsive as the local school board, though for slightly different reasons. They were still trying to get official recognition as a demonstration district. Also, since the situation in several of the other feeder schools was even worse than it was at PS 84 (with even greater educational failure and far less articulate parent bodies), they were reluctant to expend a great deal of energy on our school. However, as the crisis over Mrs. Wachtel began to come to a boil, the governing board became more interested in us, and Pete Worthem began to make pronouncements about what the governing board would do if the school board failed to act: "We will install a principal for PS 84 across the street from the school."

Most of the maneuvering between us and the Joan of Arc board went on behind the scenes, and in public we presented a united front. But Meg, in particular, had some rather hairy phone conversations with Pete, who felt she was not running the show correctly.

This maneuvering—were we using them for leverage with the school board, or were they using our situation to get power and recognition for themselves?—which was to crop up again and again in the months that followed, was put aside, however, with the appearance of a notice from the school board asking us to come to a meeting with them at our school on Monday, December 23, at which time they would give us their decision about our problems. We were angry that they were going to toss us a bombshell at a public meeting and also that they had chosen to do it the night before Christmas Eve, when many parents would be busy with tree trimming and other pre-holiday commitments. Besides, if they were going to remove Mrs. Wachtel, they did not need a public meeting to make the announcement. If they were not, then another yelling session was not worth coming out for. Thus, Meg and Pete sent a joint telegram to the board requesting that they communicate their decision regarding Mrs. Wachtel to us immediately and stating that they saw no reason why we should be kept waiting until Monday. They said, moreover, that the PS 84 parents saw no reason to attend the Monday night meeting because we had nothing further to discuss with them unless we had been informed of their decision and had had time to consider our response to it. Then we waited for some official word—which did not come.

In the absence of facts rumors began to fly. Dr. Selig and Bob Goodfellow came to the school and spent over an hour closeted with Nancy and Toni. What did that mean? On that score, at least, we were not kept ignorant long. What Dr. Selig and Bob had requested of the two teachers was that they transfer out of the school to other, separate, schools in the district, in the best interests of PS 84. That we were furious was putting it mildly. Here were two of the best teachers in the school, teachers who cared about children and education. It was they who had first given us our vision of what a school could be. It was they, more than any other teachers, on whom we counted to help us transform the school toward that vision. We wanted the school to change, to become a place where all children could learn, where learning would be a shared task for teacher and student, joyful for both. It was to this end that we were seeking the removal of Mrs. Wachtel and her replacement by a new kind of principal. What reasoning, then, could prompt Dr. Selig and the school board to remove these teachers? And if they were, indeed, removed, what would happen to the school we were seeking? True, there were other fine teachers in the school, but Nancy and Toni had acted as catalysts in the movement toward open classes. We could not permit their transfers. The question of what would happen to Mrs. Wachtel—to which we had been addressing ourselves for more than a year, suddenly took second place to the question of the teachers. Was that what Dr. Selig had had in mind? Was this still another diversionary tactic? We would not be diverted. We would continue to insist on Mrs. Wachtel's removal, but we would insist as well that the teachers must remain.

We had the entire weekend to work ourselves into a suitable rage, and it wasn't even hard. My phone rang constantly that weekend (I assume everyone's did) as we asked ourselves what we should do, how we should proceed.

"Is there any news?" was the standard greeting.

"What are Toni and Nancy doing?" was the refrain.

There was little hard news over most of the weekend. Then, on Sunday, I got an electrifying call from Meg.

"Have you heard?" she asked. "Mrs. Wachtel has requested a transfer."

"We did it?" I asked.

"We did it. Actually, it seems she wrote the school board a letter two weeks ago, giving them three choices: they could support her wholeheartedly; they could transfer her; or they could accept her request for a voluntary transfer. Apparently they've chosen the last."

"Hey, that's great news. Is it for publication?"

"Sure. I don't see why not. That's what they're announcing tomorrow night."

"What does it all mean? Is she really leaving?"

"I don't know. I guess she can un-request her transfer, too. But at the moment I guess she's leaving."

"Well, that's the best news I've heard in a long time. But how does this affect the Nancy-Toni thing?"

"I don't know that, either."

We hung up, and I began making calls. I should have been jubilant, but strangely I wasn't. Partly it was that I didn't fully believe Mrs. Wachtel was really going. Partly it was my worry over the tie-in between the transfers of the teachers and Mrs. Wachtel's departure. I didn't know whether there was a tie-in, but it worried me. It worried a lot of other people, too, so that there was a strange absence of elation that Sunday evening. Had someone told me in November that Mrs. Wachtel would shortly transfer out and that I would not be overjoyed—and that the other parents wouldn't be either—I would have been incredulous. And here she was, and we were gloomy and angry. An outsider could well have asked what was the matter with us. We had gotten what we had been working toward, and now we still weren't happy. "I'll believe it when she's gone," someone said, and that was part of it. The other part was the gnawing doubt that this was a package deal and that once the package fell apart by our refusal to let the teachers go the whole thing would evaporate. And we could not let the teachers go. We could not throw out the baby with the bath water. If we wanted Mrs. Wachtel out, it was to build a school. The teachers were part of that. So we worried and cheered our doubting spirits with the thought that if it was, indeed, true that Mrs. Wachtel was going we would treat ourselves to a big celebration bash. We would deserve it. But before that there was the school board meeting.

Before the meeting began, Meg handed Jessica a position paper which stated that the Executive Board and the Joan of Arc planning /governing board had agreed on the following points:

1. Mrs. Wachtel must be transferred immediately from PS 84 and a person must be appointed to function as Acting Principal for an interim period.
2. The committee to screen and select a new principal with the local school board be enlarged to include two members of the elected Joan of Arc board.
3. We reject the involuntary transfer of Mrs. Diamond and Mrs. Calvert from our school.
4. Decisions made by the local school board concerning PS 84 must be made in consultation with parent representatives and representatives of the Joan of Arc board before presentation to all parents.

IT WOULD SAVE EVERYONE A LOT OF TIME!

Then we sat around and waited for them to have their executive session. At 9:00 o'clock the school board gathered itself on the stage of the auditorium; and after we all settled down, Jessica opened the meeting and thanked us all for coming. She then turned the meeting over to Bob Goodfellow who said he would read us the board's report. Jessica looked visibly pained as he began:

"In the late spring of this year there was brought to the attention of the District Superintendent and the school board the fact that there was a growing unrest among parents and some teachers at PS

84 concerning the performance of the principal who had been appointed in February 1967. In response to this concern, Mrs. Dodge and Mr. Goodfellow of the school board were directed by the chairman to investigate the situation and report back.

"Preliminary meetings were held in June and July with the principal, some teachers, and parents. When school opened in September, simultaneously with the strike, the visits and conferences still continued. When the third strike ended, Mrs. Dodge, Mr. Goodfellow, and Dr. Selig continued to spend extensive time at the school with all parties concerned.

"During these past five weeks the situation has grown critical. We think it fair to say that there exists an atmosphere of extreme hostility among parents, administration, and teachers of the school. We find:

1. The principal has been unable to function as an effective administrator. This is due partly to her inability to adapt to parental participation in the affairs of the school, which has become magnified when the principal's authority was continually undermined by a small group of staff and parents reacting to the principal's inability to respond constructively to their demands.

2. There exists a deep split in the staff between those who support the principal and those who oppose her. This has been heightened by the strike, although some teachers who taught during the strike do not support the removal of the principal.

3. The UFT leadership in the school has continued to nurture this conflict with the opposition to the principal and strike as tools to oppose parent participation in the school and at the same time continue the breach among the staff.

4. The parents have overreacted to any move restricting their participation in the affairs of the school. This has resulted in their reasonable demands accelerating into the literal desire that the parents run the day-to-day affairs of the school, and, in turn, has accelerated the opposition of the principal to whatever they have had to say. What is most disturbing is that the Parents' Association has had good leadership, which has been stymied at every turn by the polarization of both sides.

5. Two teachers of the staff for the past nine months have made it their personal crusade to remove the principal. Their opposition has been so vocal and manifested at every opportunity, i.e., staff meetings, PA meetings, school board meetings, conferences with

paraprofessionals, balanced-class projects, and others, so as to only heighten the tension. This has not been responsible opposition or criticism, but opposition that has bordered upon hysteria.

"To resolve these problems, it will take more than the observation of two well-meaning members of the school board. It will take the desire of all concerned to make an honest evaluation of the roles that they have played during the past nine months without shading their eyes with a cloak of self-righteousness.

"No one concerned can be certain what action will make PS 84 a viable educational institution. But if an honest evaluation is a good start, then the school board will make such a beginning. It is hoped that this frankness is accepted and responded to in the same manner.

"The principal has already removed herself from the scene. A letter to the school board was received last week from the principal, in which she recommended as one of three alternatives that the school board request that she transfer voluntarily without prejudice out of the district. The school board has made such a request, which has been accepted. But as has been pointed out, this really solves very little with regard to the long-term problems of the school. A proper atmosphere must be created so that all parties concerned are working together. The school board, therefore, proposes the following:

1. The UFT chapter chairman in the school be put on notice that any further union activity aimed at continuing the breach between the staff and parents will be considered by the school board as acts of insubordination, and disciplinary proceedings wll be instituted against all parties concerned.

2. Guidelines concerning parent participation in the affairs of the school are to be established immediately, to be worked out in consultation with the parents, teachers, and school board.

3. The parents of the school will immediately appoint three members and the teachers of the school one member, to meet with the school board for the purpose of helping the school board select a new principal."

Bob stopped—triumphantly. He was obviously pleased at the balanced evaluation that he had just read. Who could argue with it? There was something in it for everyone. Mrs. Wachtel had "already removed herself from the scene"; the teachers were reprimanded for their hysteria in bringing to the attention of everyone the untenable situation (interestingly, no one denied the situation, but merely deplored the fact that they had so publicly and "hysterically" blown the whistle); the UFT chapter chairman got a slap on the wrist for her divisive activities; the parents, good leadership notwithstanding, got a slap on the wrist for theirs. Who could fault such a reasonable document? Certainly no one unless he was "shading his eyes with a cloak of self-righteousness." What was fascinating about the report—aside from the fact that it did not mention the punitive action intended against Nancy and Toni—was that nothing was said of the role of Dr. Selig and the school board. One could suppose that had they acted decisively earlier none of the conditions they now deplored would have come to pass. But no self-righteousness, fellows.

At this point, reasonable though the report was, the proverbial hit the fan. Jessica continued to look pained. I know she disagreed with the report; and it is to her credit that she did not take the easy way out by saying, "Look, I voted against this nonsense." It would have been a popular thing to do; but being honorable, she would abide —publicly, at least—by her board's decision. We, however, were not bound by this sense of honor, and one parent after another rose to blast the board, Bob, and the report. A succession of parents stood to recount what a marvelous job Toni and Nancy were doing in teaching all children. They told how the two of them had been able to weld diverse children into cohesive classes. They recited how children who had not been learning heretofore were learning in their classes. And so on. To all this the members of the board replied that there was no denying that the two were good teachers, but that they felt that they were a divisive force, and that therefore they must go. Only Jessica and Elizabeth Dodge did not pursue this line of "reasoning." The meeting went on for hours as successive speakers denounced the report's stupidity. I had the sense, as I sat and listened, that the board members were off in some never-never land. Did they think you could solve the problem of educational failure by removing from the scene some of the few people who were effective? I wanted to get up and shake them, and say "Goddammit, I wish you had kids in this school. Maybe then you'd understand what we were saying"; and if I had believed it would have done any good, I would have done it. I had long advocated that only parents should decide on what goes on in their schools. Now I would have liked to refine that still further, to only parents in a particular school. It was obvious to me that the board members could not conceive of the situation. But this line of reasoning was not going to change anyone's mind, and finally I rose to discuss another aspect of their report that I found particularly distressing.

"Look," I said, "if you go through with transferring these teachers, you'd better consider what you'll be saying to all teachers in the district. What you'll be saying is 'don't rock the boat. No matter how bad a situation is, don't say anything.' Is that the kind of education you want for your children? Do you want the kind of teachers who accept all sorts of horrors because it's the safe, the politic, thing to do? Do you want teachers who are yes men, who will go along with any decision because not to means to jeopardize their jobs? What sort of education is that for our children? If you judge these teachers on the *fact* that they criticized, rather than on whether their criticism was justified, then you're telling teachers from now on to shut up or else. In that case I fear for education in our district. If you go ahead with the transfers, you will effectively kill true education in this district. And then, I hope you sleep well tonight."

I sat down, and I was shaking. Everyone applauded my speech, and Jessica and Elizabeth had been nodding in agreement as I spoke, but they were convinced before I began. As for the others, I don't think I made a dent. Several of the other parents spoke after that, and then Jessica said they would meet in executive session and let us know their answer. At that we surged forward and began, individually, to buttonhole Bob, Celia Cohen, Gonzalez-Patron, and Mr. Torres. But it was hopeless. They were right and reasonable. We were—again—hysterical.

Toni Diamond summed up the whole idiocy in a three-page letter to the school board in which she blasted their attempt to remove Nancy and her for their "political" activities. The letter was quite an indictment, and I would have liked to have been present at the meeting at which it was discussed. Aside from its blast at the board, the interesting fact of the letter, to me, was that it touched on the whole question of due process for teachers. Nancy and Toni found themselves in a position not too different from the transferred—or fired—teachers of Ocean-Hill, and their response was the same. How *do* you define "for the good of the school"? In Brownsville we may assume that the teachers involved were sabotaging the will of the community. In our school in this instance they were sabotaging the will of the establishment. The outcome is the same in either case. And how can teachers have the freedom to express their views, to cry out against injustice as they see it, if, each time, they run the risk of losing their jobs? It's not an easy question, and if tenure is no answer neither is the lack of tenure. Were all men disinterested and honorable at all times then perhaps there would be no conflict. Till then I guess we have to muddle along. In this instance, of course, the teachers had the support of the community, and it saved them when the school board realized that if it was going to have any claim to acting on behalf of the community it had better listen. But what happens in a community where the teacher does not have this backing? What happens to the teacher who teaches peace in a DAR community? or brotherhood in Klan country? Then we fall back on the protection of tenure, and that leads us right to the other end of the pendulum where, because of the many legal steps necessary to remove a tenured teacher, supervisors are often unwilling to move against someone even if he commits the most anti-child, anti-educational acts. I wish I knew the answer.

In any case, whether in response to the parental clamor, to Toni's letter, or to the few voices of sanity on the school board, the board at its next meeting withdrew the offending report "in its entirety." And that left us right back where we had started.

TWENTY-THREE

Lame Ducks

The Christmas vacation ended, and upon our return to the school we learned that though the school board had withdrawn its report they had not withdrawn their acceptance of Mrs. Wachtel's transfer request. Thus we could now look forward to her departure—as soon as she could secure a position elsewhere. We scheduled a meeting for January 9 to elect parents to serve on the screening panel for a new principal, and we put a notice to that effect on our bulletin board. Shortly thereafter a second notice appeared next to ours, stating that our notice was premature and that Mrs. Wachtel was, and would continue to be, principal of PS 84. It was signed by the UFT chapter chairman. If this was not a divisive action, I don't know what was; but since the report of the school board had been withdrawn, I guess Jenny felt that she was no longer enjoined from continuing her activities. Meg wrote her an angry note asking for an explanation, to which Jenny replied that the purpose of her note was to relieve the anxieties of the PS 84 staff regarding the status of their principal. She said that the PA notice had made Mrs. Wachtel's transfer seem like a *fait accompli* when, in fact, Mrs. Wachtel had informed Jenny that she had not as yet reached a final decision as to whether or not she would remain as principal. So though according to the school board Mrs. Wachtel had removed herself from the scene, according to the UFT and to Mrs. Wachtel she was still very much a part of the scene. The UFT notice may have relieved faculty anxieties. It did little for ours.

Nevertheless, we proceeded with our meeting, and elected three parents and three alternates to serve on a screening panel: Carmen Johnson, Ronnie Rubin, and Nancy Sergeant, and Edna Garrett,

Irene Martins, and John Rollins. When the Joan of Arc board began its screening, they decided, since they were not bound by the numbers limitations imposed by the school board, that all six of the parents would participate, as well as several teachers elected from among the staff and members of the governing board. They also asked Preston Wilcox* to serve as their educational consultant, and he agreed, so the panel represented a broad spectrum.

One of the problems in the selection of a new principal was that we did not want to exchange one bureaucrat for another. Though we were quite willing to look at any person who applied, we did not want to limit ourselves only to those candidates who had passed the Board of Examiners' test and who were on the eligible list. Indeed, one of the reasons parents like Stephanie Hale and Irene Martins had opposed the profile had been their feeling that until parents had some real choice as to who could be a principal, there was no point in going through the hassle. Now Jessica had told us that the school board might be willing to consider someone off the list as well— which would widen our choice. In response to the two ads the governing board had placed in the *Times* had come applicants with impeccable qualifications, even though they had not taken the New York City exams. And we certainly wanted to consider them, as well as any promising candidates from the list. Though since then many schools have chosen principals not anointed by the Board of Examiners, at this time our position was quite radical. Only schools in the demonstration districts had, at that time, been able to circumvent the lists and appoint "demonstration" principals (a special category for which no principal's license was required). We were proposing to make ourselves a demonstration district and do likewise if the person we ultimately chose lacked a New York City license. Someone pointed out that though the school board had said they would "consider" someone off the list that was not the same as saying they would actually hire him, and they proposed that we get a firm commitment from the school board that, if the parents' choice was someone not on the list, the board would, nevertheless, accept that choice.

We also began to discuss some of the qualifications we felt a

---

*Professor at the Columbia School of Social Work and an early consultant to the IS 201 complex. He is now president of AFRAM, a firm that does educational consulting.

principal should have. Pete Worthem, speaking for the governing board, said that the final choice should reside with the community. "We feel no principal should be installed without the consent of the parents."

He also said that a candidate of his choice would be committed to community control and would be from a background the children could relate to. He said his personal choice would be for "a strong, black male." A lot of us liberated women objected to that. Walter said that he was disturbed by the tone of Pete's comments. He said that the emphasis was on the degree of interest in community control with very little emphasis on educational qualifications, to which Pete replied that the reality of the situation seemed to him to be that the educators in the system who have the best relationship with children are those who are interested in community control.

I have been giving the impression that our meetings generally presented a united front. In fact, at nearly all of them, there was always at least one parent who presented the law-and-order approach and who, in response to any action we wanted to take regarding the ouster of Mrs. Wachtel or opposition to a school board action, would tell us we were terrible people, just like those in Ocean-Hill. It wasn't always the same parent. One would come for several meetings and then give up. And since his comments were often greeted with less than polite silence, one could hardly blame him, but he would soon be replaced by a new one. They kept cropping up to remind us that there was another world. At this meeting, Pat Hollingsway arose to say that he had attended a school board meeting at which they had stated that candidates be selected on qualifications other than their position on the list, including ethnic considerations.

"I would consider an interest in community control an immediate disqualification. I would consider an interest in children learning in an orderly and calm way the prime consideration. Mr. Worthem's remarks are insulting and arrogant."

No one, till then, had made community control and children learning diametrically opposed, and in fact our interest in community control was that children were not, at present, learning. But Mr. Hollingsway felt that where children were not learning it was because of the subversive acts of their parents and that the worst thing you could do for children and education was to permit these parents to have a say in it. Mr. Hollingsway was treated to a barrage of jeers, but he remained stoically in his seat and continued to come to every meeting to present his views, always with a good deal of disdain for the likes of us. And the rest of the parents happily reciprocated his scorn.

Mike Goodman then said that sympathy for community control was not, in itself, a qualification but was indicative of an educator's leanings. The prime considerations had to be philosophy of education, competency in administration, and attitudes toward teaching and children.

WALTER: "The question to be asked is 'what kind of society does he hope these children will enter?' Should they be pegs manufactured to fit into our industrial society or should these children develop into independent, autonomous persons who can make decisions? This is an educational and a social question. A person's answers to this kind of question should be decisive."

FRED PEPPER: "We should draw up a statement or an audit sheet of characteristics. This could serve as a position sheet or a checklist, and I propose that we select a committee to do so."

It was so moved, with two opposing votes. The discussion on qualifications then continued with Pat Hollingsway still arguing that community control was no touchstone.

RAY FISHER: "If we can get a principal who can run this school, there will be no concern about community control. There won't be anyone around to do anything. Parents are only here now because it's such a mess."

At this point Jessica Malamud appeared and we gave her our list of parents for their screening panel. She then agreed to answer any questions we might have, and they dealt with what real voice the parents would have in the selection. Jessica said that the school board would not ram anyone down the parents' throats, but that there usually was a consensus. When asked whether the school board would appoint someone from off the list, she answered that she didn't know. She said that there was presently a case before the Court of Appeals, and unless they reversed a lower court decision such an appointment would be an exercise in futility.*

RAY FISHER: "Can the local school board appoint an acting principal in the interim?"

JESSICA: "I don't know. Mrs. Wachtel has requested a voluntary

---

*The Court of Appeals did reverse it.

transfer. This involves a sending and a receiving district. When she finds a school she wants and that wants her then it is implemented."

JOHN ROLLINS: "There is a dangerous situation in the school. We want her sent to 110 Livingston Street, and someone else appointed acting principal until a permanent principal is selected."

JESSICA: "There is no way the board can transfer her downtown."

MIKE GOODMAN: "I suggest the local school board recognize that an acute emergency exists and go to the Board of Education with the problem."

IRENE: "Would you object if people from the school went to the Board to reinforce your position?"

JESSICA: "No."

SELMA WOOD: "Maybe the local school board could use her."

JOHN: "Can Selig assume this responsibility?"

JESSICA: "He cannot. What it really comes down to is legal rights."

NANCY SERGEANT: "These are special circumstances. We are fast running into an emergency. The school is unsafe."

JESSICA: "We have done everything we can. Find her a job somewhere."

She then asked whether we wanted a state administrator to take over the school (as had happened in several of the Brownsville schools after the strike). We answered that this would be one way of protecting the children. Jessica said that the state administrator might mean that the parents would lose their status. Ronnie answered that we had no status anyway and so had nothing to lose. Pat Hollingsway asked whether Mrs. Wachtel was engaged in looking for another position.

JESSICA: "I think some effort is being made."

I: "What if she changes her mind?" No answer.

MIKE GOODMAN: "She is due for a rating. This could be used as pressure. If she gets an 'S' rating it would be difficult to transfer her."

JESSICA: "That is not the proper use of a rating."

As it was by then past eleven and the displeasure of the custodian was visible, we adjourned the meeting.

Following this meeting we decided to take actions on several levels: to write a letter to Mrs. Wachtel appealing to her to take an immediate leave and to go downtown to the Board of Education to see whether they could or would help us. We also decided that, if nothing changed by the end of January, we would take some dramatic action such as a boycott or a picket line.

So we sent a letter to Mrs. Wachtel and asked for a reply by January 20. Pete Worthem also asked MFY for a legal opinion as to how the services of an untenured principal could, in fact, be terminated. The answer was that Dr. Selig and the school board could remove Mrs. Wachtel if they so chose. We decided to go downtown and see whether in that way we could make them so choose, and so on Thursday, January 23, Sarah Tydings, Ronnie Rubin, Irene Martins, and I took a ride to 110 Livingston Street, above whose portals I have always felt there should be Dante's inscription: "Abandon Hope All Ye Who Enter Here." And from the treatment I had always gotten on my trips there, it was evident that the civil servants therein long had. Actually on this occasion we were well treated, at least by Milton Galamison's secretary, Lucille, who not only let us use his office as our base, but who also sent out for coffee and danish for us! And Galamison agreed to try to put pressure on Dr. Selig to do something about effecting the desired transfer.

Meg had now been acting president of the PA for over a month, and she had agreed to run for the presidency, but then her son had gotten ill and was in the hospital with an undiagnosed, worrisome set of symptoms. Consequently she withdrew from the running, and the election committee asked me whether I would run. I had come a long way from my original views regarding the PA; and considering that I am not a joiner, I certainly had joined. I agreed to be a candidate, and the election was scheduled for January 30. Normally our elections are rather unenthusiastic—to say the least—and we're generally happy if we can find one warm body for each office. On this occasion, though, on the night of the election, Pat Hollingsway nominated his wife. We had agreed that we would have balloting on the evening of the 30th and all of the following day in the community room, to enable as many people as possible to vote. When the ballots were counted, I was elected by a vote of 69 to 10, and so I became president of the PA at a time so chaotic that on occasion I might have been willing to settle for a tea-and-cookies school.

While we were engaged in the political maneuvering regarding Mrs. Wachtel's continued presence, we also continued to be concerned about the quality of education at the school. It had been decided to make the two kindergartens in the open classes into all-day kindergartens, in order to allow for interaction between them and the first grades. Ordinarily this should have been a simple matter—you simply decide to extend the day for the kids involved; you send home notices to that effect; and you proceed. But at PS 84 at that time nothing was a simple matter; and though the time extension had been planned since mid-November, it was not until February that it finally went into effect. Also it became apparent early on that one of the kindergarten teachers selected by Mrs. Wachtel to teach in the program seemed poorly suited to it. She was Mrs. Winter, the teacher in whose kindergarten Kathy had withered; and though she had agreed to the assignment, it was soon clear to all concerned—including the lady herself—that this was not her cup of tea. Nevertheless, she struggled on with it for quite a while (as did the kids); and though the subject was discussed at various meetings on the program as a whole, it was not until Easter that, with everyone's concurrence, she finally left the class and a former pre-kindergarten teacher took it over and breathed fresh life into the undertaking.

Dotty Steinberg and Millie Miller had become chairmen of the Infant School Committee, and they held several meetings to explain to parents what the philosophy and aims of the program were. Mrs. Weber attended one of these, and she was a delight to listen to. Her common sense and her enthusiasm were a refreshing contrast to the style we generally encountered from administrators. She was also most reassuring to parents who were not entirely sold on the idea that children could learn if they were happy—a recurrent theme on the subject to this day. It says something about the education we all got that so many of us still feel that in order to learn children must be miserable! Mrs. Weber, whenever she spoke to parents, said that she would guarantee that every child in the program would leave it with at least the same skills as children in a traditional class. She was sure they would leave with a great deal more, but this was the minimum essential, and for parents who worried whether their children would learn to read, this was comforting.

Some of the parents were annoyed that while we were engaged in our battles we should be spending time putting band-aids on the system. They felt we were dissipating our energies (this was basically the same argument we had had at the time of the profile and the picketing, but now it was directed against Dotty and Millie. It went: don't try to do anything about programs now. Wait till we have a receptive principal. This one will only botch things up anyway, and the whole thing will be discredited before it ever gets a real chance. While we recognized the truth of some of that and the danger in trying to work on a program the principal did not understand, we also felt—again—that there were kids in there and that while we were engaged in the political battle we could still not ignore the day-to-day education. But Dotty and Millie became known as the "Infant-School Ladies," and it was sometimes tough for them to put up with the abuse they got from some quarters. However they are both strong people who refused to give in and continued to nurse the program along, helping in any way they could, fighting whenever they had to, both with Mrs. Wachtel and with the "political" parents.

One of the problems elementary schools face regularly is that although they have gone to yearly promotion for children, staff is still hired at midyear due to sabbatical leaves and retirements. As a result, though a class remains together for a year, they may be faced, midstream, with a change of teacher. This also means that at midyear as well as in June a principal must make decisions regarding the hiring and firing of staff. Not only do people go on leave in February, but others also return then, and a substitute who gets a job in September may be out on the street in February. Because we did not feel Mrs. Wachtel was competent to make these decisions in any case and because, since she was leaving, she could have no interest in their consequences (unless, if she were vindictive, she would want to take a few last licks at the school that had rejected her), we were determined that she should make no staff changes at this time, but should leave them to her successor. We therefore wrote a letter to Dr. Selig to this effect. He replied, "Unfortunately it is not always possible to maintain a staff throughout a year for reasons of administrative necessity, or other reasons resulting in inadequate service to a school."

Though all of us—and the school board, too—agreed at this point that Mrs. Wachtel could not make proper administrative decisions and, as a lame-duck principal, should not make them, Dr. Selig was still allowing her to go on making them. And so she decided to let three teachers go. We appealed to the school board, who reviewed the cases; and one of the three was permitted to remain. It was a partial victory for us, but we continued to chafe under the rule of our lame-duck principal who was still very much on the scene. We heard via the grapevine that exists throughout those portions of the city where parents are active that she had, indeed, interviewed for several vacancies; but nothing had come of these interviews (wise parents, there!), and it seemed that her presence would continue unless we could force the issue. So we took off for Livingston Street again to see whether they could make room for still another principal down there.

This time ten of us went—a nice mixed group, black and white, male and female. As the almost-elected president, I headed the delegation. We again left our things in Milton Galamison's office (he was "the people's representative" on the Board of Education), and then decided to go to see Superintendent Donovan who, we were told, could circumvent a lot of red tape by assigning Mrs. Wachtel to central headquarters. As anyone with a knowledge of the Board of Education knows, this is a time-honored method of getting inadequate personnel out of schools. They keep their tenure but are added to the budget of 110, thus allowing the schools to limp along. What we were asking, then, was nothing that hadn't been done a thousand times before. The question was only whether they would do it for us. District 5 at that time was not their favorite district. Though to us our school board was not very militant, they had, vis-à-vis the central board, taken various gutsy stands. Furthermore, all our schools had, in some form, been open during the strikes; and since 110 is filled with UFT and CSA supporters, we were also unpopular on that count. Those people may not be able to teach kids, but they are loyal to their own. We were not sure we would be greeted with red carpets.

Indeed. We arrived at Donovan's office and were told by the head secretary that Dr. Donovan was not in. However, she would see whether Mr. Anker, Dr. Donovan's assistant, would see us.

"Fine," I said.

She stepped back into her office, which was separated from the foyer by a swinging gate, made a call, and returned to report that Mr. Anker would meet with three of us.

"There are ten of us here," I said.

"I'm afraid that's impossible. He'll only see a delegation of three."

"We're a delegation of ten," I said. "We've all come a long way. We'd all like to see him."

"He'll only see three of you."

"There are ten of us."

"I'm afraid he can't see more than three."

"May I speak to him?" I asked.

"Well . . . I'll ask him if he'll speak to you."

This whole conversation had taken place across the barrier of the swinging gate, with those other nine formidable and menacing parents behind me and the entire complement of secretaries looking up from their work in open-mouthed shock. Parents not going away nicely? Where would all this permissiveness end? The secretary returned from her desk to inform me—with wonder in her voice— that Mr. Anker would speak to me, and she opened the gate to let me into the outer office, swinging it shut quickly behind me lest she loose the floodgates.

"Hello, Mr. Anker," I said. "My name is Hannah Hess, and I'm here with a group of parents from PS 84. We'd like to speak to you about a problem we're having."

"I'll be glad to see three of you," he said.

"Ah, there are ten of us," I answered. "We'd really all like to see you."

"I'm afraid that's impossible, Mrs. Hess. I'm sure three of you could state your case adequately."

"I'm sure we could. But there are ten of us. We've all come, taken time off from other duties, and we'd all like to speak to you."

"How about four?"

"We're ten."

"I never see large delegations. I find them counterproductive."

"We're all very well behaved."

"Oh, I'm sure of that, or I wouldn't see any of you. But I find that when meetings get too large nothing gets accomplished."

"Why don't you try it this once."

There was a minute's silence. Obviously a momentous decision was in the works. Then, "Well, I won't ask you into my office, but I'll come out and speak to you in the vestibule."

"Thank you," I said and swung out of the gate, grinning. Good as his word, Mr. Anker appeared moments later, a small thin man with white hair. We spoke for ten minutes or so, and I wouldn't recognize him again if I fell over him. He looked like countless others at Livingston Street, and I've seen his twins in the corridors at Albany—in pale gray or pale brown suits, all the juices sapped from them by their years within the bureaucratic system. Still, he was very sweet. He listened politely as we recounted our tale of woe; he sympathized with us, and yet . . .

"It's really not anything we can solve. We can't remove principals."

"You could assign her down here," he said.

"But on what grounds? You can't deny principals their rights."

"What about the children's rights?"

"With due process you have the best protection of children's rights," or words to that effect.

"She can't function."

"Then let your superintendent remove her if she's incompetent."

"He won't."

"Ah, then maybe he feels she's competent. He *is* a professional, you know."

"And we're *only* parents," I said.

"I didn't say that, but perhaps he sees the larger picture."

"Maybe he doesn't see what we see."

"Maybe. You get him to act if things are as bad as you say. I'll pass your message along to Dr. Donovan; but if you want some advice from me, your best bet is with your superintendent. Who did you say that was?"

"Dr. Selig."

"Ah, yes, Selig. A good man. You talk to him. I do understand how you feel, and I will give your message to Dr. Donovan. But do talk to Dr. Selig."

We thanked him for his time and walked out of the vestibule.

"What now?" we asked each other.

Someone suggested we go to see Harold Siegel, secretary to the Board of Education, who was a resident of the upper West Side and might be willing to see us on that basis. So we trotted upstairs again, and we were ceremoniously ushered into his office by Siegel's secretary, who also expressed great sympathy with us since, she informed us, she had come up from the ranks of the United Parents' Association. The office was huge, carpeted, and curtained, and we were seated around a large wood conference table where another secretary supplied each of us with paper and pencil and took all of our names. While we were waiting for Mr. Siegel to appear, another small gray man came rushing into the office. The word of our presence was, apparently, out.

This gentleman introduced himself as Dr. Nathan Brown*, and he began to berate us for barging into offices and for daring to come to see Mr. Siegel after Mr. Anker had already given us so much of his time.

"You'd do better to spend your energies in your own district. Let me tell you something. We used to take a lot of principals from all the districts, but we don't anymore. Now that you've got decentralization, don't come running down to us. You got what you wanted. Now you have to live with it. Do you know how many extra principals we have here now?" We didn't.

"Plenty. But we don't have to take them anymore, and we won't. You go back uptown, and you tell Dr. Selig to put her in his office. He's got the power."

It went on like that for a while, and then he left. Mr. Siegel, who appeared shortly afterwards, echoed his sentiments, though more politely and sympathetically. It was obvious by then that the name of the game—again—was pass the buck. You go uptown and they tell you only downtown has the power. You go downtown and they tell you you should be uptown. It's stuff like that that discourages parents. But we were mad and decided to take their advice and go back uptown and yell some more. Somebody someplace had the power to make a decision, and we'd just go on bothering them until they got so tired of us that doing something would be simpler.

*He subsequently became superintendent of schools upon the resignation of Dr. Donovan. Mr. Anker is now deputy to Chancellor Scribner.

TWENTY-FOUR

Out of the Frying Pan

It was now February, the start of a new term. Mrs. Wachtel had not been besieged by offers for her services, and it became apparent that, therefore, she was likely to remain with us till June unless we could force the issue. At the same time we were concerned with the question of an interim replacement for Mrs. Wachtel once she was gone until such a time as we could screen for a permanent principal. Ordinarily in a school where the principal leaves, one of the assistant principals, usually the one with seniority, fills in until a replacement is chosen. In our case we felt that neither of the assistant principals was acceptable. Mrs. Young (she of the ethnic census) had seniority. She was presently on leave, and Bob Goodfellow had earlier assured unhappy parents that she would return over his dead body. Shortly before she had gone on her sabbatical, the Spanish parents had circulated a petition demanding her removal; and though the petition had never been officially presented to Dr. Selig, he, as well as Mrs. Young, was aware of its existence and of the feelings that had given it birth. She and Mrs. Wachtel had never gotten along, and rumor had it that she had felt slighted when she had been passed over for the position of principal when Mrs. Wachtel had been chosen and that that feeling had had something to do with her extended leave. Now, Meg told us, she had gotten a call from Mrs. Young expressing interest in the principal's job, and we were determined that she should not become the replacement.

What we wanted in an interim principal was someone who could begin to heal the breaches in the school, who could restore some semblance of order, who could carry on the educational programs with sympathy, and whose vision of parental involvement extended beyond hall patrol. Neither of the assistant principals, in our opinion, came close to these requirements. Certainly with the amount of polarization on the staff, neither of the two assistant principals—both identified with a faction—was likely to heal anything.

We met at my house the night before the school board meeting to review events and to discuss what we should do. Meg pointed out that Jessica Malamud had told her that on the agenda was simply an announcement that Mrs. Wachtel had requested a transfer. We all felt that that was not enough and that one of us should make a public statement at the meeting regarding our position. And then we began thinking of ways in which we could put pressure on them, in a publicly embarrassing way, to get Dr. Selig to act.

"The press won't come for just another demonstration," Tom Cabot said. "Unless you can come up with something dramatic, I won't even call my contacts."

"How about a funeral for the school?" I asked. That suggestion was quickly laid to rest.

"How do we demonstrate that we're a school without a real principal—that we have a lame-duck administration making important decisions?" Meg asked.

"Why don't we get a duck?" someone suggested. "As a symbol. And march with it to Dr. Selig's office."

"We could bandage one of its legs and carry signs saying that's our principal."

"The humane society will picket us."

"Swell. That'll make the papers."

We all liked the idea. It was just silly enough so it might work, and we had to do something. Millie was commissioned to buy a live duck. We could always make it a school mascot afterwards, or use it at a celebration banquet if we ever had cause to celebrate. Tom would call his TV contacts, and we would hope for the best. The demonstration was planned for the coming Thursday, February 6. Before that day the school board was meeting; and if they came up with a decent solution, then we could still call off our demonstration. If they didn't . . .

About thirty PS 84 parents attended the school board meeting on February 3, and, indeed, the announcement was made that Mrs. Wachtel had requested a transfer. Then the explanation followed: since the transfer was voluntary and since Mrs. Wachtel had not yet found employment elsewhere, she would remain at PS 84 until such a time as she did. Thereupon I rose to read my statement. I said that I had two statements and that I would first read the one I had written in the event that the school board acted properly:

"The parents of PS 84 are glad that it has finally been recognized that the intolerable situation at the school could no longer continue. Our energies have too long been spent in trips to Livingston Street, to Dr. Selig's office, and to school board meetings. For many of us this has become an almost full-time, albeit unsalaried, job. We have been kept scrambling up and down the bureaucratic ladders to accomplish what should all along have been Dr. Selig's job.

"Now, hopefully, we can turn these energies to the search for a new principal—to the search for the kind of principal who will achieve what this struggle has been all about: quality education for *all* our children.

"We want to thank all the school-board members who helped us and all the parents who put their time and efforts into the fight. We have proved, I think, that a parent body with a purpose can succeed, in spite of all the roadblocks that an entrenched bureaucracy can put in its way.

"With the same unanimity of purpose let us begin our search for a real principal. This time we will not accept an ersatz administrator. A principal who understands that all we want for our children is the best education will find the parent body ready to cooperate and to work hard to achieve this aim. A united administration, staff, and parent body can make PS 84 into a showcase in the district and in the city.

"Now," I continued, "I am sorry to have to read the other statement. I had hoped this one wouldn't be necessary.

"To Dr. Selig: the *only* person who has the power to remove principals under the interim decentralization bill.

"Since early last spring the parents of PS 84 have come to you because ours was a troubled school. Time after time we presented documentation, both written and verbal. You asked for facts—we gave you facts. Members of the local school board spent countless hours in the school and saw what we had seen. Finally the local school board issued its report which stated that 'Mrs. Wachtel had removed herself from the scene by requesting a voluntary transfer.'

"*But* although this may be comforting on paper it is not a fact. Mrs. Wachtel is still very much on the scene, and the result is continuing chaos. We are tired of coming to meeting after meeting with new evidence. We can no longer tolerate the unsafe and chaotic conditions in the school. We are tired of living with a principal who cannot make even the simplest administrative decision. We can no longer tolerate the undermining of programs that Mrs. Wachtel allegedly supports—be that undermining through malice or gross inefficiency. We are tired of running up the bureaucratic ladder every time a new crisis develops. We shall no longer tolerate a lame-duck administration. We do not intend, any longer, to have our children live with terror, chaos, and educational failure. The local school board has admitted that Mrs. Wachtel is incompetent. We cannot stand back and allow her to get an 'S' rating—especially when, for us, that 'S' will mean not satisfactory, but *stuck*.

"The local school board seems to be on our side but says it has gone as far as it can; 110 Livingston Street says you, Dr. Selig, have the power and the responsibility to remove Mrs. Wachtel *now*. The local school board, as your employer, must insist that you do. We have talked enough. We have been patient long enough. We have no other recourse now but to take dramatic public action."

I sat down to tremendous applause. Jessica was nodding approval. And Dr. Selig sat as though cast in bronze. Joe Dreier rose to ask whether Mrs. Wachtel wasn't due for a rating soon. Dr. Selig smiled smugly and nodded.

"When is she due to be rated?" Joe continued.

"In December," was the answer.

"You mean her rating is past due? Or have you rated her?"

"I've rated her."

"What was the rating?" Joe asked.

"Satisfactory," he answered.

There was a moment's stunned silence, a mass involuntary gasp, and then bedlam. A parent called out "Well, it finally came out."

Millie rose to her feet, furious. "How can you sit there and tell us, after everything you've heard, that you've rated her satisfactory? I want to hear your answer. You've been sitting there, meeting after meeting, just smiling, not saying anything. Well, I want to hear you speak. I think we have a right to hear your explanation. Let's hear from Dr. Selig. Let's hear whether he can speak, or whether he can only smile."

Dr. Selig rose slowly, still smiling. "I'll speak. But I will give in to no parent. I rated Mrs. Wachtel satisfactory because, with my professionally developed sensitivity, I judged her satisfactory. I've been to the school. I think she's doing a satisfactory job. I haven't seen any of the terror you speak of."

"You call kids being attacked in the bathroom normal?" I shot out.

"It happens all over the city," he answered.

"That makes it all right?" I said.

"No. But it's not something peculiar to your school."

"Listen to him still playing games," someone said. "Let's get out of here. What's the point of wasting any more time?"

Jessica tried to stop us.

"Let me try to explain," she said. "When a principal is transferred out of a district the change has to be approved by the district she is entering as well as the one she is leaving. We wrote to every district where Mrs. Wachtel might be accepted. All of them refused to accept her. Then we wrote to 110 Livingston Street. They told us they weren't taking any more principals."

A woman shouted, "Even they've had their fill of her."

"Under the decentralization plan," Jessica continued, "we have the illusion but not the reality of power against Mrs. Wachtel if there are charges to press; but our district superintendent rates her, and there's nothing we can do about the rating. There are a few unexplored possibilities, such as assigning her to the district office. We haven't discussed them yet. We just found out about the rating ourselves. But we'll discuss those possibilities."

RAY FISHER: "I was among those ten parents who went to 110 Livingston Street. And what they told me there was 'The trouble with the local school board is that they have no guts.'"

"Funny," Jessica replied, "what they tell me is that we have no power."

"Nobody gives you power," someone called out. "You have to take it."

And then we stormed out.

Outside the auditorium we were met by a reporter for the *Manhattan Tribune*, who wanted to know what our next move would be. We had had enough experience with the press by this time to trust them as much as we trusted the Board of Education, so we refused to tell her of our plans beyond saying that we would take some dramatic action and that we would take it soon. And so it was reported in the paper. I'm sure everyone trembled at the thought.

Late that night I got a phone call from Jessica, who told me that after the public meeting the board had met in executive session and had decided to transfer Mrs. Wachtel to the district office. Dr. Selig had agreed, and it was official, but she suggested that I call him the next day to confirm it.

"Hooray," I said. "Thanks."

"But there's a problem," she went on.

"There's always a problem," I said.

Jessica ignored that, and continued, "When she goes to the district office, she takes her salary line with her. That means PS 84 doesn't have a line to pay another principal."

"What does that mean?"

"Well, it means one of several things. We can take one of your APs and make her acting principal. I'd rather not do that."

"Neither would we."

"Another possibility is that we might find someone who has his own salary line and put him in the school. I've been exploring this, and there are a few people who might be possibilities."

"What about Mrs. Warner?" I asked. "She's got an AP license."

"But your other two APs have seniority over her. I don't think we can do that."

"What about Dan Harriman?" I asked. "I understand he's applied to the governing board."

"I'd be against that. He's already got a job in the district. I wouldn't want to take him away from his work and deprive the other children."

"Shouldn't that be his decision?"

"I'd be against it. But I'm working on those other possibilities. You call Dr. Selig tomorrow."

I thanked her and hung up and began to think where we were now. We were losing our principal and her salary line. To take someone else with a salary line would mean accepting someone who, for whatever reason, was on another school's payroll and working for some district or for the central board. And that meant that they were probably some other bureaucratic wonder. On the other hand, we could accept one of our APs, and that was also no solution. We had thought that once Mrs. Wachtel left, our problems would be, if not solved, at least lessened. Now it looked as though we had just gotten a different set. I still liked the idea of Dan Harriman, who had been a math teacher and chairman at Joan of Arc junior high school and had then become math coordinator for the district. He had spent a lot of time in our school during the strike, and we had been impressed with his approach to kids and to parents. Since the end of the strike, he had been coming to the school once a week to give a math workshop to parents and children; and those who were in the workshop spoke very highly of him, both as a teacher and as a human being. He had the added advantage of being familiar with the school, the children, and the district, and yet being from outside of the school and thus not aligned with any of the internal factions. And he was already being paid by the district, so that his salary line thing wouldn't present a problem. Maybe, I thought facetiously, he and Mrs. Wachtel could simply trade jobs.

The following morning at our Executive Board meeting I related my phone conversation with Jessica.

"She said that she would prefer not to make Mrs. Young acting principal, but she said that if the other possibilities don't work out that's our only alternative. But she says she won't put Mrs. Wachtel in the district office if it means that we'll scream that we've been screwed by Mrs. Young's appointment. She says we have to decide in advance."

ANNE: "We can't accept Mrs. Young. She'd be a bad principal."

I: "We can't keep Mrs. Wachtel either. Jessica said there was the possibility of someone with another salary line coming in. She mentioned a Mr. Morton who was in South Jamaica, and a Mr. Robbins, who used to be in this district and is now downtown. We might be able to work out some kind of switch that way. I suggested Dan Harriman, but Jessica said she wouldn't deprive the rest of the district of his services for us. Anyway, they want to meet with us on Thursday at the school board office to discuss all the possibilities. Mrs. Wachtel would be here through Friday. But Jessica says that before they make a decision she wants to know our reaction to Mrs. Young. I told her I could only speak for myself and for what I thought the other parents would say, and I said that I'd prefer another alternative. She asked what we'd do if there were no other alternative. I asked whether if we accepted Mrs. Young on a temporary basis it would mean that we couldn't react if she did something outrageous, and she answered that of course she didn't mean that. She just wanted to make sure that we didn't scream simply about the *fact* of the appointment, providing that was the only alternative. Of course if Mrs. Young did something awful she couldn't expect us to keep quiet."

Irene, who had not been at the school board meeting the previous evening, said that she had heard that we had been magnificent and that we had finally smoked out Dr. Selig and made him take responsibility for his actions.

"That's what we have to do here, too. Don't let them put us in the trap of consulting us and then telling us 'you made the decision.' That's what they did when Mrs. Wachtel was appointed. We should say, 'You are the professional, Dr. Selig. Who do you think will be best?' If we can make the actual choice, then we will be responsible for it, but if we can't, we won't decide for them."

ANNE: "I can't do that. I can't play that kind of game. I think we should recommend someone."

IRENE: "Don't you see, if you can't do the hiring, you have no choice. You just become the fall guy if things don't work out. We can provide criteria about the *kind* of person we want, but we can't make the decision so we shouldn't be stuck with the responsibility. I know Mr. Robbins. I think he'd be O.K. on an interim basis. He's a decent guy. I don't know Morton, but I'll check him out with my sources in South Jamaica."

Someone asked whether we should call off our lame-duck demonstration, and we decided that we wouldn't unless we heard from Dr. Selig that the transfer was actually going through. Gwen Palmer and I went off to call him, and he confirmed what Jessica had said. Then, because by this time we were most untrusting of everyone, we sent off a letter confirming our telephone conversation, which letter offended Dr. Selig, who felt we didn't trust him.

We decided to meet again shortly before the meeting with Dr. Selig and the school board on Thursday to lay out our strategy, and Irene suggested that we play things close to the vest. By this time she had checked out Morton's credentials and found them satisfactory, but she argued that we not share this bit of information with Dr. Selig and the school board lest it be taken as a sign of our compliance, to be used against us later if we found Morton unsatisfactory in fact and if the board and Selig, not wanting another scene, said that we had agreed on his choice and must therefore abide by it. Some of us questioned the wisdom of this advice; but Irene is a powerful convincer, and we agreed to follow the policy of reacting rather than acting. It had, after all, worked well in our encounters with Mrs. Wachtel. The agreed-upon strategy, then, was to listen, to caucus, and to say, "if that's your decision, do it."

The school board had just acquired offices across the street from my house in a storefront. Since it was still rather bare and unfinished, our voices echoed in the empty quarters. Jessica, Mr. Somers, Celia Cohen and Dr. Selig represented the district, while for the parents there were Irene, Ronnie, Mike Goodman, Ruth King, Violet Morton, Meg Knight, Beth Barron, and I. The meeting began with Jessica's announcement that Mrs. Wachtel would be transferred to the district office as of Monday, February 10, and that Mrs. Young would be acting principal with as brief a tenure as possible, until a successor could be selected.

"The salary line for Mrs. Wachtel remains at PS 84 until she gets another position, so there are no vacancies at the school for either principal or assistant principal."

She said she would try to get someone of supervisory status with a salary line, and she suggested Mr. Morton and asked whether we knew anything about him. Silence (uncomfortable on my part, and, I'm sure, on the part of many of the other parents).

Dr. Selig said that we were in a bind about the money line, that he had been trying to get a line, that he had spoken to the Board of Ed, and that they had no job for Mrs. Wachtel there. He said that if we could get Mr. Morton we would, in effect, be getting an administrator free of charge. He said he had checked his references and that he thought Mr. Morton had a lot going for him.

IRENE: "We will have to explore the money question and the budget line at a later time. Do you, Dr. Selig, suggest we explore Mr. Morton?"

Dr. Selig nodded yes. I asked whether the possibility didn't exist that if we accepted Mrs. Young on a temporary basis she might not, in fact, be with us forever. Both Jessica and Dr. Selig said no, it would only be for a short time.

"How short?" I asked.

"Not more than for a few weeks," Dr. Selig answered. "A month at the most." (That period of a few weeks was to stretch into nine months.)

Ruth King asked whether Friday was truly to be Mrs. Wachtel's last day. Dr. Selig assured us that it was, although he had acceded to her request that she be given a few additional days to gather up her personal effects. But he assured us that after Friday at 3:00 P.M. she would no longer be in a position of authority.

Sunday evening we had another meeting at my house. We reviewed the session we had had with Dr. Selig and the others, and I told the other parents that Dr. Selig had subsequently informed me that Mr. Morton was not interested in our school. Mr. Robbins, the other possibility, had, unfortunately, died suddenly. That left us with only Mrs. Young as a contender; and faced with that awesome prospect, we again thought of Dan Harriman, whom we called and invited to join us.

He came, a tall, slim man in his early thirties, dressed in blue jeans, and explained that he had a line at the district office—a teacher's line.

"Theoretically, I cover twenty-three schools, which is, of course, physically impossible. I work in only some schools. Some ask for me, some I seek out, some don't want my help. APs are supposed to train teachers, but they don't. I go to a school, work out a program of demonstration lessons and workshops to explore methods and materials. I have considered the alternatives, and I would take full responsibility for this decision. My reasons for being interested in the position at 84 are that there is real community involvement there. The school has the making of something very good educationally. I can see that you are in a position of not wanting the situation with Mrs. Young to take hold."

IRENE: "I am in a position of wanting someone other than Mrs. Young, but I don't want to make a parent commitment to anyone without knowing who is available. We're now looking for an *acting* principal. We haven't explored all the possibilities."

WALTER: "We don't want to lead you on, either."

I: "What would you want from us?"

DAN: "An assurance that I would be there for a reasonable period of time—till June, at least."

I: "Have you any idea how the district would react to this proposal?"

DAN, with a grin: "Dr. Selig would like to get rid of me."

The meeting was adjourned with no conclusion, and the following day dawned under the aegis of our new acting principal. On Tuesday, she asked the Executive Board to come to a meeting with her and the teachers to develop a "comprehensive plan for the school." This immediately raised some problems. Since we had been assured that her tenure was to be short, we were not sure that we wanted her working out any comprehensive plans. On the other hand, everyone agreed that the school was a mess, and that something had to be done. The issue was further complicated by the fact that we were still trying to get the school board to consider Dan Harriman, and he had asked us not to meet with Mrs. Young since he felt that would be legitimizing her position. Furthermore, since Mrs. Young had not invited any of the nonstriking teachers to the meeting, she really could not make any comprehensive plans without dividing the school yet again. I was in a quandary. I was interested in Mr. Harriman. I did not want to undermine our nonstriking teachers. But I didn't see how I could boycott the meeting. I decided, therefore, that we should go, but that our position would be that we could not discuss anything unless all teachers were represented. Mr. Harriman was, I think, disappointed, and took our going as an indication that we would not be willing to fight to get him.

The meeting never got off the ground. Mrs. Young began by introducing herself and the teachers present, and I, in turn, introduced the parents. I then requested that I be allowed to make a statement from the Executive Board: that the teachers present had been elected at a UFT meeting and that other members of the staff were displeased because they could not be represented. I said that the PA was unwilling to meet with a group of teachers who could not be considered representative of the total faculty and that the aim of the PA was not to take sides in this matter, but to encourage communication between all members of the faculty and the parent body.

Jenny Silverman explained that the UFT represented all the teachers in any school and that there had been an "open" UFT meeting called on Friday, February 7, to which all teachers had been invited by flier. At that meeting the UFT executive committee had proposed a slate (Mrs. Silverman had invited Mrs. Warner to be on the slate, and she had refused), and nominations were also requested from the floor. Mrs. Warner had been nominated and had declined. Four teachers and two alternates were subsequently elected.

Ronnie said that the parents appreciated Mrs. Silverman's efforts, but the fact must be faced that at present a UFT meeting could not include all teachers. Mrs. Young said that as soon as Dr. Selig had informed her that she would be acting principal she had proceeded to set up this committee to begin to work on solving the problems in the school. She felt that on a cooperative basis we could bring the school back to where it had been. We objected to that, and she said, "Well, to where it should be." Ronnie said again that we appreciated the effort but that the situation was still so unsettled that the most we could do would be to discuss any plans for this week.

The rest of the nonmeeting was given over to a discussion of how teachers should be chosen to represent the entire staff, which led one of the teachers to retort that perhaps they should decide how the parents for the committee should be selected. It was obvious that the oil had not yet been poured on the troubled waters.

We had promised ourselves a party when Mrs. Wachtel was truly gone. Now she was, and we went ahead with our preparations. We posted invitations to all parents and staff in the school. We rented the community room of Beth Barron's co-op. (We had decided against having the party in the school because we did not think Mr. O'Malley shared our joy in our victory, and also because we were not sure what the rules were on serving drinks—even to consenting adults—in school buildings.) We invited the governing board and the school board (the latter declined) and all the people who had helped us throughout the long months. And we went home and cooked and baked. I baked a cheesecake, which I do only for very special occasions. Everyone made something special. We put on party clothes and went to celebrate.

The community room was decorated and the mood festive. My only problem was that I was walking around with a fever of 102° and was therefore slightly dazed, but this was one party I wasn't going to miss, even if they had to take me home in an ambulance. It wasn't quite necessary. We were veterans who had survived a long and bitter battle. Much of the conversation that night had that flavor. There was much reminiscing. Do you remember when she said that "I will remain until removed under due process"? And so forth. And the time we thought she was going to have us all arrested. And the time. And the time. And throughout it all ran the refrain "We've won, we've won." If Dan Harriman was a bit cool and if in the back of our minds was the thought that Mrs. Young was now our principal, it did not dampen our spirits. We had made it, had done the impossible, and if there were further battles ahead we would fight those, too. Having won this one, we were confident that we could win the others.

I was still in bed with my flu the following Monday when I got a phone call from Mrs. Young demanding an explanation of an article in the latest issue of the *Manhattan Tribune*. I am not a subscriber to that paper and am not sufficiently interested in it to have gotten someone to get me a copy, so I had no idea what she wanted explained. She therefore read me part of an article that dealt with the reassignment of Mrs. Wachtel and that quoted me as saying, "We feel the same way about Mrs. Young as we did about Mrs. Wachtel, only more so."

I had, indeed, spoken to the reporter, but I hadn't said that. I apologized to Mrs. Young, who asked what she had done to deserve that from me. So I repeated that I had been misquoted, which was not unusual for that paper.

But the incident pointed up how shaky the peace in the school was. Though it is true that that was not what *I* had said, certainly lots of people *had* said it; and though up until this point Mrs. Young had been most cordial and sweet and warm to the children and cooperative to parents, there was, nevertheless, the memory of her whistle and her attitudes. And the feeling on the part of many parents was that we had gone from the frying pan with Mrs. Wachtel into the fire with Mrs. Young.

TWENTY-FIVE

"Anything You Say"

Mrs. Young wanted very much to be principal of PS 84. She bent over backwards to accommodate herself to the parents' wishes. Thus, when the question of the community room came up again (there were various teachers who were less than thrilled with our continued presence in the school, and some who felt the room could have been more constructively used by a teacher or teachers), it was on a most tentative basis. Mrs. Young began by saying that the school was desperately in need of space and that several cluster teachers, notably the art and science teachers, were forced to carry their materials with them. Could they, she asked, use part of the room to store their things? We thought that would present no problems. Would it also be possible for teachers to use the room for part of the day without the parents being present? That was another matter. We would very much like teachers to feel free to use the room, and to that end we would appreciate it if Mrs. Young would rescind Mrs. Wachtel's order to the staff to stay away from there. But as far as vacating it for part of each day we really could not agree, since the realities of the situation don't fit such restrictions. Parents come in and use the room when they have the time —not on a set schedule. Nancy Sergeant, who was in charge of publicity for the PA, pointed out that she came in at odd times to work on fliers and bulletins. She said we could get more and more people in if the time was flexible, but that once you had to give the room up for some portion of each day then it was no longer, strictly speaking, a parents' room.

MRS. YOUNG: "I was thinking of the children. We want to be able to display their artwork. But if you feel so strongly about it, we'll

255

forget it for now. I've done two master schedules already. I'll just do another one."

IRENE: "There's a whole bureau at the Board of Ed that does space utilization studies. I suggest we look into this service to see how we can best utilize the school."

MRS. YOUNG: "Find out who is in charge, and I'll contact them."

IRENE: "What's missing is the concept. A lot happened in the year you were gone. The role of parents is a real one in the education of their children, and this room is essential."

MRS. YOUNG: "We'll drop the matter for now, and I'll rescind Mrs. Wachtel's order. I had no idea she had issued one."

ELIZABETH O'SHEA: "It's probably not written down."

MRS. YOUNG: "When I say 'we' I want to mean parents, teachers, the total school community. We can all learn more." And we kept our room.

Things at the school began to quiet down. I think there was a great feeling of relief on the part of many of us that someone had appeared on the scene who could, at the least, push a piece of paper. Also, because of Mrs. Young's reputation, perhaps the kids—especially the older ones who had had past experiences with her—were treading softly, and so the chaos in the halls and bathrooms, the threats and actual instances of violence, began to die down; and though we never for a minute considered Mrs. Young as a permanent replacement, still we were glad of a respite from the daily turmoil.

She wanted to please us. At a meeting held in the spring for next year's kindergarten parents (of which I was one, for Maggie was entering in the fall), she spoke glowingly of the infant school and promised that every parent who wanted his child in the program would have his request honored—that if there were not enough classes she would create additional ones. Still, though she paid homage to the program, she did not seem to understand its underlying philosophy. When she went to observe teachers whose classes were run along these lines, she still expected to see a formal lesson plan and was annoyed when none was presented. Her criticisms of these teachers, moreover, tended to concern themselves more with housekeeping than with things of substance. The teachers complained that while an exciting learning experience was in progress Mrs. Young saw only that the window shades were unevenly aligned.

Again, though she verbally supported the program, she did nothing to eliminate roadblocks to its functioning. The custodian regularly called in the fire department for alleged violations of the fire laws—children working in the corridors or examples of their work on the walls—and she made no attempt to cool his ire. Whenever anything innovative was attempted, she was always ready with reasons why it was not possible; and according to various people, she had to be led by the hand through every step, and at the first difficulty she was ready to say it didn't work.

As to our community room, we complained constantly that the custodial staff bypassed it in its rounds. Garbage didn't even get taken away unless Mr. Rhodes was on duty. And we were told that if *we* didn't keep it cleaner, we would be summarily evicted.

And yet, in her own way, she tried. On one occasion a group of us went in to her to complain about the departmentalization in the upper grades. We were, again, a most diverse group ethnically. When we presented our opposition to tracking and to departmentalization, Mrs. Young seemed genuinely surprised. I think what really floored her was that a group of middle-class mothers whose children were likely, in any case, to be in the top track, should want tracking ended. She could, I suppose, understand why parents of kids on the bottom might make such a demand, but us? She wanted to hear our reasons, and we gave them—again: All children benefit from heterogeneous grouping; tracking is damaging to all children, those who get an inflated sense of their worth as well as those who are made to feel like failures; tracking tended to resegregate the school; children tend to live up to the expectations adults have of them, as studies have shown; and so forth. To all this, Mrs. Young listened attentively. When we were finished, she said,

"All right, if you don't want departmentalization, we won't have it." And it was done—as simply as that. Now if that wasn't community control, what was? Poor lady, I'm sure she couldn't understand why we still didn't want her permanently when she was being so accommodating!

Meanwhile, screening was to begin for a new principal when the local school board realized that it did not have a salary line with which to hire anyone. Their screening thus ground to an abrupt halt before it began. The Joan of Arc governing board, on the other hand, was bound by no such technicalities. Since, in effect, their entire search for a principal was extralegal (they had no power to install anyone unless the school board agreed), they simply told

each prospective candidate what the situation was. Those who were
sufficiently interested in the idea of parent control were willing to
take the gamble. The others, forewarned, were free to decline and
go through more legitimate channels in their search for a principal's
job.

I was not involved in the earliest sessions of the governing board
panel, but I got reports from the parents who were on it, and they
said that there were several promising candidates. The first two
sessions of the panel had been spent not in interviewing candidates,
but in thrashing out a set of criteria for a principal. In this regard,
Preston Wilcox, who had, in addition to his educational credentials,
several years of experience with the IS 201 governing board under
his belt, was most helpful. The questions he asked were sharp and
to the point. He was able, when the actual screening began, to cut
through a lot of the parents' reticence in getting down to important
issues. And on the subject of establishing criteria his help was also
invaluable.

The important thing to realize about criteria in the search for a
principal is that there really have never been any. In the past the
method of principal selection was simple: the candidates took a test
consisting of a written part, a performance part, and an evaluative
part (of their record of performance in their other jobs in the system). According to the rules, a candidate must have served a number of years *within the New York City system* as a teacher and another
stint as a supervisor *within the New York City system* before he became
eligible to take a principal's exam. This of course, ensures that very
few new or original ideas are likely to come from any of the aspirants
and that, having come up through the system, they will be loyal to
it. Every once in a while, nothing being perfect, even this procedure
fails and you get, in spite of the screening process, a maverick like
Eliot Shapiro* who uses the system for the kids instead of for the
professionals. But for the most part this testing process works very
well to produce a uniform set of principals, and the corollary to this

---

*Former principal of PS 119 in Harlem, who had bucked the Board of Ed
and Mayor Wagner for the sake of his children. To demonstrate the need
for a new school, he flushed a rat out of hiding and chased it across the
auditorium stage when Mayor Wagner paid a visit. He subsequently became
Superintendent of District #2 in Manhattan. (See Nat Hentoff's *Our Children Are Dying.*)

is, therefore, that any principal can be put into any school and administer it. Like rifle parts, they are interchangeable. This may have worked, once upon a time, when schools were more homogeneous—though I doubt that, too. Certainly it wasn't working anymore, as evidenced by the numerous cases in the papers of schools bouncing duly licensed and certified principals because they were incapable of functioning there. The key here is that they *were* all licensed, which the unions used as proof of their competence. The communities, on the other hand, argued that this was proof that the licensing procedure was faulty.

The tests themselves, even where the content may be relevant, prove nothing, since there are individuals skilled at taking tests who are incapable of translating theoretical knowledge into execution. It is also possible to know what the proper thing to do is in a given circumstance and yet not be able to do it. So that all the tests prove is that those who pass tests can pass tests. It does not, necessarily, mean that they can administer schools or relate to children and other forms of life. But with all this testing there is no set of criteria that anyone can point to and say this or that is essential for a principal. And this is what the screening panel attempted to do. What they finally came up with was a set of criteria:*

1. That he be able to absorb, understand, and implement educational ideas and programs.
2. That he be able to grow and develop as a professional.
3. That he be able to understand and respect children as human beings.
4. That he be honest and fair with children, parents, community, and staff.
5. That he have a sense of humor.
6. That he have an imaginative approach to school programs and be informed about new educational ideas and programs.
7. That he be informed and involved in community activities.
8. That he be committed to the idea that low-income people have the right and capacity to be responsible for their children's education.
9. That he keep the community board and general community regularly informed.
10. That while supervising his staff he
    a. is considerate of teachers' needs and wishes.
    b. is a leader.
    c. respects his staff.

*Extracts from data provided by Professor Preston Wilcox *re:* Criteria for Principals. February 6, 1969.

d. is creative in planting seeds of new ideas for teachers to accept and develop.
e. encourage and support his staff.
f. is interested in his staff as human beings as well as their classroom performances.
g. is responsible for the performance of his staff and students.
h. recruit community people to work in the school; and encourage his teachers to develop an understanding plus an appreciation of the community.

A set of questions aimed at finding out the kind of human being the prospective principal was also was drafted. These were the questions and we used them not only in the Joan of Arc screenings, but also later when the school board began its search anew. It is surprising how much came out about the various candidates as a result:

SCREENING COMMITTEE QUESTIONS

1. Is the candidate a human being? (more an area than a question)*
2. How will the candidate relate to the community, to parents, and seek out community resources?*
3. What does the candidate know about PS 84? Has he visited the school? If not, why not? Why is he applying to PS 84?*
4. How does the candidate feel about being interviewed by a screening panel of parents, teachers, and paraprofessionals?
5. How would the candidate feel if he were called at 11 P.M. or 1 A.M. to deal with a school problem?
6. Does the candidate live in or near the PS 84 community?
7. Has the candidate interviewed for other schools? Is he being discriminate, or does he just want to be principal anywhere?
8. To what does the candidate attribute lack of learning in children?*
9. What can be done to help teachers, especially those who are working in experimental programs (such as the Infant School)?
10. What do you think of the Bereiter-Engelman† system of learning?
11. What is your position on discipline?*
12. How do you think tests (of all kinds) should be used and evaluated?*
13. What are your criteria for evaluating teachers and teaching?*
14. How do you feel about the initiation of a bilingual school?*
15. Where, in your view, does the buck stop if the children aren't learning?*

*Asterisks denote priority questions.
†A highly structured rote-learning method that has found favor in some quarters.

The Joan of Arc panel was willing to interview anyone, on or off the eligible list. Thus, to our amazement, they soon got an application from Mrs. Young. Since she had, in the past, hardly been a strong advocate of community control, it came as something of a shock; but it illustrated again how badly she wanted the job. Obviously, if the governing board was the route, she would take that, too. She was duly scheduled for an interview, and we were all determined that she be treated with the same courtesy afforded to all the other aspirants.

About this time I began to attend the Joan of Arc screening sessions, since I was now president of the PA. In addition, since neither Edna nor Carmen had been able to attend most of the sessions, I appointed Jenny Romero and Norma Hill in their places. The first session I attended we were screening a man by the name of Jack Molloy. A short, muscular man in his late thirties, and the father of nine children, he had been a principal and a superintendent in an upstate suburb. He had left those posts to become a coordinator of an agency providing training and employment for blacks and Puerto Ricans, in particular for teen-aged migrant workers. We asked him why he was willing to take a demotion—not to mention the risk of casting his lot with our powerless group—and his answer was that he felt that community control was the last answer to save the dying public schools. He feared the rise of industry in the education field (the proliferation of firms getting into the performance-contract business) and felt that unless public education could succeed we would find, in a few years, that we had bought a package we could not control. As an educator that scared him.

What impressed us about Jack Molloy from the outset was his strength. Although his general philosophy seemed in tune with ours, we did not get the impression that he was saying things simply to please us. On several issues he had definite ideas that did not coincide completely with ours. But in general he was looking for the kind of education we were. Nancy Calvert asked him what he would look for when he passed a classroom.

"Let me tell you what I wouldn't look for. I wouldn't want to see the kids sitting quietly in their seats. If I passed a room and there was dead silence or only the sound of the teacher's voice droning on, I'd worry about that class. Kids don't learn that way. I'm not saying I'd want to see them hanging from the chandeliers, but I would want to see them alive, excited, participating actively in what was going on."

His answer on the reasons kids fail was equally satisfactory. Unlike Mrs. Wachtel, who had cited as the cause for failure everything but the school, Mr. Molloy believed that if the business of the school was education then it must be held responsible for the failure to educate.

"I know it's popular in educational circles to say that if children don't learn it's their fault, or their environment's fault, but that's nonsense. Schools have to take children *as they are* and somehow, teach them. If one method doesn't work with particular children, you can't change the children, so you change the method. And that means teacher retraining, too. That's one of the areas I feel a lot of work has to be done in."

"What would you do with a teacher who was hopeless?"

"I'd work with her. I'd support her. I'd get someone in there every day to show her the way. And if, after a reasonable period of time nothing changed, well then, I'm afraid she'd have to go."

"But that would get you into a fight with the UFT and the Board of Education if she was tenured."

"Look. I'm an Irishman. I'm not afraid of a fight, or I wouldn't be here."

"What's your opinion on suspensions?"

"What do they solve? You suspend a child and then what? Is there any place for him to go after that? What educational purpose is served by suspending him? You've got to do two things: you have to look at the class situation that makes a child act out. Maybe he's bored. Maybe he's not being properly handled. If that's the case, then you have to work with the classroom situation and improve that. If that's not the cause—if you're dealing with a seriously disturbed child—then suspension is still no answer. Then you have to get help for him; and in the meantime, because even if he gets help his problems won't disappear overnight, you have to find the kind of school situation that will sustain him. Because even troubled children have a right to an education. If you suspend them and they lose their chance at learning, then you merely compound their problems when they return."

We asked him what kind of a commitment he would want from us if we selected him. Here, too, his answer was a refreshing change from most of the "professionals" we had dealt with in the past. He said, "If I can't do the job you want, I wouldn't expect you to keep me. All I'd ask would be two months' notice to give me a chance to get another job. I get more offers than I know what to do with, so I'm not worried. If I can't be the kind of principal you want, then I shouldn't stay."

After the formal interview ended, he stayed around for a while to chat, and our impression of him as a solid, decent guy, with a sense of humor and an open mind, was strengthened. After he left we discussed our impressions. We went around the room and each of us gave our views, and the consensus was that he was worth investigating further.

NANCY: "I like his ideas on what he'd look for in a class."

NORMA: "He seems straight. I didn't get the feeling from him that he uses black in quotation marks the way so many people do. He seemed very comfortable."

PETE: "I liked his views on community control."

I: "I think he could unite the staff. He seems like a strong guy, and his educational ideas are the kind I'm interested in. But he's got enough degrees and credentials to soothe some of our more traditional staff members. And he seems fair."

We decided that a group of us would take a ride to his community, to talk to parents there, to talk to the teachers and principals with whom he had worked, to see whether he looked as good on his home grounds as he had during the interview. Since we didn't want anyone coached in advance we didn't tell Mr. Molloy of our forthcoming expedition.

Dan Harriman had been interviewed by the panel earlier. I had not been present at that interview, but those who had been were impressed by his humanity and by his feeling for children, as well as by his views on education. He was very much interested in the infant school—individualized instruction—as a way to reach all children. He felt teacher-training (which was what he did as math coordinator) was essential to improving schools and saw that as his chief responsibility as a principal. He said that under the present setup principals had no time for this, but that he would rather neglect paper work to work with teachers.

His manner during the interview, I was told, was hesitant. He had no easy answers. The thing that bothered the parents about him, mainly, was his lack of experience, and though they felt he could learn on the job, they worried whether this particular job—crisis-laden as it was—would permit the luxury of on-the-job training. In spite of this reservation, he was certainly a serious contender.

Several others had also been seen. Mrs. Young, though she had been given an appointment, did not come and told someone the following day that she had heard that the panel had already made up its mind and so her coming for an interview would have been wasted effort. This was not the case. We had not yet chosen any candidate and we had intended to interview her fairly. However, from that moment on the tone of the school and Mrs. Young's attitude toward parents began to change. She was no longer so accommodating. We got several nasty comments about the filthy condition of the community room. We were told that we should stay out of classrooms as our presence was disruptive of the educational process. We had had a meeting of parents of Kathy's class, and one of the topics was the desirability of introducing Spanish into the curriculum. The suggestion had been made to start slowly, by labeling certain familiar objects—such as the door, the window, the books—with both the English and Spanish word and increasing these labels weekly so as to give the children a certain basic vocabulary. Since Mrs. Austin's paraprofessional was Spanish-speaking and since at least one-third of the children were too, it seemed like a natural opportunity for them to learn in this manner. We had all been excited by the prospect, and Mrs. Austin had gone home and written up a detailed, week by week, plan of the experiment. She took it to Mrs. Young, and, as she later told me, "I felt as though someone had thrown cold water on me." Mrs. Young said curtly, "No, you can't do it." When Mrs. Austin pressed for a reason, she was told, "This is America. The children should learn English."

With the prospect of parent approval of her hopes slipping away, the honeymoon came to an end.

TWENTY-SIX

The Governing Board's Solution

The flier for a parents' meeting for Tuesday, March 25, read:

WILL WE HAVE A PS 84 PRINCIPAL IN SEPTEMBER?

1. Local School Board #5 *is not screening* candidates

2. Joan of Arc Governing Board *is screening* candidates BUT . . .

DISCUSSION: *WHAT DO WE DO NOW?*

At the meeting we informed the parents of the school board's refusal to screen until the question of a money line was resolved. They said they were still trying to find Mrs. Wachtel a job, but without success to date. They were also continuing to put pressure on the central board with equal lack of success, and so they felt there was no point in going through the screening. We then told the parents about the screening the Joan of Arc panel had been doing and that there were several promising candidates. We said, further, that when the panel made its final choice that candidate would be presented to the parent body for their approval before the selection became complete. No candidate would be selected unless he met with the approval of the parents. However, once the selection was made, we still had the problem of installing that person as principal, and this would be where the fight would come in. The school board was unlikely to act unless it was forced to. Therefore, how could we force them to accept our choice after it was made? It was suggested that we write to the school board again and ask them to proceed with their interviewing, which I did. The answer was that they "could not,

265

in all fairness, request that candidates come for an interview for a position that does not yet exist."

So we decided to go back to Dr. Selig, who still was the person with the power to do something, and to point out to him that his contract ran out in June. What we would ask was that they go downtown with us to support our demand that a line must be cleared so that, come September, we would have a new principal and would not lose another year in the kind of turmoil we had had. One way or another—and this we must make clear to Dr. Selig—we would have a new principal in September. We set our demonstration for April 16 ("Do we still have the duck?" I asked) and sent out a flier asking all parents to join us.

"We demand that Dr. Selig find money to pay full salary for a new principal—chosen by the parents and the elected governing board, and accountable to them. NOW!"

Interestingly, Mrs. Young cheered us on. She still considered herself a contender, and I imagine she wanted the pay to go with the position when she got it.

Wednesday, April 16, dawned cold and gray. We assembled in the community room and waited for a while for latecomers to join us. In addition to the PS 84 parents, Otis Grace, an organizer recently hired by the Joan of Arc governing board, was also there. We marched, about fifteen strong, from PS 84 to PS 75, joined along the way by Violet Morton and Phyllis Miles who were waiting in front of their house. When we got to PS 75 it was raining, but still we marched outside of Selig's office for a while, chanting that we needed a principal. We had called the press and the various TV channels, but no one was there. A few curious onlookers watched us for a few minutes, then passed by. One man muttered something about crazy radicals and that we should all be locked up. A squad car stood by, its dry occupants watching us getting soaked. It was now raining steadily. Some of us had umbrellas which we shared as best we could, but it was raw and the rain cold, and no one from inside the district office gave any indication that they were aware of our presence. Finally I decided that this was silly. Our purpose had been to embarrass Dr. Selig publicly, since that was the one thing that seemed to move him; and to that end, to get the press and TV to cover our demonstration. Apparently, though, parent demonstrations were no longer news, even if they were integrated demonstrations as ours was, and we couldn't even raise the *Manhattan*

Tribune. Thus, since at the moment only we were getting public exposure there seemed no further point in our catching pneumonia. On the other hand, we were not ready to give up so easily.

Had it not been raining, we would probably have remained outside. Going into Dr. Selig's office had not been part of the game plan. But the rain made it clear that we would soon lose our line, and so I suggested that we go inside. Thus, the rain which we had cursed, turned out to be a good thing. We filed into the district office, past several startled secretaries. Mrs. Wachtel, now working at the district office, was nowhere in sight. (Someone must have warned her of our demonstration for she had taken the day off.) We were stopped by Dr. Selig's assistant who told us that he was not in. "Fine," we said, "we'll wait," and before she could say anything else we had walked past her into Dr. Selig's inner sanctum. We seated ourselves around his large conference table, and those who couldn't get seats stood against the wall. Otis, a large, handsome man in a dashiki, seated himself in Dr. Selig's swivel chair and announced, amid our laughter, that he had just fired Dr. Selig and that he was our new superintendent, Superintendent X.

"What can I do for you?" he asked.

"We need a new principal for PS 84, but we don't have a line to pay for one. We want you, as superintendent, to do something."

"Well," he said, "I have good news for you. The Joan of Arc governing board has come up with a solution. Since you need a principal, and since there's no money, the governing board is willing to offer the Board of Education the salary to pay for a principal of the parents' choice for four months."

We applauded this news and asked for further details. Otis told us that the governing board had voted the previous evening to make the PS 84 parents this offer, which he was now doing. If Dr. Selig and the school board accepted, we could finish our screening process and install the new principal. If they did not accept, we could expose the superintendent and the school board when they said there was no money to pay for a new principal. We would also then have the additional option of trying to install him without official sanction or of installing him across the street and making that PS 84 in exile. But hopefully the school board and Dr. Selig would agree to accept the money, and we would get a community-control principal who would, since he would be hired by the parents rather than by the establishment, be accountable to the parents.

The idea of being Superintendent X tickled Otis, and he sat back in the swivel chair, arms folded comfortably behind his back and began to make some phone calls to people he knew on various newspapers, announcing that a group of PS 84 parents had taken over the superintendent's office and would not leave until they got what they wanted: namely, a new principal for their school. Still no one from any paper showed up. Dr. Selig did though, after a while, and he seemed somewhat ruffled to see so many of us in his office. He asked what we wanted, and we told him. Otis also told him of the governing board's offer.

"Who are you?" asked Dr. Selig.

"I'm Superintendent X. I've taken over your job."

Dr. Selig smiled wryly. He sat down at another chair near his desk and began reading through some papers. We sat. Someone had gone out for lunch and coffee, and we now began to eat. After a while, Dr. Selig left. We stayed.

I had made arrangements for the kids to spend the afternoon with friends, so I was under no pressure to get home. Some of the other parents couldn't stay, but they sent others to take their place, and so though the cast of characters changed throughout the afternoon the numbers remained fairly constant. Sue Neal and Father Cody from Stryckers Bay came to pay us a visit. Various governing board members also dropped by, as did parents from some of the other schools in the district. One of the things that had happened throughout the year had been that whenever one school had been in trouble the others had rallied round. Thus, when one school had been boycotted by its parents to demand that an acting AP be given the permanent position, a group of us had gone, in the bitter cold, to augment their picket line. Now they were doing the same for us —dropping in to show their moral support.

Dr. Selig came back and fiddled some more with the papers on his desk. After a while he said, "I'm afraid I'll have to ask you to leave. I have work to do."

"Sorry," we said, "we can't leave till we have an answer."

"I can't give you an answer," he said. He left again. It continued like that throughout the afternoon. Dr. Selig would come in for a while, ask us to leave, and retreat again when we refused. At no point did he threaten to call the police. I don't know what would have happened if he had. I for one did not intend to get arrested, at least not at that point.

The mood in the office was festive. Visitors were greeted joyfully. People went in and out to get refreshments. Each new arrival was introduced to Superintendent X. Outside it continued to pour, but we were in out of the rain and enjoying ourselves. We were all really very civilized law-abiding citizens; but we had been given so many runarounds, treated with such a lack of respect for our opinions by Dr. Selig, that none of us felt in the least guilty at this takeover. If someone had said to me two years earlier that I would be involved in such a sit-in, I wouldn't have believed it, and yet here I was, with no intention of going away quietly. Thus the system makes its own militants. And since in the end it always gives at the point of greatest pressure, one would think that by now they would have learned to do what is right, simply because sooner or later they are forced to do it anyway. But the amount of energy that is wasted, both in the pressuring and in the resistance, is enormous, and could more usefully be applied to improving the schools.

The afternoon wore on.

"How long are you going to stay?" Dr. Selig asked at one point.

"Till you give us an answer," we said.

"I don't have the authority to make that kind of decision."

"Who does?" we asked.

"The school board."

"Then get them down here," we said.

"I can't," he said and left again.

"Why don't we call the school board?" I suggested.

We did, one member after another. Several had other commitments. Bob refused to knuckle under to pressure. Celia was sick. But Jessica said she'd come after work, and she did.

She was mad when she came in, "I ought to be home making supper for my family." A while later she was furious, because Otis' position was that either you're with us or you're against us; and if you're on the school board, you're probably against us. He treated her in the same cavalier manner he had been using on Dr. Selig. Now Dr. Selig had it coming, but Jessica really didn't, and I was somewhat annoyed that Otis couldn't make fine distinctions. However, we had agreed that he should be our spokesman, and speak he did. Jessica listened as he outlined the governing board's proposal, and she asked a couple of practical questions as to how the money was to be paid to the person, who would hire him, and so forth. When she said she couldn't make any unilateral decisions but must consult with her entire board, Otis again was less than gentle. At one point she turned to me and said,

"Why are you letting him do all the talking? Why don't you say something?"

"He's our spokesman," I answered, feeling about three inches tall.

She turned her back on me and went into the other office, where a proposal was drafted by her and Otis, which proposal they then came back to read to us. Jessica made it clear that her board would have to approve, but that she would sign the draft and urge the other board members to accept it too. The proposal stated that

1. A demand is to be made of the Board of Education that it allocate an additional position to PS 84 for the purpose of providing an acting principal to be funded by a contribution by the Joan of Arc governing board to the Board of Education earmarked for this purpose only.
2. The Local School Board will interview and nominate a person to fill the position of acting principal, the interviews and evaluation to be done with three parents elected by the parent body and one staff member elected by the teachers.
3. Accountability procedures for PS 84 will be worked out by the local school board, district superintendent, parents, staff, supervisors, and community along these lines:

A committee of PS 84 parents, staff, and community will be established to review regularly with the principal the school program and problems.

Thus, having wrung this agreement out of the school board, we went home. Jessica did send a telegram to John Doar, President of the Board of Education, and to Dr. Donovan, Superintendent of Schools, and in due course the answer came: we have no additional positions for the school, but you can use one of the assistant principals in the school. It completely ignored the offer of the governing board to provide the money.

Meanwhile, back on the homefront all was not sweetness and light either. During most of the fight about Mrs. Wachtel, the governing board had been inactive. They had come in only at the tail end. Then, with the hiring of Otis Grace, the governing board began to rouse itself, but there were constant snide remarks from its members about those PS 84 parents who seemed more interested in getting a new principal than in the principle of community control. This had taken the form of attacks on certain parents, as well as of their exclusion from certain governing board functions. For example, the board had invited Gordon Hill, an expert on the British Infant School visiting in the States, to address interested parents after a dinner in his honor. I had been invited to the dinner, but neither Millie nor Dotty, the chairmen of the PS 84 Infant School Committee, had been invited. Neither had Mrs. Weber. In addition, when the governing board had been looking for a writer organizer, though they had solicited applications from the community, they had chosen someone from the "in group" without so much as the courtesy of a reply to the other applicants. Though these may both have been small slights in the larger scheme of things, they seemed to us to be symptomatic of an attitude on the part of the governing board and its supporters that either you were part of them or you were nothing. And since the whole point was the involvement of *all* parents it seemed a poor way of proceeding. As these feelings intensified, I felt it was necessary for us to meet with the governing board and to thrash things out, because if we were going to go forward together this kind of antagonism could not continue. I spoke to Irene about this, and to Ronnie, and I made some phone calls.

We met at Gwen Palmer's house one evening in April and had a group therapy session. I said that I hoped we could discuss the meaning of community control to the PS 84 parents and to the governing board and that we could also discuss the direction both bodies should take from here. I said, further, that I was personally disturbed at the criticisms leveled at some of our parents because they were interested in the quality of a principal. "The Board seems to feel that accountability is more important than the quality of the individual. To me, community control is only a tool to get good education. It is not an end in itself."

DOTTY: "A distinction has been drawn between groups in the neighborhood: educational versus political. Being educational seems to preclude being militant in some people's minds."

I: "You are the planning/governing board. Has educational planning been done by you? Have you planned for the future? People seem to be losing sight of the fact that education is what this is all about."

MIKE GOODMAN: "If there is a split between the educationally oriented and the militants, there shouldn't be. I couldn't answer which one I am. I am interested in education and only in the political area because of necessity. I have learned about education and about politics. They must be considered together. We are all interested in education."

DOTTY: "I'm tired of people who feel they have the corner on radicalism. Up to now I've been more interested in politics. I've been an organizer for years. I'm aware of the difficulties at PS 84, and I know you can only organize around an educational idea. The infant school is the only program I have seen that can get parents to come out."

IRENE: "Anyone who has worked with a bureaucracy knows you need a political movement. Until you fight the bureaucracy question, you can't achieve any program. No bureaucracy is as corrupt or as complex as the Board of Ed. You have to organize parents around their needs, their children. They can get co-opted because they fight singly and lose every time. You can't win as individuals or even as one school. They beat you every time. There's never any significant change. Basic changes are needed for every kid, but especially for the black and Puerto Rican kids. Until all parents understand that no kid can go to junior high reading at 2.4, you can't win. We fail until we stop letting any kid fail."

DOTTY: "No one disagrees with you."

MILLIE: "I see the bureaucracy for what it is. Community control offered a way to smash the bureaucracy. But it is not enough to shout community control. Community control means to take power and give it to a new group. What they do with that power is crucial. And I'd like to know what the governing board plans to do."

What the governing board planned to do was to organize the entire community, and it was to this end that Otis Grace had been hired. There was some resentment on the part of our parents, both black and white, that he had never been formally introduced to them, and the question was also raised as to whether he could unite the entire community if he only organized the black parents. That led us into another can of worms: Were we really an integrated community or were we merely an interracial one? And was it desirable to have an integrated community at this time? Was it even possible? None of these questions, obviously, was resolved, but I think the air was somewhat cleared, at least temporarily.

And it was decided that Millie, Dotty, Beth, and I should go up to Mr. Molloy's town to investigate his past performance. We went, and came back still very much interested. We spoke to three parents, two of them past PA presidents who had served under Mr. Molloy, and they had nothing but good things to say of him. They all said he was a human being and that he had his failings, but that he listened to parents, consulted with them, was truly interested in their children. They said he was not only interested in the academically gifted, but in all of them. We got much the same report from a man who had worked first with, and then over, Mr. Molloy. The only negative thing he had to say was that paper pushing was not his highest priority, that if he could delay paper work to deal with children and staff he would do so. To us that was not necessarily a negative, and we went home feeling we had found a live one. There were still two other candidates in the running, Mr. Harriman and a Mr. Forman. It was now up to the screening panel to decide which of the three to select and then to present their choice to the parents and to the school board. The governing board would provide the money, and the reign of Mrs. Young would come to an end.

TWENTY-SEVEN

The Course of True Love Never
Did Run Smooth

On April 28 the local school board sent a letter to PS 84 parents speaking of our sit-in and saying that "a group of PS 84 parents and outsiders" had made a proposal to pay for a principal's salary and that that proposal was illegal. The letter went on to ask whether there were problems in the school; they had had no complaints. It ended with a plea for peace, saying it was late in the year, and that another change in the school would be damaging to the children. We felt we had been stabbed in the back. They had called a special meeting at and about our school at 7:30, to precede the regular monthly school board meeting that was to take place uptown at 8:30. They were giving us a whole hour, but that was more than enough time for them to slit our throats. We were determined not to give them the opportunity. We filibustered.

I began the meeting by objecting to the inflammatory tone of the notice they had sent, which played into parental fears of further disorder and which was designed to stampede the parents into accepting an unacceptable status quo. I objected to their reference to the PA president and Executive Board members as "a group of PS 84 parents" and to members of the governing board and its staff (parents, elected by parents) as "outsiders." I pointed out that the school board was appointed, and that not one of them had a child at our school. I pointed out, further, that though they referred to the proposal to pay with governing-board funds for a principal as illegal, they had omitted to mention that Jessica Malamud had agreed to this illegal proposal (and that the board had, in fact, sent a telegram to John Doar and to Dr. Donovan to implement it).

274

Finally, I said there *were* still problems in the school, and though the school board claimed to have had no complaints we had, in fact, sent them many, including data showing that Mrs. Young was continuing the pernicious practice of tracking in the school. Yes, I concluded, it *was* late in the year, but that was all the more reason to settle things now so that the next year could start without the chaos the children had had as their daily fare.

When I finished, Pete Worthem, Otis Grace, and John Rollins rose to blast the board, with the result that they never had a chance to tell us why they had called us out so early. We suspected that, their letter having done its dirty work, they had hoped that the "responsible" parents would rise en masse to repudiate us. We never gave them the chance, and so they left for the second part of their evening, and though some of us followed for the regular meeting, this time we were simply spectators.

The school-board letter had made it plain that we were up the creek without a paddle as far as getting our principal in the front door. But we weren't about to quit, having achieved results through back doors before. Thus, the screening panel met again to decide which of the three remaining contenders to select. Mr. Forman, whom I had never seen, was quickly out of the running. That left us to decide between Dan Harriman and Jack Molloy, and in the end we chose Molloy. The reasons: though we all liked Dan Harriman and knew he was good in many areas, he had had little administrative experience. Molloy, on the other hand, had proven himself as a principal and superintendent. Moreover, we were slightly scared of the staff reaction to Harriman and felt that Molloy, being older and more experienced, would be easier for the conservative teachers to swallow and to work with. A chicken-hearted decision, maybe, for all of us who had been yelling power to the people, but it's not as though we felt we were settling for second best with Molloy. It was just that, weighing things, we felt his experience gave him a slight edge. Pete gave Mr. Harriman our decision, along with our regrets and called Mr. Molloy to tell him that the final phase of the selection process would be a series of small meetings with parents around the community and a final large meeting with the parents and staff of the school. Molloy said fine, and the meetings were set up for the first week in May.

On Wednesday, May 7, the first of these was to take place at the offices of the governing board, with the members of the Joan of Arc board and the PS 84 Executive Board. Eight o'clock came and went, and then nine. At nine-thirty Pete called Molloy's home. His wife said he had been slightly delayed in starting but was on his way. We waited some more. Ten passed, and still no Molloy.

"Maybe his car broke down," someone suggested.

"Maybe the CSA kidnapped him," offered someone else.

"No. But maybe they got to him, somehow. Threatened him, blackmailed him."

"He didn't look like the kind of guy who'd knuckle under to threats," I said.

So we whiled away the time with wild speculation, only half jokingly. And worried. And got edgy. "If he's not here by eleven . . ." And got nervous at the step we were contemplating. Assurance was easier in the presence of Jack Molloy. In the flesh we were swept away by his reality, and the question of his installation blurred in our minds. He was real. We would install him. All obstacles would crumble. In his absence all the doubts cropped up. Would the parents accept him? What would the school board do? the teachers? Mrs. Young had already announced that the governing board and the Ford Foundation were planning to install Mr. Molloy on May 14, and she had so informed John Doar and the police. What about the parents who wanted only a legal principal? What about the parents who were content with Mrs. Young because she had restored—if not education—at least order? What if, at the meetings to introduce him, he fell on his face and the parents then rejected him? What if . . . ? Specters. And the specters dissolved the uneasy truce between us and the governing board.

"Are you people committed to community control or just a principal of PS 84? If that's all, don't waste my time. You've wanted us when you've needed something."

"And vice versa," countered Walter.

"You play both sides against the middle," said another member of the governing board. "You listen to the school board when it suits you."

"We're going to pay the bill for the principal. Suppose Selig says 'I want him out.' Who will be protecting our money? There won't be six of you."

"That's not true," I said. "When we started, we were the ones doing all the work while the governing board made grand pronouncements. You call the PS 84 parents bad guys because they're just interested in our school. But we're the ones who supported you and picketed with you at other schools in the district."

"Parents at 84 should decide which board they want to work with. If we always have to wait around while you go back and forth between the local school board and us . . ."

"Look," Pete said, "it's after eleven. He's not coming tonight. We might as well go home. But it shouldn't be a condition imposed on 84 parents to give up their feelings about the school board in order for us to help them. We can't ask parents to commit themselves for life against the school board. I think what people are saying here, though, is that they have the sense that the governing board is only as strong as the parents make us. As far as staff and money are concerned, we're ready to go down the line. But if there isn't strong parent support on confrontation day, we'll all look silly."

It never came to confrontation day. The following day, after a series of unreturned calls, Pete finally reached Molloy, and he said he had withdrawn his name from consideration. Period. (It subsequently developed that he objected to our unauthorized visit to his home territory—so much for parent control!) Nevertheless, certain machinery having been set in motion, Molloy still had some effect. When our parents' association had decided on a no-dues policy (every parent is a member by virtue of his parenthood), we had to find other means of support. One of these was a buffet supper, which would combine socializing with fund-raising. This supper had been set for May 9, and it had seemed like a good time for Jack Molloy to be introduced informally to the parents and staff. Fliers had gone out announcing his coming—this before his defection—and consequently there was a large turnout of parents and a boycott by a large segment of the staff.

At the supper ham hocks and collard greens, stuffed cabbage, lasagna, Indian meat pies, arroz con pollo, and pastellitos steamed side by side on the serving tables. We could not dish out the food fast enough, and a long line formed as people waited good-naturedly to be served. Children darted about, played tag in the empty spaces. Fathers who had slept in the school together sat and reminisced over beers. For that evening we were any church-group barbecue and fish fry. For that evening we were not crazy militant parents. We were simply mothers who, after sweating over hot stoves to prepare the various dishes, sweated to feed everyone who had come to eat and enjoy the sense of community. It was, all in all, a smashing financial and social success in spite of the boycott. Delicious, too.

On May 14, again in honor of Molloy's expected appearance, the school was crawling with cops. Poor Mrs. Young. Someone had forgotten to tell her to call off the troops. Someone had forgotten to tell the school board, too, because they sent another letter to all the parents at PS 84 on the subject of illegal actions by the Executive Board to replace the acting principal.

"We want to assure you," they said, "that the local school board and district superintendent will use whatever means are necessary to ensure that the only principal or acting principal at PS 84 is serving under legal appointment. We will not allow any illegal placement."

On the heels of that forthright position came a summary of our fiscal difficulties. Mrs. Wachtel was still on our payroll, though the school board was making efforts to change that and wished the PS 84 parents would support their efforts. Then they pointed out that there were parents at the school who had expressed their support for Mrs. Young. (That had, of course, also been true of Mrs. Wachtel, whom they had nevertheless allowed to transfer.) Therefore, "it would be unfortunate for the school . . . if one group sought to 'install' its choice without regard to legal procedures and over the expressed opposition of other parents. This is not community control, but community destruction."

They ended by pledging allegiance to community control (their definition thereof) and urged all parents at the school who disagreed with such illegal action to oppose it (and us?) and to "understand that such acts will create tremendous disturbance in the school, harm its educational program, and seriously upset the children." I promptly sent an answer.

I said that in searching for a suitable principal for the school parents had done nothing illegal or immoral and that it seemed more immoral to us that we were short an administrator because Dr. Selig couldn't buck the system that had produced him.

"The local school board," I continued, "cannot and will not screen candidates for principal until there is a vacancy. They show their belief in community control by 'inviting' three parents to sit on a *nonexistent* screening panel. They say they will consult with everyone before *they* make *their* decision. This may be their definition of community control. But it says nothing of accountability. If *they* decide wrong, *our* children are stuck with the decision, as we have learned to our sorrow. That's not community control, but control of the community."

I concluded by deploring their efforts to pit parent against parent and to create further division in the school by misrepresentation and innuendo—as though we did not all want law and order. But, I said, "some of us want law and order as only part of the educational picture. We want *education*, too. Law and order as an end is only a polite term for repression, as most civil libertarians well know." All of which may have relieved our anger, but it left us, as before, with the status quo. Mr. Molloy's withdrawal left us not only without a candidate (we could, I suppose, have gone to our second choice), but more important, it took away our momentum. We had been primed for Molloy's installation. With him gone it all fizzled out into rhetoric.

TWENTY-EIGHT

June Is Busting Out All Over

Organization for the fall was in progress, and we were back where we had been in January—with a principal we did not want and did not trust, making decisions regarding our children and our teachers. There were certain untenured teachers she wanted to get rid of. We fought her on it. Then came the subject of the community room again: we would have to vacate because she would need the room for a classroom since she was expecting hordes of new children from the buildings that were opening. We questioned her figures. She remained adamant. We went to Stryckers Bay and got projected figures of new children. We said if we got twenty it would be a lot. Mrs. Young insisted there would be over one hundred. She planned her organization based on her figures and put a teacher into every classroom, including room 134. She ended up with ten first grades; and though one of them had no chidlren in it and the others had ridiculous registers, she assured us that come September, children would materialize to fill those registers. We went to the school board and got from Bob the assurance that before we could be bounced from the room those children would have to be there in the flesh and not merely in Mrs. Young's imagination. We could keep the room until registration figures were reviewed in late September.

Also on the subject of reorganization, Nancy and Toni had submitted a proposal for a combined fifth-sixth grade, taught by them and run along the lines of an open class. Mrs. Young had agreed to the preliminary proposal, as had Dr. Selig, and they had received foundation funding. Thus the open classroom was extended into those grades. It was also being extended up to the third grade,

280

thereby leaving only the fourth grade with no choice of program. When parents objected to this, pointing out that it was that particular group of kids who had been short-changed since they had entered the school, Mrs. Young said she would see what could be done. At a meeting held with parents and teachers on the subject, Mrs. Young spoke of the need to move slowly and to evaluate the program. In the same breath she promised that every child who had started in the program would continue in it, providing the parents of the child so desired. To that end request slips were distributed to all parents in the school. This question of voluntarism also posed a problem: if all the children who requested the program were white, what would happen? Would we go back to unbalanced classes, or would we balance the "voluntary" classes with black and Spanish children even though their parents had not requested the program? And at what point does a voluntary program cease to be voluntary and become an accepted part of the school, with placement of children made according to the judgment of the staff? If that happens, what happens to parent control—for that brings us right back to the old concept of the professionals knowing what is best for your children. You can go round and round with that one, too, and though we now have a principal whose judgment we trust, we still have no simple answers to these questions. At the point where Mrs. Young was still the professional of record, the answer was easier. We did not trust her to know what was in the best interests of our children.

At the meeting on organization for the fall, Mrs. Young promised that to accommodate all those children who wanted open classes she would find the teachers to staff those classes. Good as her word, she did, even though it meant twisting an arm here and there. The result was that, on paper, the organization looked beautiful. We had at least one infant-school class in each grade and several in some. In reality, of course, things were not quite so beautiful. Some of the teachers whose classes had the E (for Experimental) designation knew and cared as much about the program as my cat. But E they were designated, and E they became, and it caused a lot of headaches for a lot of parents and children the following year.

In addition, there were some members of the staff (Mrs. Rudley, the fastidious kindergarten teacher being the most glaring example) who openly tried to sabotage the program by not giving out the request slips or by discouraging parents from requesting the program. And though this was pointed out to Mrs. Young, nothing was ever done about it.

Another bone of contention was the manner in which teachers would be assigned to rooms. One of the essentials of the infant school* was that the classes involved share a common corridor or corridors so that the children and teachers could interact. The whole point was to go from a self-contained class into one that moved outward, and to this end it was important that these classes were near each other. We understood this, but apparently Mrs. Young didn't, for in her master schedule the classes were scattered all over the place without rhyme or reason. The teachers got hysterical and met to make up a master schedule of their own. It was rejected. Mrs. Young submitted another schedule. The teachers got hysterical again and went back to their drawing board. And so it went as the term drew to its end.

Meanwhile, election time was coming up again. I had been elected to finish out Carmen's unexpired term, but now the annual elections were upon us. We had proposed a constitutional change whereby from now on officers would be elected in January so that a new set of officers would not come in with the new term (which, we had found, meant that while all sorts of problems were cropping up, inexperienced people were being called upon to deal with them. Midyear elections would avoid that). This change was to be approved by vote along with the slate of officers. I was running unopposed this time, so my election was a foregone conclusion. But because of the constitutional change I would, if I wanted to go on serving as president, have to stand for election again next January. I joked that nobody trusted me since I was the only president in the history of our school who had to get a new mandate every six months, but it at least helped answer the argument of whether we really represented the parent body. We certainly gave them lots of chances to throw the bums out.

On the next to the last day of the term, Theresa Hunter, Ronnie, Nancy Sergeant, Beth Barron, and I decided, upon the advice of

*Mrs. Weber detested that phrase since she felt we were not slavishly copying the British system but adapting it to our own particular needs. She called the program the expanded-environment program. That mouthful never caught on, and it next became the open classroom, or the open-corridor program.

Jessica, to make another pilgrimage to 110 Livingston Street to see whether Dr. Donovan, who was leaving the system, might not as a final gesture, transfer Mrs. Wachtel out of our district and thus clear our line. We had also been advised to see Dr. Meade, who handled personnel matters for the board; and, in fact, she did meet with us and seemed very understanding, promising to see what she could do. We then went down to Dr. Donovan's office with a sense of "this is where we came in." The secretary, the same one who had argued numbers with us on our last visit, said that we couldn't possibly see Dr. Donovan. This time she didn't even offer us Mr. Anker.

"Is he in the building?" we asked.

"Yes," she answered, "but he's got several meetings, and he really can't see you."

"Couldn't you squeeze us in between meetings?"

"I'm afraid not."

"If you'll tell us where he is, we'll wait and talk to him on the elevator. Surely he can spare that much time."

We would have suggested the men's room, too, had there been a male among us.

"That's impossible," she said.

We might have been stymied at this point had Dr. Donovan, unwarned, not made the mistake of coming out of his office just then.

"There he is," I said.

The secretary didn't even look embarrassed; but since she had just lost her excuse, she did go to him and ask whether he would see us—briefly—and he agreed. So we were ushered into his office and seated around his table, and we asked him, once again, to remove Mrs. Wachtel from our payroll. Dr. Donovan seemed quite irritated by us and by everything about our situation. He criticized the entire handling of the matter, but he did tell us that Mrs. Wachtel would be transferred as of September. We tried to press him on specifics, but that was all he would say, that she would no longer be in our district when the fall term opened. He said that the chairman of the school board could call him to confirm this. We had to be satisfied, thanked him, and left with the hope that the millstone would, finally, be taken off our necks.

Jessica did call him the following day and he confirmed to her what he had told us. To make sure nothing got lost in the shuffle, she then sent him a letter confirming their conversation. We weren't the only ones who didn't trust anyone anymore. But at least the term ended with some assurance that, come fall, we would have a line and that screening for a new principal could now begin legally.

The other event that was to have major consequences for us was the resignation of Dr. Selig. Whether the resignation resulted in part from parental pressures, as a social scientist who did a study of our school and our district for his doctoral dissertation asserts, or whether he felt it was time to move on in any case, I have no way of knowing; but it was good news to us because Dr. Selig had acted as an impediment to everything we had tried to accomplish over the past two years, and anything that had, finally, been gained had been over his resistance. We felt we had led him kicking and screaming into the twentieth century, and maybe he felt it too.

His impending departure necessitated a search on the part of the school board for a replacement, and they convened a screening panel of PA presidents, community leaders, and board members. The man they chose, Dr. Milton Rock, had been a principal in a Harlem school for several years and had made a name for himself as a bucker of the system. He had substantially raised the reading scores of the children in his school and was well thought of by his teachers and his community according to the reports the school board got. When he took office, he lined his wall with his citations and with plaques from his school, as well as with inscribed photographs from Robert Kennedy and other notables.

He was a short, square man with big blue eyes, a ready smile, rapid-fire style of delivery, and an open manner—quite a contrast to the cool, aloof, professional Dr. Selig. His first appearance before a school board meeting left me slightly dubious. In his introductory speech he told of his battles against the establishment and concluded, "They want me to fail. We've all got to work together, because if I fail it will be a victory for the forces who oppose community control." (Translation: If you work against me you're giving aid and comfort to the enemy.) Though this made me less than gung ho for Dr. Rock, I certainly was not going to damn him on that score; and I, and a lot of other parents, adopted a wait-and-see attitude. We had seen other miracle workers come into the system. We would wait for the miracle before we made a judgment.

In spite of all the problems we would face come September,

though, we were hopeful. We had a new superintendent who said he would fight the system; and we had assurance that we would have an opening for a principal in the fall. We had come a long way since last summer, and if we still had a way to go, at least we were moving in the right direction.

TWENTY-NINE

A New Term and Some Old Problems

September came, and school reopened. The first thing that greeted us when we entered the school was that our community room was occupied by Mr. Trumbull, the bat-wielder. This was a direct violation of the agreement Mrs. Young had made with us, and we went to see her at once. She looked at us blankly, as if she didn't know what we were talking about, and said that the agreement, as far as she recalled it, was that the room would be a classroom until the registration figures were reviewed in late September. Then, if her estimates proved incorrect, we would get the room back. This was a complete reversal of what we had been told, but no amount of memory-refreshing on our part could sway Mrs. Young. She told us kindly that we were welcome to use the PA closet that had been ours in the past and that, further, we could use the dressing room behind the auditorium (which was windowless and airless, and small, and could be reached only via a flight of steps—a great place for the kiddies, and most conducive to parent activities in general)! A cynic might have suggested that perhaps Mrs. Young was not terribly interested in fostering PA activities, but we were not cynics. Obviously, it was only the welfare of the children that she had in mind, while we . . . We went yelling to Bob Goodfellow. Bob agreed that the compromise had been as we had remembered, and he promised to come over the first thing in the morning to straighten out the matter. And come he did. Mrs. Young sighed, swore that she remembered it the other way around; but, "Very well, you can have the room back until we do the registration check. But I should tell you, Mr. Goodfellow, that it isn't only the classes. I've had numerous complaints from the custodial staff about the filthy condition of that room. This *is* a school; and if that room is vermin infested it will affect the other rooms."

At that we exploded. We suggested that if she told the custodian to clean the room when he cleaned the classrooms—since it was part of the school that did not seem like an unreasonable request to us —then perhaps the room would be a bit cleaner.

"And we do clean it," I said. "I've mopped the floor myself, because the custodians wouldn't, and so have many of the other parents. And at that we had to bring cleaning supplies from home because we couldn't get them from the custodians."

"All right. Just keep it clean," said Mrs. Young, "and we'll wait and see what the figures say. But you'll have to give Mr. Trumbull a day or so to move his class. It really is a shame to move children, especially when they may be moving back."

"You shouldn't have put them in there in the first place," we said. No answer. So we got our room back, and whenever we met Mr. Trumbull in the hall he scowled at us.

The next problem that cropped up, and it was really related to the issue of the community room, was the organization of the classes. In her zeal to oust us, Mrs. Young had set up ten first-grade classes, hoping, no doubt, that she could somehow fill them. The registers, therefore, were absurd, with only three classes having fifteen children (the legal minimum), some having three or five, and one having no children at all. It was just as we had said. But the fact that we had been right gave us small pleasure, since it was obvious to us that the classes could not remain the way they were, and that meant that children would have to be moved again. We had hoped that after the upheavals of last year the children could have a stable year for once. And here we were, hardly into the term, and already the first-graders were going to be shifted. It was such a flagrant example of Mrs. Young's using the children to get back at us that we were furious. And in those days we were no longer silently furious. We called in the authorities again.

Dr. Rock, upon assuming the superintendent's job, had replaced many of Dr. Selig's people with those with whom he could work. One of the few he had retained from the old staff had been Dan Harriman, and what Dr. Rock had done was to divide the district along the lines of the junior high school complex. Since Dan was most familiar with the Joan of Arc complex, he had been put in charge of us—and it was he whom we summoned on the matter of the reorganization of classes. It got to be comical. Every morning Harriman would come in to review what Mrs. Young had done the night before (we were now up to "Tentative Revised Schedule #7"). We would meet with him and with Mrs. Young; we would point out how impossible this solution was, and she would be sent home to do it again. The following morning the same thing would happen again.

The situation was further complicated by the fact that Mrs. Young had, in overestimating her registers, gotten more teachers than we were entitled to, and we therefore faced a reduction of staff as well as a reshuffling of teachers. And, naturally, our views on which staff members were expendable did not coincide with Mrs. Young's, so that we had some battles to save some of our good young teachers again. In that whole scene her theme was, always, that we could not possibly judge which teachers were good—parents' evaluations could not be put on a par with professional evaluations. It was a rerun of an earlier scene with Mrs. Wachtel, but after much struggle, and with Mr. Harriman's assistance, we were able to come up with five reasonable classes, and I hope the kids weren't too traumatized by the switches. But since most of the younger ones were used to terms starting with chaos (mine had been surprised that there had been no strike this year; they thought that was how school was supposed to start), perhaps they took it in stride. After all, in the words of that great educational authority, "Children are flexible."

Being well-mannered, I sent Dr. Rock a thank you note during this period. To wit:

"On behalf of the PS 84 Parents' Association, I would like to thank you and Mr. Harriman for all your efforts in solving the daily crises at the school. We are truly sorry to be taking up so much of Mr. Harriman's time, but as he can tell you, problems that seem resolved on one day, and solutions that are mutually arrived at and agreed to, come apart the next and must then be re-resolved."

There was, of course, method in my politeness. It was a cool way of getting into the record a description of life at PS 84. We weren't going to let anyone forget that we still needed a new principal.

At the same time I sent a note to the school board suggesting that three parents were too few to serve on the forthcoming screening panel. They thanked me for my suggestion (I think I had suggested twelve parents) but said that they had decided that three parents plus the PA president seemed like a swell number. That answer notwithstanding, at the end of October the school board issued a new policy statement on screening panels. Henceforth, one parent would be elected for every one hundred children in the school. In addition, the PA president, two teacher representatives (elected by the teachers), one paraprofessional (elected by the paraprofessionals), and one school-board member would round out the board. Since we had about nine hundred and forty-five children at the school, we would be entitled to nine elected parents plus me; and that is how the panel finally shaped up.

If we wanted Dr. Rock and the school board to know that all was not roses at PS 84, Mrs. Young was determined to help us prove it. One day as we were sitting in her office with her, she mentioned that she really needed an acting AP for the third floor.

"As you know I used to be up there, but now that I'm down here there's no one to keep order. So I've decided to ask Mrs. Ruppert whether she'll take the job."

Mrs. Ruppert was an old friend of Mrs. Young's, and she was cut from the same mold. It was she who had said to Nina Gossens, at a meeting discussing balanced classes versus IGC classes, that she had never seen a black or Spanish child who was capable of being in an IGC class. Nina's son was, at that time, in Mrs. Ruppert's IGC and was doing splendidly. This did not kill her stereotype. It simply never occurred to her that Ned was Spanish. Perfectly reasonable! Of course her comment went over big with Nina and with everyone else to whom she told it. In addition to this attitude, Mrs. Ruppert was a rigid, authoritarian type who rarely smiled, whose children marched down the halls in tight lines, and whose relationships with the Parents' Association were simple: nonexistent.

So when Mrs. Young told us that she was thinking of Mrs. Ruppert as acting AP we gave a collective gasp. Irene recovered first and asked, "What about Mrs. Warner. She has an AP license, you know, and she'd be very good."

"I don't think she'd be interested," Mrs. Young answered. "I once asked her whether she would like to be acting AP a few years back, and she declined."

"Why don't you ask her anyway?" I asked.

"She's absent and won't be back till Monday," said Mrs. Young.

"Can't it wait till Monday?" we asked.

"Well . . . I really need someone up there."

"We've struggled along for this long. Today's Wednesday. I

hardly think a few more days would make that much difference," Irene said.

"You could call Mrs. Warner," I suggested.

"Yes."

The conference ended with Mrs. Young's promise that she would make no appointment until she had spoken with Mrs. Warner. Meanwhile, I spent the next couple of days, trying, unsuccessfully, to reach her. It wasn't until late Sunday night that I talked to her, and she told me she would be interested (had, in fact, in the spring sent a letter to Mrs. Young asking to be considered for the next administrative position). She said that Mrs. Young had known where to reach her; she had been ill and at her daughter's home. She told me, moreover, that the refusal Mrs. Young had spoken of had, indeed, occurred but that it had occurred because on an earlier occasion, during another of Mrs. Young's leaves, Mrs. Warner had been made an acting AP by Mrs. Wachtel. At that time she had been given none of the duties or powers of an AP but had been given scut work, lunchroom duty, garbage detail. In spite of this, though, she said she would now be interested.

On Monday morning Mrs. Warner arrived at school. According to her account, Mrs. Young met her in the outer office and said to her:

"Sylvia, I just wanted to tell you that I'm appointing Katherine as acting AP."

There seemed nothing more to be said, so Mrs. Warner had turned and gone upstairs.

Again we were boiling—it seemed to be an almost permanent condition. Not only was this a violation of a promise to us, but, in addition, it was a slap in the face at a fine, qualified lady who did not deserve such treatment. Moreover, the racial implications could not be overlooked. Mrs. Young was bypassing a licensed *and* qualified AP who was black in favor of someone who had no license and who, we felt, was less qualified (she had never, to the best of my knowledge, had any administrative training) but was white. And this after the school board had issued a directive saying that, wherever possible, appointments should more closely reflect the ethnic composition of the school. And if all that wasn't enough to make us mad, the appointment of Katherine Ruppert as acting AP would mean that she would have to leave her class, and though I wouldn't have wanted any kid of mine in her class, still we were opposed to this kind of change being made once the term had begun. We did not want the kids constantly having to make these adjustments. Mrs. Warner, as the corrective-reading teacher, did not have a class, so from that point of view as well her selection would have been the more sensible one.

This time our outrage took us straight to Dr. Rock, who met with us on September 16 in the teachers' cafeteria (we had not yet gotten our room back). We reviewed the situation with Dr. Rock, told him of Mrs. Warner's splendid performance during the strike, pointed out all the implications, both educational and racial, and asked for his intervention. Dr. Rock, who called us "girls" a lot, asked us to give him a couple of days and to trust him. Having no other choice, we agreed. In the interim we got a notice, via the children, stating that Mrs. Ruppert had been appointed acting AP as of Monday. We waited. And we waited some more. Then I called Dr. Rock.

"Give me a little more time," he said, "I'm working it out." We waited some more. What he worked out, it transpired, was to offer to Mrs. Warner an assistant principal's job in another school in our complex. And since there was, then, no hope of an AP's slot opening in our school I really couldn't blame Mrs. Warner for accepting a concrete offer. Mrs. Young, once we got a real principal, would go back to her old AP job (though I had a hunch that if she wasn't made principal she would leave for pastures where she would be more appreciated). But that was iffy, whereas Dr. Rock's deal was a bird in the hand. Still, we were terribly sorry to be losing Mrs. Warner. We could have used her skills and her warmth and her humor. She is a rare lady, and our school was the poorer for her leaving it.

So Dr. Rock had messed that one up, for us at least, by his wheeling and dealing. After a conference with Mrs. Young, Dr. Rock did order her to rescind the appointment of Mrs. Ruppert, and returned the lady to her class; and the third floor was again without a supervisor. This, in turn, led again to the chaotic and unsafe situation there, for the lull that had accompanied Mrs. Young's coming had passed, and things were pretty well back to normal on the third floor.

One of the things we had found out during the strike and our occupation of the school was that normal, for many of the kids on

the third floor, meant that they roamed the halls all day. The standard operating procedure for years, it seems, had been that when a
kid acted out he was simply put out, and so there was a contingent
of these kids who spent most of their school days out there. We had
controlled the situation pretty well while we were in the school. It's
tough for a bunch of kids to zip around when there's a parent (and
one he knows and who knows his parents) at every corner. But once
we left the wanderers had returned, and though they had been kept
somewhat in check when Mrs. Young had first returned, they were
now back in full force. In fact, it was these roamers who finally led
to Mrs. Young's undoing.

Early in October we were in the community room when Mickey
Preston came flying in. He was close to tears and shaking with rage.
Irene, who is friendly with his mother, went over to him and asked
him what had happened. He said his teacher had kicked him in the
shin, and he pulled up his trouser leg and exhibited a good-sized
bruise. Irene asked for details, and the story that emerged was as
follows: Micky had been sitting at his table at the front of the room
with his leg on the crossbar. Mr. Conrad had asked him to remove
it. He had, but a few minutes later it was up there again. Repeat.
This time Mr. Conrad had said that if he didn't remove his foot he
would kick it off; and since Mickey, like the Southern schools, moved
with all deliberate speed, Mr. Conrad proceeded to kick him in the
shin, according to Mickey—vigorously, one could presume from the
bruise on his leg. At that he ran out of the room, whereupon Mr.
Conrad locked the door behind him. Mickey ran to the gym, looking
for Mr. Ryan, a teacher he liked and trusted; but Mr. Ryan was not
there, so he went to the guidance office where, likewise, the guidance counselor wasn't. But there was a tennis racket in the guidance
office, and Mickey picked it up and returned upstairs and began
banging on the door with the racket. At this point a note went down
to Mrs. Young saying that Mickey had used profane language and
had threatened Mr. Conrad with the tennis racket. No mention was
made of the fact that Mickey had been kicked. Mrs. Young did not
call Mickey to ask what had happened but did call his mother to tell
her that if she did not come to school the next morning her son
would be suspended. (Mickey also said that the week before this
episode Mr. Conrad, angry at him over something else, had stamped
on his foot with the heel of his shoe; and since Mr. Conrad was no
lightweight I imagine Mickey got the point! Of this first incident

Mickey had not even bothered to tell his mother. He thought she'd be angry with him.)

Helen, Mickey's mother, came to school the next day with him. By this time she had seen his bruised leg and had taken him to the doctor, and she was pretty angry. Mrs. Young read her the account Mr. Conrad had written of the incident. When Mickey tried to interject that he had been kicked, she called him a liar and told him to shut up. When Helen asked that Mr. Conrad be called so that he could give his account in her and Mickey's presence, Mrs. Young said that wasn't necessary; Mr. Conrad had already given his description. At that point, Helen walked out, but before she did she made it clear that she didn't want Mickey back in Mr. Conrad's class (and since the feeling was mutual that posed no problem) and that Mrs. Young hadn't heard the last of this. Then she came to us.

We decided to move on two fronts: We would go with Helen as members of the grievance committee when she asked Mrs. Young to take disciplinary action against Mr. Conrad; and we, the Executive Board, while making no judgment of the actual event, would go on record as expressing our concern at this kind of conduct, if true, and asking for an immediate investigation of the incident on behalf of all the children in the school.

When we tried to see Mrs. Young about the matter, she refused to see us, but she said that if the mother wanted to see her she should make an appointment. So Helen called and made an appointment for the following Monday morning, and she asked Irene, Jenny Romero, Gwen Palmer, and me to accompany her. When we got to the office we cooled our heels for a while. Then Mrs. Young came out and said she would see Helen now. When we all started to enter, she stopped us.

"I have an appointment with Mrs. Preston," she said. Helen said that she wanted us present. Mrs. Young refused.

"I'm not seeing any delegations," she said.

"We're not a delegation," we answered. "Mrs. Preston has the right to bring along anyone of her choosing."

"And I," said Mrs. Young imperiously, "have the right to refuse to see you. I'm tired of mob scenes in my office. They serve no purpose. If Mrs. Preston wishes to see me, I'll be glad to talk to her. And if she wants to bring along one parent, I'll permit it. But I will no longer meet with a mob."

"It's up to Mrs. Preston," we said. "If she wants to meet with you on those terms that's up to her."

Helen said, "They're my friends. I want them to be there. I have nothing to hide from them."

"Very well," answered Mrs. Young, "if that's your decision. But I won't meet with them."

"You refuse to meet with us?" Irene asked.

"That's right," she snapped.

"Then I'm afraid we'll have to go over your head," Irene said.

"Do that." And she wheeled and marched back into her office.

We marched, too—directly to Dr. Rock's office. He greeted us jovially and offered us coffee from an urn he had. Then he left, saying he'd be back in a few minutes. The few minutes stretched into an hour and a half (superintendents seem to have a poorly developed time sense), and I called Millie and asked her to pick up Kathy from school. Maggie and Sammy were, fortunately, playing with friends.

Dr. Rock finally returned and apologized for the long delay, and we proceeded to tell him why we had come. After hearing us out, he said that those were very serious charges and that he would appoint Mr. Harriman to look into them.

"You understand, don't you, that I must investigate this. Mr. Harriman will talk to your son; he'll talk to the other children; he'll talk to the teacher. And then he'll give me his recommendation."

"What if he finds that Mickey told the truth?"

"If he recommends charges, I'll bring Mr. Conrad up on charges. If it's true, he shouldn't be teaching."

"One other thing. If Mr. Harriman recommends charges against Mr. Conrad, then we'd like to have Mrs. Young brought up, also, on the grounds that she tried to cover it up and that she wouldn't even listen to the boy's side."

"Let's see what Mr. Harriman finds, first."

"Of course, but if he finds that charges are warranted we think Mrs. Young should be included."

"Okay," he said, "I'll certainly consider it."

"Thank you," we said.

"Thank *you*," he answered.

A week passed, and during that time Mr. Harriman did, indeed, talk to all the parties. Then he made his recommendation. The recommendation then sat on Dr. Rock's desk. It took a while to find out what it was, because Mr. Harriman had been told not to give us any information, and Dr. Rock suddenly wasn't around. Finally we reached him, and he said he wanted to have an all-parties conference to help him to make his decision. He said that Helen could bring anyone of her choosing and that he would so inform Mr. Conrad as well. The conference was scheduled and we arrived. In addition to Jenny, Irene, Gwen, and me, Helen had asked a lawyer and a social worker to come along. We all met at Helen's house to review our strategy, then walked over to the district office where Mr. Conrad, Mrs. Young, Jenny Silverman, and Mrs. Johnson, the UFT field representative, were already assembled. So we waited in the hall.

Finally Dr. Rock came out and told us there was a slight problem. Mrs. Johnson refused to allow the meeting if people who weren't directly involved were included.

"Is *she* directly involved?" we asked.

Dr. Rock went back inside. He then moved their whole party into the conference room and ushered us into his office, then scurried back into the conference room and the negotiations continued. He came back, saying that they remained firm—only those directly involved in the controversy were acceptable to Mr. Conrad and company.

"But you told Mrs. Preston she could bring anyone she chose. Didn't you tell them that?"

"Yes. But what can I do? They just won't meet with all of you."

"Tell them we'll explain why we should all be there."

"Okay . . . but they're not being very cooperative."

Off he went again, to return a few minutes later. He was, by this time, perspiring profusely.

"They'll listen," he said, and we followed him into the conference room and took seats around the table.

"Do you all know each other?" he asked, and since some of us shook our heads introductions were made all around. Mrs. Young and Mr. Conrad looked straight ahead, without the least sign that they had ever seen any of us before. I was sitting next to Mr. Conrad, and he sat stiff and erect as though he was afraid his arm might accidentally brush against me and contract—what?

"I object to the presence of these outsiders," Mrs. Johnson said.

"They're not outsiders. They're friends of mine. Dr. Rock told me I could bring anyone I wanted to, and these are the people I wanted to bring," Helen retorted.

"I don't see why a lawyer and a—what, a social worker?—are necessary," Mrs. Johnson said.

"I asked them," Helen answered.

"And all these other people—who are they? I can understand—maybe—that the PA president has a right to be here and even the chairman of the grievance committee [that was Irene], but not all those others."

"I asked them," Helen repeated. "You're here. You weren't there when it happened, so you're an outsider. And Mrs. Young wasn't there either. Neither was I. Maybe we're all outsiders. This whole thing is silly. I thought we wanted to sit down together and hear the whole story from everyone's side. If Mrs. Young had let us do that in the first place, maybe none of us would have to be here. But this arguing is foolishness."

"I'm afraid I can't agree to a meeting if the lawyer and social worker and those others remain," said Mrs. Johnson.

"They're remaining," said Helen. "Unless you want to throw them out, Dr. Rock."

"Who, me?" he said. "I said you could bring anyone you liked."

"In that case," said Mrs. Johnson, standing up, "there's no point in our staying."

"All right," said Dr. Rock, "but then I'll have to make my decision without hearing directly from you."

The Conrad party departed, looking straight ahead still. None of them, except the UFT, had spoken a word during the entire exchange. Dr. Rock then asked whether Mickey would tell his story again, and whether anyone objected to its being taped. We looked at the lawyer, and he said there were no objections on his part if Mickey and his mother didn't mind. So Mickey told his story for posterity, Helen filled in her part of it, and then we recounted our involvement with Mrs. Young. Dr. Rock asked some questions during Mickey's part, and for the rest he puffed on his pipe. When we were finished, he thanked us and said he'd let us know his decision in the next few days.

A week passed, and Helen called him. He was still weighing all the pieces. Another week passed, and Helen, impatient by this time, called again. Finally he told her Mr. Harriman had recommended bringing Mr. Conrad up on charges, and he was now going to proceed. And what about Mrs. Young? "Well, one step at a time."

He obviously stepped slowly, because by December 1 we had still heard nothing, and so Helen sent him a letter saying that it was now two months since she had brought the incident to his attention and that during that time he and members of his staff had investigated the charges. A recommendation had been made, and she was now asking him to act on that recommendation because the fact that nothing had been done was having a very demoralizing effect on her son. She said that she had told the PA that the matter was now out of the hands of the parents, teachers, and acting principal and that if she did not hear from Dr. Rock by Friday, December 5, she would be forced to take further action.

And still it dragged on, and when I confronted Dr. Rock he said that he had not yet sent the papers through. Dr. Rock never did act on it. And then we wonder why kids take things into their own hands. Here was a case where a child was wronged and where he waited for the adults to protect him and punish the guilty, and the adults flubbed it. Who could blame him if, on the next occasion, he would act on his own?

While all this was going on, the school continued on its course. We elected nine parents to serve on the expanded screening panel, and it looked as though, by golly, they were really going to screen. In fact, before the expanded panel had been elected the original panel actually screened three people. Two were standard types, and no one had gotten excited at the prospect of having either of them as our next principal. The third was Dan Harriman. It was interesting to us that although in February the school board could not dream of depriving the entire district of his services, they were now willing to do so; but we weren't going to complain about that particular inconsistency. The panel expressed interest in Mr. Harriman.

On October 30 we met with Dr. Rock to discuss the forthcoming screening for a principal and to explore just what the possibilities were for our school. Specifically, we wanted to know about the applicants from the principal's list. Was there a timetable? What were the procedures? Did we have to choose from the list? If we didn't, what would happen? Dr. Rock said that if a candidate were not on the list he could be appointed an "acting" principal (something that the school board, when Dr. Selig had been the superintendent, had not been willing to consider). An acting principal must have state certification, or special qualifications such as completion of the Fordham Intern Program.* He said that an acting principal could be assured of a reasonably long stay in the school if the school was "plugged."† Our school, in fact, had been plugged by Mrs. Wachtel as long as she sat in the district office. When the central board took her downtown, we came unplugged. Now Dr. Rock was suggesting that we get plugged again (but this time by someone whom we wouldn't actually have to pay) so that we could, if we chose, select someone from off the list as acting principal.

"What if we decide on someone on the list?" we asked.

"Then we'll unplug the school again."

"What's the procedure with the list?" we wanted to know.

"The way it works is like this: if there's a vacancy in a school, the Board of Ed notifies everyone on the list of the vacancy. If they're interested, they must reply by a certain day. If they don't reply, they waive their right to that spot. In addition, the Board sends notices to all principals in the city who have transfer rights, because transfers take priority over people on the list. When we get the names of all the people who want to transfer or who are interested in being considered, then we begin to screen them."

"How many names are on the list now?"

"About two hundred and forty."

"And how many of those have said they're interested in PS 84?"

"Maybe about thirty."

"So we'd have to screen at least thirty people?"

"No. I could prescreen them and send you only the ones I could recommend."

"But we want to do this right. We want to follow the proper procedure. If we end up with someone from off the list, that'll be extremely important. We can't know if he's the most qualified unless we've really gone through everyone available."

The opinions of some people notwithstanding, we were very responsible.

---

*A program that had been set up jointly between Fordham University and the Board of Education as a method of getting more black and Spanish principals into the city's schools.

†A new term for some of us. What it means is that a school with an actual vacancy lists as its principal someone who is duly licensed but who, for some reason (e.g., he is on leave), does not serve for the moment.

And still the school limped along. Relations between the parents and Mrs. Young were by now extremely strained. When we had business to transact we did, but when she passed us in the hall, she didn't see us. And the chaos continued. We were, essentially, back where we had been during the last days of Mrs. Wachtel.

On Friday, November 8, Celia Cohen, who was then chairman of the local school board, came to the school to deliver a message to a friend's child. The child was in a third-floor classroom, so Celia went upstairs. What she saw—the corridor dwellers in full swing—horrified her, and she went down to Mrs. Young—barged right into the office—and said,

"The third floor is in bedlam."

Mrs. Young, a cigarette dangling from her lip, answered, "What do you want me to do about it?"

Celia's jaw dropped.

"You don't understand, Mrs. Young. I said the third floor is in a state of absolute bedlam."

"Well, Mrs. Cohen," Mrs. Young said, "why don't you tell *your* Dr. Rock about it?"

Celia left, shaking with rage. She did tell "her" Dr. Rock about it.

THIRTY

"So That We Can Begin to Move
Forward Together"

"Dr. Rock and Dan Harriman are locked in the office with Mrs. Young. What does that mean?" asked Marge Weill, one of our teachers, when I met her in the hall early Tuesday morning. I knew because I had gotten a call from Dr. Rock the previous day, but I had been sworn to secrecy, so I shrugged and went into the community room to wait.

"Hannah," the voice over the phone had said, "this is Milton Rock. What would you say if I told you I was removing Mrs. Young as of tomorrow and putting Dan Harriman in as interim acting principal?"

"I'd say hooray. Are you going to?"

"Yep," he answered, the smile detectable in his voice. "But don't say anything to anyone yet, because I want to tell Mrs. Young first."

I assured him I wouldn't, and I asked why he was doing this. He said because he found the school to be so chaotic that he didn't feel it could continue thus until we finished screening, and he didn't want to pressure the screening panel to hurry and select the wrong person simply because life in the school was unbearable. Therefore he felt it best to make the switch now and let the screening continue at a normal pace. He also wanted to assure me that his putting Mr. Harriman in now in no way committed us to him as the permanent choice. Mr. Harriman understood this. At the same time, he said, this would give us the opportunity to see Mr. Harriman on the job, which would give us a better chance to evaluate him as a candidate. I thanked him for telling me, and he again swore me to secrecy. Walter, who was still home, saw me grinning, and I did tell him, but

I told him, too, that if he breathed a word to anyone I'd break his neck. I waited around joyous and bursting all day, but I didn't tell another soul. It was that phone call, though, that had brought me so early into the community room, and now I waited impatiently to be able to share the good news. Fortunately I didn't have to wait too long.

Shortly after nine o'clock, Dr. Rock and Mr. Harriman came into the room, and Dr. Rock said,

"Mrs. Hess, I'd like to introduce you to your new principal."

"It's official?" I asked.

"It's official."

"Congratulations," I said, and extended my hand to Mr. Harriman. "Or maybe I ought to offer condolences. We're very hard on principals around here. And I don't know whether anyone has warned you, but the PS 84 parents are crazy."

"I'll risk it," he said, smiling.

"Let us know how we can help," I said.

Dr. Rock said he was going to take Mr. Harriman around to every room and introduce him to the teachers and to the children, and I wished them luck. In some rooms their welcome would be cool, to say the least. Shortly thereafter people began to stream in, teachers who had a prep period, and then parents as the news spread. There was a lot of kissing, and a lot of people spent the day at least three feet off the ground. This elation was not, of course, unanimous. There were some teachers who were loyal to Mrs. Young and who had, in fact, sent a petition in her support to the school board in September. There were also some parents who felt she was the embodiment of law and order and that only she could hold back the flood of community control and keep us crazy parents in check. But those of us in the room were grinning. It looked like pennant day in the Mets' locker room, minus the champagne.

My elation was cooled, somewhat, when Mrs. Young passed me in the hall. She looked absolutely shattered; and though I had never wanted her as our principal and could not be sorry that she no longer was, seeing her made me realize anew that here was a human being who had been hurt. And it did not make me happy. I was well aware of all her faults and blindness, but she was in the wrong place at the wrong time and it destroyed her. Unlike Mrs. Wachtel, she was a bright and capable woman, and I think that, in a different school, with different parents and children, she could have been a competent principal. It was clear proof that principals, unlike rifle parts, are not interchangeable. A few days later Mrs. Young went on sick leave and never returned. She subsequently was appointed to a school in Riverdale as principal; and from what I know of Riverdale, everyone may live happily ever after there, unless they realize that the schools are failing their children, too, and begin to demand a voice in the programs of the school.

On November 14, Dr. Rock sent a letter to all the parents in the school:

On Tuesday, November 12, I appointed Mr. Daniel Harriman of my office as interim Acting Principal of PS 84 Manhattan. I did this because, in my judgment, it served the best educational interest of all the children of PS 84.

This interim appointment in no way affects the screening process, which is now under way, to select a principal for PS 84 Manhattan.

Mr. Harriman is intimately acquainted with PS 84 since he represented my office as coordinator of the elementary schools feeding into Joan of Arc JHS. I have complete faith and confidence that Mr. Harriman will bring a fine educational program to your children.

I sincerely ask your cooperation in this matter so that we can begin to move forward together.

It was official. It was legal. We hadn't installed anyone—either across the street or in the school. The school board had approved, and we could all move forward together. And for the first time in the two years Kathy had been in the school, we had someone in the principal's office who understood what we had been talking about. It was a good feeling.

Mr. Harriman was determined to be a "community principal." To this end he asked the parents to set up a series of meetings around the community so that he could meet with parents who, traditionally, do not come into the school unless they are summoned for some dereliction on the part of their children. At these meetings he would answer questions about the school and what he hoped for it, and he would ask the parents what their hopes for the school were as well. Several of these meetings were held, but the turnout was rather disappointing. I guess everyone was tired; and unless some crisis was brewing, people were just not coming to any more meetings. Although others had been planned, they weren't held; and instead Mr. Harriman began to turn to the considerable problems of PS. 84.

One of these was discipline, or the lack thereof. Over the past two years the kids had been through an enormous amount of turmoil. They had gone from a weak principal to an authoritarian one, and now they had a principal who felt that discipline was not something that could be enforced from outside, but that had to come from the kids themselves. He is a quiet, soft-spoken man, and he believed that children would act properly if they understood the reasons for the rules they were supposed to obey. But the fact of the matter is that there were no uniform rules, and the kids were confused. The incident of Mickey Preston had been a case in point. I'm sure there must be any number of children who put their feet on the bar of their table. How many of them get kicked? And is there anything wrong with it in the first place? Mr. Harriman felt that if rules were reasonable and the kids understood them they would obey them—not blindly, but because they made sense. And this, after all, is what we wanted, too. We wanted kids who were well-mannered and who respected themselves and each other and their teachers. We didn't just want them to obey because someone was standing over them with a whistle. We were well aware that once the whistle was gone so would the obedience be. But to convert children who obey a whistle into children who have inner control takes some doing, and Mr. Harriman and the teachers decided to discuss which rules made sense and to give a copy of a set of basic rules to each child so that he would know what was expected of him.

We were concerned, too, about a recurrent theme in the school: that teachers were afraid to stop a child from doing *anything* because "the parents don't want us to discipline them." This was obviously not true. We didn't want them to kick them or hit them or prevent them from going to the bathroom so that they wet their pants or using other cruel and unusual punishment, but we certainly wanted them stopped if they were being antisocial. This was an area of misunderstanding that we would have to try to remedy. This feeling on the part of some teachers, alas, persists to this day, in spite of all our pronouncements on the subject. But at least no one has been kicked lately.

Our primary concern, of course, was education. We had all become involved because of our realization of the massive failure of so many children, and we were appalled at the blithe acceptance of this fact by an "educator." Now, we hoped, we could begin to turn to the kind of programs and approaches that would give all kids a chance, and it was to this that Mr. Harriman wanted to address himself as well.

Meanwhile, the screening panel went on with its work. Of the thirty or so candidates who had originally expressed interest in the school, many had, when called for an interview, lost that interest. Some had gotten other jobs. Some had, perhaps, been warned of us by their knowledgeable friends or by the item that had appeared in the CSA newsletter:

HANKY-PANKY

District 5 is at it again. PS 84M was listed as a vacancy in September. Letters were sent out to eligibles on the Principal's list. Meanwhile, Mrs. Cora Young, the senior Assistant Principal, has been acting Principal. She is on the eligible list for Principal. Now, a Principal who is on sick leave from his school in the Bronx, has been shifted for payroll purposes to PS 84. No longer is there a vacancy for principal. Dr. Rock, the community Superintendent and the Local School Board are now putting a teacher into the school to be the Acting Principal.

Such outraged virtue! Obviously no one had ever plugged a school before Milton Rock invented it. But apparently some originally interested applicants thought better of working in a district where hanky-panky was going on.

The screenings took place in the offices of the school board. The procedure we followed was that we would get the applicant's résumé, read through it, and then interview him or her. We generally scheduled three or four people an evening. After we had spent a half hour or so with each candidate, we would sit around and discuss our impressions. Sometimes, if one seemed interesting, we took longer. At other times a half hour was interminable, because we could tell after the first five minutes that this one was hopeless.

One of the curious things that happened is that there was very little disagreement among any of us. The parents, of course, pretty much reflected a similar philosophy, though here, too, there were degrees of "militancy"; but of the teachers elected to the panel not all were, by any means, in agreement on anything. But the fascinating thing was that though educational philosophies might differ, our feelings about most of the prospective candidates did not.

We had our first screening session on November 19, and six candidates were scheduled. Of these, only two appeared, and we interviewed them. One of the first questions we asked each candidate was why he or she had applied. Every one of the "list" people answered, "Because I was told there was a vacancy." Now I have, over the years, read many articles that give advice to job applicants, and one of the first things always mentioned is "Find out something about the company you're applying to." Rudimentary good sense, then, would have been for these people to do so, but they didn't. One after the other, they showed ignorance of the school. No, they had never visited it. No, they did not know the kind of population it served. No, they were not familiar with its programs. What is more, given the opportunity to talk to parents and teachers from the school in which they were allegedly interested, few saw fit, even at the interview, to ask us any questions that might have given them a clue to the kind of school it was and, therefore, to the kind of answers we might have wanted to hear. The impression, then, was that they were either so confident that they could do a job in any situation, or they were suicidal.

My impressions of all these candidates tend to blur—to run together—so that I have the feeling that we really interviewed only one person in diverse shapes. Sometimes he was tall and stout, other times short and thin. Sometimes he was a she. Some seemed more competent than others. Some were mousy, some dogmatic. But under all these superficial differences breathed the same soul: Mrs. Wachtel.

On the subject of heterogeneous grouping, they were also all united: it wouldn't work. Though some said they were for it, when we probed it developed that within these groupings they still felt children must be tracked. They were all unfamiliar with the philosophy and workings of the infant school. They believed in suspensions. They were wary of the role of parents, except in the most circumscribed way. Why do children fail? That varied, somewhat, according to the "individual," but they all agreed that if parents would send children who were receptive to learning they would learn.

One fellow did not appear for his original interview. At our next session he arrived. The interview had not yet started, and, to make small talk, I asked how he was feeling. (He had been sick at the last session.) He flushed and said he had had a bad cold, he really had, and I could check with his principal. Shortly afterwards Nancy Sergeant came in and also asked him if he were feeling better. Again he replied that he really had been ill and she could check it out with his principal. During his interview, he boldly stated in response to some question that he disagreed with his principal's handling of something or other—and, by golly, he didn't care if it got back to his principal. A brave soul.

On the subject of how to deal with ineffective teachers, they were also uniform. They would try to work with them. What if they were hopeless? Well, if they're tenured, what can you do? One of them suggested that he would try to get hopeless personnel to take a "rest leave." A couple thought that perhaps pressure could be exerted to get them to transfer. None of them questioned their right to be there if they were incompetent.

All in all they were a sorry crew. Now, it is possible (and some people have so charged) that we went into these interviews with a bias against anyone on the list and that we were determined to find all of those candidates wanting. Certainly on a conscious level I don't think this was so, and even on a subconscious level I doubt it. After all, had we found a candidate on the list, we could have saved ourselves considerable headaches. We would have gained a principal who was legitimate in everyone's eyes, and we would not have been living under the Damoclean sword of an unlicensed person. Had an outstanding candidate appeared from the list, I think we would have grabbed him. The point, though, was that not only were none of the Board of Ed people distinguished, they weren't even distinguishable.

Dan Harriman stood heads and shoulders above all of them. Part of that, of course, was that we knew him and he us. But it was more than that. The most refreshing thing about Mr. Harriman was his lack of glibness. He had no easy answers to tough situations. But he had an attitude—of wanting to work things through with parents and teachers, and even with children.

A case in point was lunchtime. Traditionally, the lunch hour was a bad scene, and most kids who had a choice refused to eat there. Those without a choice bolted their lunches and then, in good weather, went out to hang around the yard. In bad weather they were sentenced to the auditorium to watch movies. For some reason it was always the same movie; and since the time for showing it was always approximately the same and they always began at the beginning again, the kids never got to see the film past the same point (which, if the film had been worth seeing in the first place, would have been extremely frustrating). As it was, the auditorium was the scene of constant bedlam, with flying missiles, fights, and half-hearted attempts to curb the more glaring offenders.

Mr. Harriman was determined to improve the lunch hour, and with a group of volunteer parents, teachers, and children, he formed a committee. This committee came up with various suggestions to make the cafeteria itself more hospitable by rearranging the tables into a less prisonlike atmosphere and by decorating the walls. In addition they suggested a club program whereby the older children, after they ate lunch, could go to various activities such as arts and crafts, knitting and crocheting, cooking, chess, stamp collecting, gym, or instrumental or choral music. The interesting thing in all of this was how sensible the suggestions of the children were, how responsible they were about carrying out their end. Money for supplies was provided by a special school fund. The club program began, and the lunch hour was tremendously improved. The kids began to look forward to the lunch hour. It was no miracle, but it was an example of how, by involving all parties, bad conditions to which everyone had become resigned could be ameliorated.

The other thing that made Mr. Harriman so attractive to us was his attitude toward the children, and theirs to him. It was clear that he saw them as human beings and that he treated them with respect. This was not to say that he was wishy-washy. When a kid ran down the hall and Mr. Harriman called "Stop!" the kid stopped. But he was able to do this without harshness or brutality. The proof was that his office was always filled with kids who wanted to talk something over with him. They realized, too, that for the first time they had a principal who listened and who would try to help. This posed certain problems, too, because it meant that it was often difficult for teachers or parents to get to see him; but he felt that he had to establish a relationship of trust with the kids, and he did.

He also began to use teachers more in line with their abilities and interests, to seek their advice on school problems, and, the other side of the coin, to remove from the classroom and put into less sensitive spots the most glaringly ineffective ones. Altogether, from the two months he had been on the job, we all got the feeling, not of solutions, but of a moving forward together; and the panel voted, therefore, on January 15, 1970, to recommend Mr. Harriman as its choice.

This was not unanimous. One teacher felt we should look further before we cast our lot with Mr. Harriman, but the rest of us felt that we had advertised widely, both by newspaper and by word of mouth, and that though there was the possibility that somewhere, sometime, there might be someone more qualified than Mr. Harriman, we had not come across him. And we were afraid that if we delayed too long while we continued our search, the conditions might change (because of the forthcoming elections for a local school board and because of increased activity on the part of the CSA in trying to prevent the appointment of acting principals), and we would lose our mobility and would end up with one of the "list" candidates.

Thus, on January 21, Mr. Harriman was formally introduced to the parents at a general membership meeting as the choice of the screening panel. When he spoke, he outlined his objective for the school: to create an atmosphere where kids can be happy and learn.

"School needs to be a positive experience for the children, not a place to avoid. I hope, with your help, to make this school into what its potential promises: a community center where all of us can come together. This can be accomplished by getting to know each child and where he is and how we can extend his abilities; by getting to know and support teachers—regardless of educational styles. We have to take teachers where they are, too, and extend them. A teacher-training program must be established. I have tried to make it clear what I expect of teachers: they must be responsible for the curriculum, and they must not mishandle children."

He had, he explained, also changed the role of the cluster teacher, from one where, as a "specialist" in art or science, she saw as many as twenty classes a week (while their regular teacher had a prep period) and therefore could never really get to know any of the children, thereby creating discipline problems, to one where each cluster teacher covered the same four or five classes daily, worked closely with the classroom teacher, and thus got to know both the children and the style of the classes. This still left the teachers their free periods, but it meant that he had eliminated the specialists. However, it was doubtful that anyone had ever profited very much from the small taste of the specialty, even where it was taught well, and certainly from my one observation of the art period—when Kathy had been in kindergarten—I would not argue for this kind of coverage.

Someone then asked why there were still so many children in the halls, and he answered that this was an area where he was pressing his teachers to be more responsible. Someone else asked about the change in the library program, and he explained that, here too, he and the library teacher had sought new ways to utilize the facilities better. They had decided that, rather than having whole classes come for a library "lesson" (where it was doubtful that anyone learned anything), they would change the library to permit it to be used on a need basis. That is, any child, with the permission of his teacher, could come to the library during hours and take out a book or work on a research project. Again, it seemed like a most sensible solution.

The local school board, in due course, appointed Dan Harriman as acting principal of PS 84, and we had, for the first time in the history of the school, a principal of our choice and, moreover, one who felt accountable to the parents and the children. We had gone, in the space of a little more than two years, from a Board of Ed school to a community school.

THIRTY-ONE

All Our Troubles Are Over—
But Not Quite

We were ready to turn to education—the thing that school is supposed to be about. We wanted, together with Mr. Harriman and the teachers, to begin planning so that the open classroom program could proceed in a sensible fashion, and so that, come September, we would not again have the mess we traditionally faced with the new term. To this end we formed an organization committee, of parents and teachers, that began to meet regularly to discuss ways in which classes should be formed, problems could be avoided, and so forth.

We also began to question both the content and the use of the tests that are used in schools to determine the children's academic future, and we had an interesting meeting on the subject at which Mrs. Weber, as well as an expert on testing, spoke. Many people had long felt that these tests were culturally biased, that they served to reinforce the children's negative feelings about themselves, and that they were not used diagnostically, but merely to label children. IQ tests were no longer given by the Board of Education, but now we were beginning to ask whether the Metropolitan Reading Tests might not also do more harm than good. We felt that if we were no longer going to educate children in the old ways, what sense was there in testing them in the old ways? If our aim was to individualize instruction, could we still accept standardized tests as valid indices of their achievement? We had no easy answers there either, but we certainly felt this was an area that needed further exploration. Obviously there must be some way to measure both student achievement

310

and school success in fostering it, but we no longer believed that these tests could do either.

In the midst of trying to address ourselves to these problems, we were abruptly brought back to reality. While we were busy trying to be a community school and trying to solve the problems relating thereto, other people were busy trying to turn back the clock. Specifically, a bill had been introduced in Albany that would deny schools the right to appoint as acting principal anyone who was not already an appointed and licensed supervisor. The bill stated further that the highest ranking supervisor in the school must be made acting principal where a vacancy existed. What this would do, of course, would be to slam the door on schools such as ours that had found it necessary to go outside standard procedures to get their kids educated. It would also kill the Fordham Intern Program which had opened the door a slight crack to let some minority supervisors slip in. And finally, by making this a legislative action, it would take away from the city the right to decide who should administer its schools. Thus, in addition to all its other faults, the bill was a clear violation of home rule.

The intent, apparently, had been to slip the bill through while nobody was looking. Fortunately we were alerted to it, and we immediately mobilized not only our school but the entire district (as well as other districts active in the community control movement); and, for once, we and the school board were on the same side of a fight. The school board called a press conference, because we all felt that the only chance we had was to blow the thing wide open so that enough legislators might be sufficiently embarrassed to send the bill back to committee (which would, in effect, kill it). There are never enough votes in Albany to pass anything that is good for the city or to defeat anything that is harmful.

At the press conference, which was televised, I said, "For years the rules have existed to protect the professional staff. When parents began to use the rules to protect children, they changed the rules. Black people have long been invisible in our society. Now, when we refuse to use the rules and play the game as it has been played, we are becoming the invisible whites.

"But we will be neither invisible nor silent on this issue. We have, at PS 84, a fully qualified, able, sensitive principal who is beginning to restore order and education to a school where both were lacking.

We will not allow him to be removed. We will fight this bill by all legal means. If the law will not protect us, the parents of PS 84 will not be bound by the law. We shall take whatever steps are necessary to protect our children and our principal."

Those were fighting words, and apparently they were a little too hot for the network, for just at the point where I spoke of becoming invisible whites the sound suddenly went dead and stayed that way till the end of my statement. But though my immortal words were denied to all the good folk in television-land, our activity had the desired effect. The offending bill was resubmitted to committee where it died for the year.* Our principal was safe for the moment. However, as determined as we were to have the principal of our choice, the CSA was equally determined to give us the principal of theirs (no doubt for our own good).

At a meeting of the local school board on March 23, where the school board was to appoint Louis Mercado as acting principal of PS 75, the CSA served a show-cause order on the board, answerable in Brooklyn Supreme Court, as to why they should not be enjoined from appointing Mr. Mercado and *other nonqualified persons* to principals' jobs. Albany having failed the CSA, they were now trying the courts. The suit was filed by the CSA "on behalf of all Supervisors licensed by the Board of Education of the City of New York whose rights, duties, and obligations are directly affected in this proceeding."

Louis Mercado, a teacher and graduate of the Fordham Intern Program, had gone through a screening procedure at PS 75 that was similar to ours. He had been the choice of the panel, and the school board intended to implement the school's choice. The CSA intended that they should not. In spite of this the board appointed Mr. Mercado; and although he had trouble getting into the school and then didn't get paid for months because the central board held up his paycheck, he is now principal there.

All the parents' associations in the district realized the danger to their schools. Though this suit was aimed specifically at Mr. Mercado, the next one could be aimed at their acting principals. Even those schools that, at the moment, had regularly appointed principals realized the danger, for even Board of Ed principals are mortal

---

*It appeared again at the next session of the legislature, where, again, intensive lobbying on our part got it recommitted.

or find other jobs; and should they suddenly have a vacancy, if this suit succeeded, they would be bound once more to the lists. As a result, all the PA's decided to try to intervene in the suit as *amicus curiae,* whereby they would be permitted to file a brief outlining both the screening procedures and the necessity for going outside of regular channels for principals for our schools. It seemed reasonable to us that we should be allowed to present our side. It did not, however, seem reasonable to the judge, and we were denied this right. But it did keep us busy for a while when we would have preferred to worry about our schools. That lawsuit is moribund somewhere in Brooklyn.

In the fall of 1970 the Board of Examiners scheduled a regular exam for principals of elementary schools. After much soul-searching, Mr. Harriman, Mr. Mercado, and Mr. Seabrook (acting principal of IS 44 in our district) decided against taking the exam. They had several reasons for this. First, they believed the tests were pointless in evaluating the ability to be a principal. Second, the tests had, for years, effectively kept blacks and Puerto Ricans out of the supervisory ranks.* Third, the three men felt that, as community principals, they owed their allegiance not to the Board of Examiners but to the communities they served, and they said that they did not want tenure granted by some outside agency. They said they wanted to stay only as long as their schools thought they were effective, and therefore they could not, in conscience, take the exam. We supported them in this position. Two days later the school board got slapped with another show-cause order, this one aimed specifically at Mr. Harriman "and others in a similar position." This one sought to remove him, and others like him, immediately and forever, and to appoint in their stead duly licensed people who were being deprived of jobs due to the presence of these interlopers. This order was brought on behalf of all the people on the list, some of whom we had interviewed for the position. The fact that under the decentralization law all these people had, in fact, been appointed as prin-

*At the moment there are only eleven blacks and one Puerto Rican who are licensed elementary school principals. On the grounds that these tests were, in fact, discriminatory, the NAACP had just filed a lawsuit on behalf of Mr. Mercado and Boston Chance enjoining the tests. As of this writing, Judge Mansfield has sustained the suit and has enjoined any lists from being promulgated.

cipals as of April 1, 1970, with pay to match* and that, therefore, they were being deprived of nothing but the chance to run our school into the ground did not seem to occur to the CSA. They were men with a mission: get Harriman.

The specific allegations in the order were outrageous and would have been funny had there been less at stake. They alleged that Mr. Harriman did not have state certification (he has). They alleged that a group of militants (us) had forced our choice on an unwilling school. And on and on in that vein. They dredged up every piece of garbage they could find, every disgruntled letter ever written by a teacher or parent in the school, and threw them all into the pot. Again we sought to enter the case as *amicus curiae.* Again we trekked down to court through various postponements. The judge finally heard the arguments shortly before Thanksgiving of 1970, and nine months later finally rendered his decision: that there was nothing illegal in Mr. Harriman's appointment and that, further, the courts should not deal with questions of educational policy, but only with questions of law. Hurrah! So we won that one, too, but again, all that time and energy could have been more profitably spent on education. And then they accuse us of being political!

*The law states that all persons on the list would get the pay of principals even though in some cases, where there were no jobs for them, they would not perform the duties.

THIRTY-TWO

The Open Corridor at PS 84

On my first visit to PS 84, many light years ago, I had looked for signs as to the kind of school it was. I was a different person then, looking with the bias of a teacher who had come through the system. What I had looked for then was order, quiet, and children in their seats. Finding these as I passed through the halls and peeked into classrooms, I mistook them for education and decided that we could entrust our kids to the school. I was, of course, subsequently awakened to the fact that the order and quiet were sometime things and that only certain kids got educated. I look at a school with a different eye today. I've been in quite a few in the last several years, and those that look like the PS 84 of old make me shudder. One of the first ways I now judge a school, before I even go in, is by the windows. If they are blank or are filled with uniform cutouts (of rabbits or Santas, depending on the season), then I know that when I walk around I will find silence or the voices of teachers echoing through the halls. I will see children sitting at desks with the teacher at the front. I will see children raising their hands to be called on or scrunching down in their seats to escape attention. I will, if I am allowed into the classroom, see neat examples of spelling tests or math papers with stars tacked on the bulletin boards, perhaps some drawings or paintings all on one subject, and maybe even a composition, carefully and correctly recopied. And I'm sure some of the kids there are learning. If they're lucky and the teacher is first-rate, maybe most of them will be. But I'm also sure that most of them don't look forward to school and tear out as though released from prison at 3:00. And I'm also sure that most of them don't learn (as the statistics show) and that even those who do separate learning and enjoyment into two distinct categories.

PS 84 today has few resemblances to the school I first saw. The windows are crammed full of children's art, all different. In some of the rooms the windows themselves are painted (to the everlasting horror of our custodian). A visitor to most schools will see tiled corridors, gleaming and bare. At PS 84 the walls are endless bulletin boards, filled with stories, poems, and pictures, on topics ranging from ecology and peace to monsters and rockets and trips to the zoo. The stories may be scrawled in magic marker with the letters climbing uphill and sideways, but they say clearly that children live here. When the kids run out of wall space or when there has been a rash of work being torn off by passing kids, enterprising teachers have even utilized the ceilings for display. And you can tell, by stopping to read the stories, what the kids are learning and the progress of the different grades. Outside a first-grade classroom you might read: "We measured the animals. The rabbit is eighteen inches. The hamster is seven inches. The father mouse is four inches. The mother mouse is three inches. The new babies are too small to measure. They look like cocktail frankfurters. We made a chart." And below this there would be a bar graph headed "Animal Sizes" with the measurements duly transformed.

Outside a third-grade class you would also find pictures and stories, but here they would be more complicated, the writing neater, the story longer. But again, as you read about the class brownie-baking project, "When we added the melted chocolate, the batter looked gooky, but it tasted good when we licked it," you would know that here were living children at work.

The open-corridor classes at our school have been set up in communities. There are presently three lower-grade corridors, each grouped to contain a kindergarten, a first, and a second grade. There is a third/fourth-grade corridor, and there are also several open upper grade classes, but they are not part of the official program.* The children work in their own rooms, but they are also free to go into one of the other rooms as the need arises. This may be to work on material unavailable in their own room or to show the children or teacher some project they have completed. A first-grader may feel the need to work out something with blocks. Or a

*Supervised by Lillian Weber and her staff.

kindergartner may want to participate in a science project or a reading period in one of the upper grades. In each case he takes a name tag from the wall, indicates in which activity he is engaging and where, and goes about his business.

The children also meet in the corridor for songs or for activities that would disturb the peace of the classroom—gymnastics, dramatics, or woodworking, for example. Children from various grades also come together to work on handicrafts—needlepoint, macrame, knitting, or crocheting. In all these activities they are supervised by a corridor teacher, and they learn from her and from each other. Thus the children come to know not only the other children in their class but all the children in the corridor, and this brings about a feeling of family—of older and younger children learning from and about each other.

One of the ways in which children learn is by talking, not only formally to the entire class, but to each other. Classes run along these lines are not deathly silent. There is, most of the time, a steady hum of conversation, but this does not distract the children who are reading or doing math. It is simply a background sound that everyone accepts. What this accomplishes is twofold: it obviates the need for the teacher to enforce absolute silence (which rule of silence actually creates discipline problems); and it enables the children to learn from each other. Since one of the basic skills that children in the lower grades must master is reading, this type of organization recognizes that speech is a step in the process of learning to read. By encouraging speech it therefore encourages learning. Of course this is not the only way in which reading is encouraged. The children tell stories and the teacher or an older child write them down. The youngster then "reads" back his own story. The room is full of words—written words. Everything is labeled, so that the child sees words all the time. There are books, and he is encouraged to look at them. Since his world is full of words, he wants to learn them. In addition the teacher also spends some time each day working with small groups, or with individual children who need it, on phonics or on other reading skills.

Children in the corridor program are free to follow their own interests. Thus, a child who is on a baseball binge may be working on that, but his teacher will make certain that he is learning his basic skills. It really doesn't matter so much what the content is at this stage—the important thing is that the skills are mastered. If a child

can learn math—fractions, percentages, division, what have you—
from baseball and if he can learn to read and to write about what
he's read through baseball, then why not teach the skills through
that? Too often schools insist that kids read about what the school
thinks is important but the kid doesn't, and the school simply ends
in turning the kid off without ever teaching him to read. In the open
classroom the teacher starts where the child's interests are and goes
on from there. Now, it's true that every education course I ever took
stressed that, too; but then in practice the curriculum never allowed
for following the child's natural inclinations. In the open classroom
the curriculum becomes secondary to the child.

Basically, what this system says is that all children are different,
that they grow and develop and learn at different rates of speed and
in different ways, and that just as you can't expect your nine-month-
old child to walk because your friend's nine-month-old child is
walking, so you cannot expect your six-year-old child to learn to
read *today* because the boy in the next seat has learned to read today.
What this program does is to provide the materials and the encouragement so that when he is physically and emotionally and intellectually ready to read he will want to and he will read.

When I walk into an open classroom at our school, I often have
trouble finding the teacher. I'm still conditioned to expect her at the
front of the room, too. Sometimes she even is there, with a group
gathered for some joint activity. But more times than not she'll be
sitting at a desk with one or two children working out some math
or reading problem. The role of the teacher has changed, from that
of the source of all learning and information to that of a master
planner. In a way, I think of the teacher's role in this type of class
as that of a conductor of a symphony orchestra. She must know
every minute what each instrument is doing and help those who are
off key or who have lost the place. But she isn't playing for them.
She must plan the day. She must provide the materials. She must
ask the question that sets the child off to seek the answer. And she
must know, at each moment, what each child is doing, what he
knows and doesn't know. In order to do this she must keep accurate
records of each child's progress, not the traditional kind of record
that says "Johnny got 85 percent on a spelling test," but things like
"he still has trouble with his short vowels," or "he hasn't mastered
the five table." When the kids work in the corridor with a teacher,
the corridor teacher also notes this kind of fact about the child, so

that a real picture of his abilities and deficiencies begins to emerge.

These classrooms look very different from ordinary classrooms. Not only are the children not sitting neatly in rows—they may not even be sitting—but the rooms themselves seem transformed. Mobiles and paintings are strung from the ceilings. Shelves are lined with books. There may be a couch, or an easy chair, or just a soft rug in the reading corner where several children may be sitting or lying (or even hanging practically upside down) completely oblivious to the other activities around them. Microscopes, scales, magnifying glasses are available—and in constant use. (In the old days all our microscopes lived locked up in the school basement.) There is a profusion of math material, some of it fancy and store-bought, some of it handmade by the teacher or a parent. There are containers of buttons and beads for counting. There are blocks. There is a water table with various sizes and kinds of containers. All these help the child to master, concretely, the concepts of math. He can add and subtract blocks (which the teacher encourages him to do while he is building). He can find out about fractions. He can establish, by constant repetition, that when you pour a quart of water into a larger container, and then back into a smaller one, it still remains a quart. And that when you take two buttons away from ten you get eight. That sort of repetition, which may look like play, is necessary for a child to understand what a quart really is, or what ten minus two really means.

Nevertheless, parents who have been taught in the traditional way still get jumpy when their children come home and tell them they played with beads. That's not how mother learned her math; and even though she may have trouble balancing her checkbook because of the way she "learned" math, chances are that she still wants her child to learn the same way.

In these classrooms there are usually plants and live animals—rabbits, guinea pigs, mice, gerbils, turtles, snakes, or fish. One class even built an incubator and tried to hatch some fertilized eggs. These animals are also an important part of the child's learning experience—both for observation and for teaching responsibility for living things. The children see baby animals born. They watch the babies grow and have babies in turn. One morning I came into Maggie's first-grade class, and there was a sign on the board: "Shh. Our mice had babies." The teacher had explained that if there was too much noise the mother might get nervous and eat the babies.

That day you could have heard a pin drop. The babies all lived.

In all of these areas—math, science, cooking—the child is encouraged to write about what he does or to read to find out more on the subject. When a teacher doesn't know the answer to a question, they look it up together. One of the beauties of this type of classroom is that the teacher is not expected to be an expert on every subject, so children see that learning never stops, and that even adults (authority figures) aren't omniscient.

A visitor to the school might wonder at the fact that most of the children walk around with a small note pad attached to a string around their necks. These are individual dictionaries the children make, recording new words they have mastered. And as they work over a story, they will ask someone how to spell a word and then painstakingly they will add it to their collection. Neither of my girls has ever had a spelling test. Yet their spelling is far better than mine was at their age—with none of the drudgery of writing *elephant,* or whatever, ten times.

One of the things that still concerns parents is the question of discipline. They wonder whether children can learn with all that diverse activity and whether they wouldn't learn more if they all sat and listened to the teacher teach. (And even the best teachers in open classrooms admit that, on a bad day, they pine for the old days when they stood up front and everything was church-quiet.) The thing is that the fact that everyone is quiet doesn't guarantee that everyone is learning, or even listening. And anyone who's ever taught, or who remembers his own school days, is familiar with the scene where the teacher says, "We won't begin until *everyone* is perfectly quiet." One kid talks, or squirms, or gets up. The teacher waits. And waits, and waits. Meanwhile nobody is learning. By the time the first kid settles down (under the teacher's scowl), someone else can't sit still anymore. So everyone sits some more, and no one is learning. And by the time everyone is finally quiet, no one feels very happy any more. The teacher is mad. The kids are resentful, and that makes it hard to learn. This kind of situation actually creates discipline problems. When each child is doing his own work —work that he's interested in—there are fewer discipline problems, and they're less serious because the whole class isn't forced to wait for one kid to settle down. And the kid doesn't get the same ego trip out of acting up if he doesn't have the whole class for a captive audience.

This doesn't mean that anything goes in this kind of class. Obviously some rules are still necessary, and usually the class and the teacher formulate a set of rules by which to live. Not silly ones such as you can't get a drink of water unless you raise your hand, but rules such as you can't hit, you can't destroy someone else's work, or you can't take someone else's property. And the kids are much harder on those of their classmates who break these rules than a teacher might be, because the rules make sense to them. They create respect for the child, for his work, for the teacher. And they create real discipline—self-discipline. We want them to learn self-control, but that comes from feeling good about themselves, from knowing they can behave even if no one is watching, from knowing they can learn even if no one is shoving it at them. It's the kind of discipline that creates human beings instead of automatons, and though this kind of growth isn't readily measured on tests, it's the kind of growth that fosters learning.

These classes are as diverse as the children in them, and just as no two children are alike, neither are any two teachers, and the style of each classroom differs according to the personality of the teacher. The thing that pleases me most about these classes is that the teacher sees the class not as a mass, but as individuals doing their own work in their own way. Thus the open classroom is offering to every child in it a chance to be himself—a unique person with skills and good qualities, and with weaknesses. It's not going to turn every child into a genius, but it will give him a chance to be as good as he can be. And it will give the teacher that chance, too. That's a great deal.

So where are we now? We have a principal of our choice. We have a school that is open—to parents, to visitors, and, most important, to children. We have, in fact, become something of a showcase school, with visitors coming from all over the country to see the open corridor at work. We have children returning to us from private schools. We have become the shining example for the district. When another school was trying to remove an unsatisfactory principal, the school board told them they were going about it all wrong, and that they should do it the way the parents at PS 84 had. Life's little ironies!

But these things are superficial. What we have now at PS 84 is a school where education is in process and where the principal cares about the progress of each child. We have a school where, when a child is seriously troubled, the principal spends long hours in conference with the child, his parents, teachers, the guidance counselor, and other experts to find a solution that will help both the child and the other children in the school. We don't have easy answers, but we have a school where we believe we all have to work together to look for ways to solve our problems. We have an open-corridor program that is thriving, and to walk into one of these classes is a joy. The children are absorbed. The classes are still heterogeneous, and though one child may be reading a book on astronomy while another is reading a preprimer, the important thing is that each is working on his own level without depriving the other of his right to learn. The attitudes of the children toward each other have also changed perceptibly. Where, in the past, they were played off against each other and achieved success at someone else's expense, they now do their own thing without worry about where their neighbor is. This was brought home to me recently when, as we were riding in the car, Maggie suddenly said, with great pride in her voice, "You know, Mommy, Tony knows the whole alphabet and can do numbers to ten." She told it in the tone an older sibling would use when telling a neighbor that her baby brother had just learned to walk. And since Tony came into the class unable to distinguish red from blue from yellow, or one letter of the alphabet from another, it was indeed a cause for pride. But the point is that in other days the report would have been that he could *only* do numbers to ten. What has happened is that a class pride has developed, so that children care about and for each other. And the fact that Tony is not reading on Maggie's level makes him no less worthy of joy than another child who is. What is more, they don't keep each other from progressing, each at his own pace. As Maggie put it on another occasion, "The thing I like about my class is that when I finish a book, I don't have to wait for everyone else to finish. I can keep going as far as I can." Indeed she can, and so can every other child there.

We have not yet had an impartial evaluation of the program, so there is no way of knowing, objectively, what the overall results are. But from a subjective point of view they are most encouraging. The kids in the open-corridor classes seem to score somewhat above those in traditional classes on standardized reading tests. They are certainly happier. More important, as two parents put it when they were discussing what their children had accomplished in the preced-

ing year in an open-corridor class, "They didn't really learn anything. Except how to learn."

If all of our children can really learn how to learn then we can
consider ourselves a success. Obviously we still have problems.
Some of the open classes function better than others—depending
on the skill of the individual teacher. This will always be true, regardless of methodology. But because the teacher in an open classroom is no longer the center of all learning and because the children
are much more responsible for their own learning, even where one
teacher is less effective than another, the results are less disastrous
for a child. And where a teacher is good, everything really takes off.

We have also found that children entering first grade from an
open-corridor kindergarten are already far ahead of their counterparts from traditional kindergartens. The first-grade teachers, time
and again, remark that the kids are much smarter than they were a
few years back (we no longer have any traditional kindergartens). I
don't believe that the kids are smarter, but I do believe that they
have become more open, that they have, indeed, learned to learn.
And I am confident that when these children reach the upper
grades, they will not be suffering the massive failure with which our
kids used to be handicapped.

Nevertheless we still have teachers who are not convinced that
children can learn unless they are sitting in their seats, and we still
have parents who share this conviction. For parents who continue
to feel this way, the school must continue to provide alternatives
(and it does still have some traditional classes); for if we are, truly,
a community school then we cannot impose our philosophies on
them, either. But I hope that in time, as the success of the children
in the open classes becomes more clearly documented, this attitude
will also begin to change. A parent stood up at a meeting and said
of the program, "In the past when I told my child to jump, she
jumped. Now when I tell her to jump she asks why. And I don't like
it."

That is her right, but if she sees children learning, perhaps she
will also see that to learn they must ask "why?"

If there is one thing all parents want, it is that the school will
educate their children. Education has been the one force in our
society that has permitted upward mobility for successive waves of
immigrants. Up until now it has, by and large, failed to do the same
for our black and Spanish-speaking children. If the open-corridor

program can reverse this failure, then I think that the parents who worry that their children no longer jump on command will worry less. It is, after all, less important that a surgeon jump on command than that a sergeant does.

What we are trying to get away from is an education that produces people who follow orders blindly. We are trying to provide an education where people think for themselves, are responsible for their actions, and develop themselves to their maximum potential. Obviously we will not produce an entire class of surgeons, but hopefully those who do not become surgeons will also become—at least—human beings and that the surgeons will be human beings as well. And, hopefully, each child will become what he is capable of being and will not assume the role that society predestines for him by virtue of his skin color or his background. That is a tall order, and we have only made a small beginning; but when I first became involved in the school, I would not have believed it possible that we would even make this small beginning, so perhaps the tall order is not impossible either.

Has it all been worth it? When I see that every child in an open classroom leaves the first grade reading at some level, when I see children happy as they work, when I see children with open alert faces asking hard questions, and getting honest answers—when, in short, I see the joy of learning at our school—then my answer is yes. When I think of Jorge, or of Tony, and that they will make it, then my answer is yes. When I think of the conversation I overheard between Kathy and three other kids from traditional classes about what they'd do if they were ghosts and the other three said, "When I had a test, I'd make myself invisible and go up to the teacher's desk and look at the right answer," and Kathy looked at them with incomprehension, then the answer is a resounding yes. And when my friends' kids in other schools read or do math because they have to and mine do it because they want to, then my answer is yes, it's been worth it.

Maybe parents in other schools (even those whose children are "successful" by today's standards) will also begin to realize that their children are only being trained to jump, and hopefully they, too, will begin to demand that their children have the right to ask why. But if our kids at PS 84 can stay turned on to learning, if they can continue to learn how to learn, then they will survive anywhere, and then it will have been worth everything.